The American Utopian Adventure

A POPULAR VIEW OF THE DOCTRINES OF CHARLES FOURIER
DEMOCRACY, CONSTRUCTIVE AND PACIFIC

A

POPULAR VIEW

OF THE

DOCTRINES OF CHARLES FOURIER.

BY PARKE GODWIN.

"If I have spoken evil, show me wherein I have erred; if I have spoken good, why smitest thou me?"—JOHN, xviii, 23.

"All human interests, combined human endeavors, and social growths in this world, have, at a certain stage of their development, required organizing: and WORK, the grandest of human interests, does now require it."—PAST AND PRESENT, BY CARLYLE.

WITH THE ADDITION OF

DEMOCRACY, CONSTRUCTIVE AND PACIFIC

PORCUPINE PRESS INC.
Philadelphia 1972

Library of Congress Cataloging in Publication Data

Godwin, Parke, 1816-1904.
  A popular view of the doctrines of Charles Fourier.

  (The American utopian adventure)
  Reprint of the 1844 ed.
  1. Fourier, François Marie Charles, 1772-1837.
I. Godwin, Parke, 1816-1904. Democracy, constructive
and pacific. 1972. II. Title.
HX704.F9G5 1972   335'.2'0924 [B]   77-187451
ISBN 0-87991-006-2

First edition of *A Popular View of the Doctrines of Charles Fourier*, 1844 (New York: J. S. Redfield, 1844)

First edition of *Democracy, Constructive and Pacific*, 1844 (New York: J. Winchester, 1844)

Reprinted 1972 by Porcupine Press, Inc., 1317 Filbert St., Philadelphia, Pa. 19107

Manufactured in the United States of America

TABLE OF CONTENTS.

	PAGE.
PREFACE.—DESIGN OF THE WORK	5

PART FIRST.

1. INTRODUCTION
   - Chap. I.—Social Architects, in general 7
   - Chap. II.—Charles Fourier, in particular 18

2. GENERAL PRINCIPLES.
   - Chap. III.—Of God and of Evil 29
   - Chap. IV.—Formula of Social Movement.... 33

3. UNITY OF MAN WITH HIMSELF. (1st section.)
   - Chap. V.—Of Man and his Essential Faculties 42
   - Chap. VI.—The Organization of the Township 50
     - § I.—Material Arrangements 50
     - § II.—Passional Arrangements......... 54
     - § III.—Consequences of these Arrangements................... 56
     - § IV.—Education................ 60
     - § V.—Division of Profits............. 65
     - § VI.—Property 69
     - § VII.—Order and Liberty............. 70

INTERMEDIATE.—DISTINCTION BETWEEN THE TWO PARTS OF THE WORK.... 73

PART SECOND.

4. UNITY OF MAN WITH HIMSELF. (2d section.)
   - Chap. VII.—Organization of Society......... 75
     - § I.—Hierarchy 75
     - § II.—Atmospheric Equilibrium........ 79
     - § III.—Equilibrium of Population....... 82
   - Chap. VIII.—Manners and Customs 84

5. UNITY OF MAN WITH GOD, AND WITH THE UNIVERSE.
   - Chap. IX.—Cosmogony 91
   - Chap. X.—Universal Analogy 99

POSTFACE.—OBJECTIONS ON THE SCORE OF MORALITY AND RELIGION 110

NOTES 118

PREFACE.

DESIGN OF THE WORK.

A CLERGYMAN once said to the author, that he had an *instinct* against all schemes of Association; we do not write for such. There may be men whose natures are so sublimated that they can discover truth by instinct; yet the probability is that the larger part of our fellow-mortals prefer the old-fashioned faculty called reason, when they have occasion to decide upon grave and important matters. It is the latter faculty to which our remarks are addressed.

We hope, however, that no class of men will be so silly as to mistake their *prejudices* for their instincts, and therefore conclude that our remarks are not intended for them. Every science, particularly every new science, conflicts with our more vulgar impressions, so that it is the first duty of a man who would come to the knowledge of truth, to guard against the influences of prejudice. According to Bacon, we can not approach the temple of science, without first demolishing the idols or false images which beset all the passages that lead to its sacred chambers.

Sir John Herschel, in the introduction to his treatise on Astronomy, gives us this advice: " In entering upon any scientific pursuit, one of the student's first endeavors ought to be, to prepare his mind for the reception of truth, by dismissing all such crude and hastily adopted notions respecting the objects and relations he is about to examine, as may tend to embarrass or mislead him ; and to strengthen himself by something of an effort and a resolve, for the unprejudiced admission of any conclusion, which shall appear to be supported by logical argument, even should it prove of a nature adverse to notions he may have previously formed for himself, or taken up, without examination, on the credit of others." " *There is no science, which more than Astronomy stands in need of such a preparation, or draws more largely on that intellectual liberality which is ready to adopt whatever is demonstrated, or concede whatever is rendered highly probable, however new or uncommon the points of view may be in which the most familiar objects may be placed.* ALMOST ALL ITS CONCLUSIONS STAND IN OPEN AND STRIKING CONTRADICTION WITH THOSE OF SUPERFICIAL AND VULGAR OBSERVATION, AND WITH WHAT APPEARS TO EVERY ONE, UNTIL HE HAS UNDERSTOOD AND WEIGHED THE PROOFS TO THE CONTRARY, THE MOST POSITIVE EVIDENCE OF HIS SENSES."

Now, we wish to rest the claims of the Social Science of Fourier upon precisely the same grounds on which Herschel rests the science of Astronomy. Fourier and his disciples hold that his social principles are entitled to rank as a science, being capable of that rigorous demonstration which only wilful prejudice rejects—as the Italian philosophers denied the existence of Galileo's telescope, although he gave them the opportunity of looking through it, or as the chemists of Europe scouted the system of Lavoisier, for more than fifty years, although they might have satisfied themselves of its truth, by a few simple experiments.

The object of the present volume is to furnish the public with a brief synthetic view of all the doctrines of Charles Fourier, who professes to have discovered the Science of Social Organization. Our limits, however, have enabled us to give *results* only and not discussions. Readers who may desire to see any subject fully developed are referred to the works of the master and his school. This book contains all that is required to enable an impartial mind to determine whether the subject is of sufficient importance to need a profounder investigation.

During the last few years, the spread of the *practical* doctrines of Fourier in France, Germany, Great Britain, and the United States, have been most rapid ; and it has therefore become important that the public should be in possession of a manual, containing a short account of the whole science, as now taught by the followers of the discoverer. It is doubly important, in this country, because the doctrines of Fourier have never received a complete exposition, and because they have been subjected, on the part of enemies, to the grossest misrepresentations. The practical parts of the system and some of the higher questions have been fully explained by Mr. ALBERT BRISBANE, to whose indefatigable energy we are indebted for the introduction of the science into the United States, and to whose works we refer; but the abstruser points of inquiry were judiciously left until public sentiment was prepared to distinguish between the practical and the purely theoretical doctrines. Most of these points will be found treated of in the following pages.

An interesting part of the subject, *viz.*, its bearing upon the religious researches and controversies of the day, we have postponed to another work which we are preparing with exclusive reference to the Moral and Religious Aspects of the Doctrine of Association.

It only remains for us to say that this work professes no higher character than that of a mere compilation from the larger works of the school to which it belongs. The arrangement and the substance of most of the chapters have been translated from the " Vue Synthetique" of Renaud, one of the most clear and admirable of the French works on the subject, and the facts of the Memoir of Fourier and a few pages in the latter part of the book have been furnished us by Hugh Doherty, of London, one of the most profound and brilliant writers of the day. In all cases, however, in which we have borrowed from others, we have modified the language in such a way that the author alone desires to be held responsible for what is said.

A POPULAR VIEW

OF THE

DOCTRINES OF CHARLES FOURIER.

CHAPTER I.

SOCIAL ARCHITECTS.

"Thinkers who are inspired with the hope or knowledge of a better social state,—Utopians in the best acceptation of the word, have a right to the respect and attention of men. Some of them are fools; but some are Revealers of Truth; and all are useful, because Time, the Refiner, will separate the gold from the dross."—REYBAUD.

BEFORE entering directly upon the consideration of Fourier's social system, there is an interesting preliminary inquiry, which may prepare our minds for the reception of his teachings.

In the history of human society, there is one peculiar and significant fact—a fact that stands out with signal and striking prominence in the current of its opinions. It is this: that a set of men have appeared from time to time, who have been led by the oppressions and disorders of society, into a position apart from others, as the projectors of an entirely new and radical reorganization. We see them springing up at such regular intervals, and possessing such a strong resemblance, that we are irresistibly compelled to regard them as members of the same family. They are characters of an altogether novel and impressive kind. They are not simply reformers, who have come with single thoughts which they labor to infuse into the ways and feelings of the race. A much higher, broader, deeper relation to us is the one which they assume. They are not mere tinkers or tailors, who would mend our old wares and garments, by here putting on a little solder, and there sewing a ragged patch; but master-mechanics rather, who would create us new utensils and cut us clothes out of whole cloth. Not as crude jack-planers or carpenters do they present themselves, who when our old buildings have been undermined by the rats or grown rickety by age, or become too narrow for the offspring of our growing thoughts and desires, would build us lean-tos and outhouses, in the manner in which the Italian style of villa is made, by adding one structure to another, until the whole becomes a rude conglomeration of ill-shaped and inconvenient tenements. No; but as true and noble architects they stride forward, who would roughly strike the old edifice into the earth, leaving it to perish in the mire and dust, while they unfolded their plans of more glorious structures, worthy to be the habitations of men of a larger stature and movement. In short, the men of whom we speak may be called SOCIAL ARCHITECTS—a class which has never been satisfied with any measures in the sphere of social reform, short of a most thorough, vital, and permanent reconstruction of the very fundamentals of social existence.

This class, we say, has been marked by characteristics which were common to all its members. They have been, for the most part, men of superior intellect; they have been men of broad and living sympathies; men of boldness and hardihood of thought; men of indefatigable zeal; men of a free sincerity, suffering willingly for their convictions; men of a high, can we not say, of an almost sublime consciousness of the imperative claims and moment of their own mission. In fact, in many cases, they were men who aspired to somewhat of a universal character; who have looked upon themselves as consecrated to a grand and deathless work; who embraced within the scope of their ambition all arts and all sciences; who were at once philosophers, legislators, teachers, economists, generals, and even prophets; and who, in some instances, not confining the sweep of their genius to the narrow limits of the earth, sought to ascend to the throne of God, and to penetrate the secrets of Providence and Human Destiny. Truly not without force does the French language speak of them as the *Témerétés* (the Audacious Ones), since they rush with so impetuous a boldness over the entire domain of possible knowledge.

These daring and original spirits, arrange themselves in three classes; the mere theoretical,—the simply practical; and the theoretico-practical combined. In other words, the Social Architects whom we propose to consider, may be described as those who ideally plan the new structure of society; those who set immediately to work to make a new structure, without any very large and comprehensive plan; and those who have both devised a plan and attempted its actual execution.

I. THE THEORETICAL CLASS is one which is most numerous, but whose claims are the least worthy of attention. Although the most insignificant of these have had some influence in moulding and vivifying their day and generation, only a few of them are sufficiently commanding to arrest our notice in this brief and hasty review. We might speak of St. Pierre, with his sentimental "*Dream of Perpetual Peace;*" of Hall, whose goods were stripped from him on account of his "*Mundus Alter;*" of the monk Campanella's "*City of the Sun*" (civitas solis); of the "*Basiliade*" of Morelly, a long while supposed to be the production of Diderot; of the good Fenelon, in his "*Salente*" and his "*Voyage to the Isle of Pleasure ;*" of Retif de la Breton in his "*Australian Discovery,*" and of a hundred others of kindred tastes, but that their works are rather curiosities for the antiquary than utilities for the student. With still greater propriety, we might refer to the School of Pythagoras, the most extraordinary and advanced mind of antiquity; to that prince of wits and satirizers, Rabelais, who is supposed in the "*Pays de Teleme,*" with which his famous Pantagruel closes, to have sketched the outlines of his own ideal of a perfect society; to Daniel De Foe, the author of Robinson Crusoe, whose "*Essay on Projects*" became the inspiration of our all too practical Franklin; or to gigantic Bacon, whose towering and capacious genius, had not his manifold pursuits prevented, would have extended the "*New Atlantis,*" now an imperfect draught of a philosophical school, to a full development of the right constitution of all human relations. Our space, however, will not allow us to dwell upon these men. We must pass to three, Plato, Harrington, and More, who have made a more decided and lasting impression on human opinion, and who may serve as a sample of the rest.

(1.) Plato, the brilliant and profound philosopher of Greece, was among the first, as he is among the most sublime of social architects. His "Republic," which is only a part of his larger treatise on the "Dikaiosuna," or Justice, the storehouse and magazine of so many that have come after him, in the same line, merits a more elaborate study than we can give it here; for rightly to understand it, we ought to be familiar with both the age in which he lived and the peculiar character of his philosophy. He was a man formed under the influences of the imaginative theology of the East, and the practical teachings of Socrates. Like the latter he gave his investigations the direction of Morals and Happiness; but like the Pythagoricians and Orientals, he considered them under the light of a lofty ideal of Virtue and Beauty. Living too, in that period of Greece, when her greatest munificence and splendor were contrasted with great degradation and outrage, his political work is a mirror, not only of his philosophy, but of his age. From the ethereal regions of his high metaphysics, it drew the grandeur of its conception, and the mighty genius and exquisite grace of its execution; while to the spirit of his times it owes those perpetuations of Injustice and Wrong, which disfigure and disgrace its practical provisions. Thus Plato, in the midst of many winning and impressive declamations, constituted his republic on an inexorable basis of caste. Magistrates, warriors, and mechanics, are the three classes of men whom he never confounds; which are separated by insuperable barriers,—which have each their peculiar social virtues; and each of which is bound to its sphere by the hand of iron necessity. The race of gold—the race of silver—the race of iron—these are the elements of his social mechanism. A shepherd, a dog, and the sheep, are the three agencies out of which he is to form a true social relation! It were an impossible task; for at the very outset he introduces two of the most active dissolvents that could be found to any harmonious aggregation of men; we mean the implacable division, the selfish rivalry, of castes. In the older nations, these elements had long before struck their forms of civilization with a deathly immobility. Bramas, Zatyras, Soudras; priests, fighters, workmen; the three organs of head, heart, and hands,—were the materials which in India and Egypt had smitten their societies with palsy; which had made Labor the trodden and torn victim of fraud and force. Plato was not unaware of this fundamental error, where, seeking to escape from it, he cries out, " You are all brothers, but God has made the Rulers, who are most precious, of gold; the warriors of silver; and artisans of iron and brass. Yet a citizen of the golden race may have children of silver, another of the silver race may generate brass, while the descendants of the iron race may become of the purest gold." A felicitous sophism, but wholly at war with his frontal principle! Where a fusion of castes is thus rendered possible, the continuance of castes becomes only a question of time. Again; he falls into conflict with his original principle, when he institutes community of goods and promiscuous intercourse. "Let the women," he says, "be held in common, let children be in common, and on no consideration, in the transactions of trade, let even the name of property be heard." Now, to abolish the relation of family, to extinguish the titles of individual possession, and, at the same time, to preserve a rigid distinction of ranks, is a contradiction which it requires all our respect for the philosopher to consider with seriousness. It is a fault, however, that must not blind us to the prodigious excellences by which it is redeemed. When we consider the era in which Plato lived, before the Revelation of Christ had shed the sunbeams of its life and light upon the world, seeing only a foreshoot of the glorious day about to open, and conjecturing obscurely as to the true relationship and destiny of men, we are astonished at the beauty and justice of his sentiments, and his deep devotion to the laws of Eternal Order and Duty. It was a penetrating, expansive, magnificent nature with which God had endowed him, and the "Republic," esteemed by some short-sighted scholars as the feeblest of his works, will remain an enduring monument of his penetration and wisdom. When mankind shall have learned to read the riddle of history aright they will see in that work a profound use and significance.

(2.) Next to Plato, we choose to speak of the chivalric and glorious Sir Thomas More,—the most illustrious of English Chancellors,—one of the bravest and heartiest of English Men. His clear and noble intellect, made an impression in that dark reign of the Eighth Henry, which is still felt in the remotest seats of English Literature and Law. It is to him that we are indebted for the name which characterizes the entire class of bold and independent thinkers that we are now discussing. Utopia, is one of the indestructible words of our mother tongue. The romance in which it took its origin, is one of our most indestructible books. Its chaste, silvery tone, its upright manly spirit, its treasures of criticism, will long make it a source of delightful and profitable reading. We see in it, everywhere, the unequivocal marks of More's high, cheerful, transparent nature. As a work of art, it possesses the rarest merit. With so much skill and simplicity, says a biographer, "are the dialogue and narrative conducted, that many people did not suspect the writer had imposed on them a production of his own fancy. Some envious critics even went so far as to affirm, that to their certain knowledge, Hythlodaeus had not only furnished the materials but had actually dictated the whole; while the mere Scribbler, who carried off the reputation, had acted as only an amanuensis. Some grave and zealous divines, on the other hand, strongly moved by the virtues of the Utopians, had actually determined to embark in an attempt to achieve the good work of their conversion to Christianity!"

In regard to the spirit of More's imaginary society, as compared with Plato's, we immediately perceive the influences of Christ's religion. Community of property is preserved, but we hear no longer of a community of wives; we are not indoctrinated into the efficacies of impassable distinctions of caste. It is true, he allows the iniquity of slavery, which is one of the few blots on his work, otherwise consistent and elevated. But in general he recognises and respects the rights of Man, disposing his political arrangements so as to confirm the interests and give force to the will of the masses of his community. The government he described was republican, established only to maintain the general good. Public lectures, he says, were instituted for the enlightenment of the popular mind. All kinds of productive labor, but especially agriculture, were held in the highest esteem and made the duty of every member of the race. Idlers of all sorts,—priests, lawyers, book-worms, and gentlemen, were not endured; yet the hours for labor were moderate in length, and alternated with agreeable recreations. The punishment of death was abolished, and provisions made for the reformation of offenders, on the ground that crimes more often spring from the injustice and wrong of society than the inherent vice of the individual.

Every city in Utopia had a well-supplied market; every house, the most airy, large, and comfortable apartments. At the tables, it was an ambition to make the conversation lively and entertaining; " They never sup without music, and there is always fruit served up after meat; while they are at table some burn perfumes, and sprinkle about fragrant ointment and sweet waters; in short they want nothing that may cheer up their spirits; they give themselves a large allowance that way, and indulge themselves in all such pleasures as are attended with no inconvenience." To use all things as not abusing them was the rule of life. Contempt of the precious metals, as signs of wealth, the most perfect religious tolerance, manners at once soft and peaceable, simple habits, laws founded on natural right, completed the beautiful theory of existence in the ever-blessed island of Utopia. The conception of it, is the rare manifestation of an exquisitely fine and benignant soul.

We can not, therefore, be surprised at the strong hold which this celebrated work has taken of the minds of scholars and reformers. If it had no other merit than the beauty of its style, it would be worthy of a lasting remembrance. But its claims to respect rest upon better grounds than any trick of art. It was for the time in which it was written, a keen and cutting criticism of the worthlessness of statesmanship and the fooleries of morals. The foremost minds and best hearts of that day saw in its rude outlines a pleasing fulfilment of their noblest aspirations. All that their faculties had idealized, in the deep longing for a better social state, they found embodied in it, with crystal clearness of style and logic, and the rare ornamentings of a lively and brilliant fancy. Even now, after the lapse of centuries, it may be read with instruction, and certainly will be read with delight. A work which has so long escaped the oblivion jaws of Time, which in the darkness and void confusion of the darkening past, still shines clear and glittering like a star in the sky, must possess many of those perdurable properties which fit it for the guidance and illumination of all times. Sir Thomas More himself was one of those pure and celestial spirits which give a lustre to their generation, and his Book, as all good books are, was the record of the purest and best feelings of his purest and best moments.

(3.) After Sir Thomas More, came Harrington, the author of Oceana. He lived in the time of Cromwell, and was a man of various learning and high character. His life was spent in the consideration of the question of government—the flower and fruit of all his studies being the Oceana, which he offers to us as the model of a perfect and Christian Commonwealth. It is written in the manner of a Romance, the assumed names of persons and places answering to persons and places in actual existence, as Adoxus for King John; Olphaus Megaletor, Oliver Cromwell; Panthenia, Queen Elizabeth; Leviathan, Hobbes; Neustrians, Normans, &c., &c. The book consists of Preliminaries, or dissertations on the objects and generation of government; the Model, which makes the body of the book, where the principles are unfolded; and the Corollary or conclusion, which mostly relates to forms. In the first part, he manages under the fiction of a Council of Legislators from all the world, to give the most elaborate history of the various governments of the Past; in the main treatise, we have definitive propositions, enforced with considerable vigor of logic and eloquence; while in the closing division, we find many, and some of them admirable suggestions, for remodeling the offices of the state, for the encouragement of trade, for the discipline of armies,—the establishment of religion, and the right constitution of the degrees of Nobility. On the whole, it is a remarkable work. Although it merely professes to deal with the question of government, it treats that subject in such a large sense that it becomes in effect a plan for the complete reorganization. of society. There can be little doubt that the author so regarded it; for he esteemed it " an equal government, completely framed in all its fundamental laws, without any contradiction to itself, to Reason, or to Truth." In the outset, he apostrophizes, in the celebrated description of Pliny, " The most blest and fortunate of all countries, Oceana! How deservedly has Nature with the bounties of Heaven and Earth indued thee? Thy ever-fruitful Womb, not closed with Ice, nor dissolved by the raging Star; where Ceres and Bacchus are perpetual twins. Thy woods are not the harbor of devouring Beasts, nor thy continual Verdure the ambush of Serpents, but the food of innumerable Herds and Flocks, presenting thee, their Shepherdess, with distended Dugs and Golden Fleeces. The wings of thy Night involve thee not in the Horrors of Darkness, but have still some white feather, and thy Day is (that for which we esteem Life) the Longest." And again, in the Corollary, following Plutarch's closing up of the story of Lycurgus, he says, " When he saw that his Government had taken root, and was in the very Plantation strong enough to stand by itself, he conceived such a delight within him, as God is described by Plato to have done, when he had finished the Creation of the World, and saw the Planetary Orbs move in their spheres. For in the Art of Man (being the imitation of Nature, which is the Art of God), there is nothing so like the first-call of Beautiful Order out of Chaos and Confusion, as the Architecture of a well-ordered Commonwealth."

Harrington's fundamental principle was that the balance of power always follows property, and the centre of his system, consequently, is an agrarian division of property, in order to keep the power in the hands of the many, and a hierarchical distribution of the people into regularly-organized orbs or orders, possessed of the Ballot. It is wrought out with infinite ingenuity and learning; and contains a vast number of suggestions greatly in advance of his age; but it has a fatal defect in the fact that it is both fanciful and arbitrary. Yet let Honor be done to the memory of the man, since he labored sincerely in the cause of his race, and suffered manfully for his faith. Less poetical than either Plato or More, he is more scientific; his plans have more of an every-day air about them; while his principles seem to us quite as liberal in their sentiment as those of the latter, and more practicable, if not more profound, than those of the former.

But these men were mere speculative thinkers, who resorted to these ideal republics, not to propose any actualization of them, so much as to acquire an inoffensive and, at the same time, effective mode of bringing what they esteemed important political and social truths before the minds of their contemporaries. In this light their criticisms were of high value; and we should like to dwell upon them, did not our plan compel us to turn to another class, who sought to teach kindred truths in a more direct method. We mean,

II. THE PRACTICAL ARCHITECTS of society, or the communities instituted to exemplify a more perfect state of social life. These have existed in all ages of the world, expressing a sort of living protest against the frauds, the corruption, the disorder, and the injustice of prevalent society, and opening an asylum for the refuge of those disappointed and unhappy spirits, or those ardent devotees, whom misfortune, principle, or enthusiasm, had driven into exile. In the former part of our inquiries, we had to deal with speculations; our business now is with speculations transformed into facts. From individuals we pass to bodies.

(1.) The most ancient community, of the sort with which we are engaged, was the Essenian, instituted among the Jews. Their sentiments were so exalted that it is yet a question among the critics whether they lived before or after Christ, whether they drew their notions from his religion, or whether he had passed a portion of his earlier life among them—the fact that he does not denounce them in the gospels, as he does the other Jewish sects, agreeing equally well with both hypotheses. They are minutely described by Pliny, Philo, and Josephus,—from the latter of whom we learn that at that time they were four thousand in number, " united only by the ties of mutual affection. They are the most moral of men, agriculture being their chief occupation, and a complete equality prevailing among all the people. Property is in common among them ; they marry no wives ; they allow no servants; yet they adopt children, and by turns serve one another. The elders, chosen freely from the best among them, take charge of their revenues and prepare their food ; their dress is plain and white ; they have no cities ; they neither buy nor sell; and at the end of their labors, at the fifth hour, they cleanse themselves and partake of a Communion Feast, which is begun with prayer. They avoid oaths, as marks of perjury, and admit no strangers to membership, without formal initiation and preparatory trials." To these interesting particulars Philo adds that they did not sacrifice animals, lived upon vegetables, and though skilful in the arts, were never known to make any warlike or destructive instrument. They avoided cities, because they thought them infected with both moral and physical disease; they had no slaves because they esteemed domination of any kind injurious to both master and servant, and because all men were brothers ; and they worshipped God, in a simple manner, as the Creator of the Universe, and a Lover of Purity, Justice, and Truth.

We see in this remarkable community, either a foreshine or a reflection of Christianity, modified by an ascetism which suppressed the splendors of dress and of outward comforts, and almost annihilated the existence of woman; yet it cherished many manly virtues and lofty sentiments.

(2.) Similar to the Essenians, in many respects, are the Herrnhutters, or God's Watchmen, better known as the Moravians, of Germany. Their history is familiar to every child, since every child must have read the memoirs of their noble founder, Count Zinzendorf, and in every land, where their miracles of missionary enterprise have planted the seeds of civilization and Christianity. They differ from the Essenians in that they have less asceticism and more enthusiasm. Unlike the more ancient sect, too, while they live in common, and profess to be guided by the law of Love, maintaining a complete equality between their members, they do not hold property entirely in common. They marry and confer separate households on such as are married. They are given to music ; they cultivate the finer arts ; their ceremonials and intercourse are marked by tenderness ; and their religion, while it is decided and strict, allows for the play of the gentler affections. But it is in the zeal of propagandism that they have displayed their most extraordinary characteristics. A few men, descendants of the Waldenses, nurtured in persecution, retire from the world to a wild, silent, and distant retreat, where they cultivate the earth and exhort each other to a high religious life. In a few years, they find themselves spread over all nations, and penetrating the most inaccessible deserts. It was not more than a century from the time that the munificent and pious Zinzendorf opened his arms to embrace the outcast Moravian carpenter at Dresden, to the period when his community thus begun, numbered its sixteen settlements in Germany, its three in Denmark, its five in Sweden, its twenty-two in Great Britain, its one in Russia, and its twenty in North America, each or all connected with missionary stations in Greenland, Labrador, the West Indies, among the Northern Indians, in South Africa, in Patagonia, and among the fiercest Kalmucks of the steppes of Asiatic Russia—thus extending their influence over millions of human souls.

(3.) The Shakers of this country are another instance of exclusive communities, in which, however, with great external prosperity, there is a rigid internal discipline. They sprung from the Quakers in England, and still retain many of their peculiarities of speech, dress, deportment, and thought. They reject civil and ecclesiastical authority and military service : they take no oaths ; they deny the obligation of the sacraments ; and they believe in the immediate inspiration of the Holy Ghost. Mother Anne Lee was their acknowledged founder in the United States ; but since her time, they have assumed a more definite organization. All their possessions are common : they live in common, except that there is a separation between the sexes ; they labor in common, with a uniform dress ; and they worship in a kind of wild, monotonous jumping dance, which they accompany with the voice. It is understood that they are frugal, industrious, and wealthy, although they are ignorant, prejudiced, and despotic.

There is another community in this country, which took their origin from the Quakers, established at Zoar, in the state of Ohio. The settlers were originally from Wittemberg, in Germany, whence they were driven by religious persecution. Only eighteen years have elapsed since they purchased their 8,000 acres, then the midst of a wilderness, but now a thriving and populous village. They allow of no rights of property ; their government is entirely democratic; and, tolerating all religious opinions, they maintain only the public inculcation of the rites commonly recognised by all sects and nations.

(4.) But not alone among Christian people has the impulse towards associated efforts and life been manifested. Mr. Urquhart gives us an account of a most extraordinary association at Ambulakice among the Turks ; but as that is rather a commercial corporation, in which the interests of labor are united, rather than a community, we shall not now dwell upon its results.

These partial and imperfect attempts at social harmony deserve one or two general reflections. The first is, to use the discriminating language of Miss Martineau, speaking of the Rappites, that "whatever is good among them, is owing to their economical principles, and that whatever they have that excites our compassion, is owing to the badness of their moral arrangements." The second remark is, that if, in spite of their ignorance, their mistakes, their imperfections, and their despotisms, the worst of these societies, which have adopted, with more or less favor, unitary principles, have succeeded in accumulating immeasurable wealth, what might have been done by a community having a right principle of organization, and composed of intellectual and upright men ? Accordingly, the discovery of such a principle has become an object of earnest investigation on the part of some of the most acute and disinterested men the world ever saw. This inquiry has given rise to our third division, called

III. THEORETICO-PRACTICAL ARCHITECTS OF SOCIETY, or those who have combined the enunciation of general principles of social organization with actual experiments, of whom the best representatives are St. Simon, Robert Owen, and Charles Fourier. This class will extend the basis of our inquiries, and demand a more elaborate consideration. We shall begin with—

(1.) *St. Simon.*—"Arouse yourself, oh count! for you have a great work to do !" were the words with which a young Frenchman sprung out of bed, on one of the mornings of his seventeenth year. "Arouse ! for you have a great work to do !" said Claude Henri, Count de St. Simon, a descendant of Charlemagne and the bearer of one of the most illustrious names in the annals of France. But it is not to the virtues of his ancestry that we must look for his title to our regards : he was a bold, original, self-sacrificing, and lofty genius ; in himself worthy of our close and sympathizing study. His earlier life had been passed in the midst of sounding cannon and clashing swords—a soldier of independence under our own majestic Washington—a Colonel at twenty-three years of age, in the corps of the patriotic Bouillé. But the destructiveness of war was not his vocation : " I was destined," he says, " to no such repugnant labor,—rather to advance the human mind and perfect civilization." He accordingly devoted his next years to the acquisition of fortune, not for the sake of wealth, but that he might found houses of industry and schools of science. It was a grand project, executed with the energy of genius. By the year 1797 (about seven years in all), he closed the commercial period of his life, with a property of 144,000 livres.

His next task was to perfect himself in all knowledge. He took a house near the Polytechnic school, the doors of which were ever kept open to the professors of the natural sciences, whose lectures he constantly attended, and of whose private instructions he became a complete master. Three years were thus occupied in the study of inorganic nature, when he removed to the neighborhood of the medical schools, where his pursuits related to the higher subjects of the organic and animated creation. He was the friend of the most accomplished *savans* of the French metropolis, and his table was free to whoever was able to contribute to the enlargement of his knowledge or the elevation of his sentiments. Seven years more were thus consumed in acquiring the philosophy and science which were then current. A tour in England, Germany, and Italy, either in the investigation of industrial processes, in the visitation of learned universities, or in the study of art, completed his inventory of the intellectual treasures of Europe.

But he was not yet ready to undertake the work of communicating the result of his researches to the world.

The larger field of actual humanity had yet to be explored. Associating with him a woman of congenial taste, he abandoned himself to the refinements and pleasures of society. It is not enough, he reasoned, that I know the men of science : I must know the operation of the various passions, in all their modes of development. He frequented balls, dinners, and soirées, that he might enlarge the basis of his experience. Calm in the midst of every vortex, silently judging others while he was himself unobserved, following all common practices, evil as well as good, gaming and license no less than elevated conversation and instructive debate, he sought the knowledge to be acquired by every character and in every condition. "A gourmand, a debauchee, and a profligate, from principle more than inclination, by system rather than by instinct, St. Simon," says Reybaud, "lived five years in one ; he acquired the experience of an old man even while a youth ; he used and abused all things, that he might prepare the elements of his future calculations ; he inoculated himself with diseases, that he might the better understand the methods of their cure. His life was an experiment, and therefore not to be judged by the rules of ordinary morality."

It was, however, in our opinion, a mistaken experiment, and by its costliness introduced its author to a round of experiences of a very different sort. His funds were exhausted, and he shortly fell into the condition of absolute want. The parasites that had fed on his bounty, deserted him ; his professed friends and admirers fell away, and he wandered homeless and pennyless about the streets of Paris. But destitution and suffering could not suppress the ardor of his enthusiasm. From the thickest of his distresses, he sent forth work after work, filled with the severest criticisms of life, and with the boldest suggestions of reform. "This fortnight," he writes in one place, " I have subsisted on bread and water ; I have labored without fire, and I have sold all, even to my wearing apparel, to defray the expense of some few copies of my work. It is the passion for science and public happiness—it is the desire to find the means of terminating in a gentle manner the frightful crisis in which all Europe is now struggling—that has reduced me to my present distress ; so that it is without a blush I avow my present destitution, and solicit the aids I need, in order to be able to go on with my work." Thus, in tribulation and anguish, too, was he prepared for the great task to which he had been called from his early sleep.

The work here referred to is doubtless his " New Christianity," in which he assumed, more distinctly than he had done before, the character of Evangelist and Prophet. This was an extraordinary production, although it was neither very new nor very original. The name of *new* Christianity was only relatively true ; for it was not so much a new form of religion that the writer propounded as a mere republication, in a new and vivid light, of the moral precepts originally advanced by Jesus. It was an attempt to show what had been often before attempted, that the spirit and practice of religion were not at one ; that there was a wide chasm separating the Revelation from the Commentary, the text from the gloss, the Master from the Disciples. Nothing could have been more forcible than its attacks on the existing Church, in which the Pope and Luther received an equal share of the blows. He convicted both parties of errors without number and heresies the most monstrous. But he did not carry the same vigor into the development of the positive portions of his thought. He ceased to be logical, that he might be sentimental. Yet the truth which he insisted on was a great one—perhaps the greatest, *viz.*, that the fundamental principle in the constitution of society should be Love. Christ teaches all men, he says, that they are brothers; that humanity is one ; that the true life of the individual is in the bosom of his race ; and that the highest law of his being is the law of Progress. The perpetual aim of religion is to ameliorate the condition of man, by which is meant, of "the most poor and the most numerous class." And in the spirit of this saying, he appealed with startling eloquence to all the votaries of science, of literature, of art, and of Religion. " Young men! let us unite then! Poets, artisans, theologians, literary men, men of industry, men of science, our career is marked out for us, since to-day we can occupy ourselves directly with the elevation of the Mass. Let the Past, to which we have paid ample obsequies, repose in peace : let there be no more funeral orations over its tomb ; yet let us not disdain it, but honor it, since it has brought us to the Present, and opened us an easy route to a brilliant Future. Let us all have but one wish and but one hope. Let us, according to the beautiful expression of the author of the book of Judges, march *as one man*, having inscribed on our banners, 'PARADISE ON EARTH IS BEFORE US!' The age of Gold, which a blind tradition has hitherto placed in the Past, is in the Future, and the Future shall henceforth show itself to men, not as a breaker, but as a secure and noble haven."

But, alas ! the magnanimous spirit which could utter these thrilling words was not destined to see their realization. The long process of starvation finally brought St. Simon to his end ; but in the sufferings of death, as in the agony of life, his mind retained its calmness and sympathy, and he perished with these words of sublime confidence and hope on his lips : " The future is ours."

The few devoted friends who stood round that death-bed took up the words, and began the work of propagation. The doctrine rapidly spread; it received a more precise and comprehensive development under the expositions of Bazard and Enfantan, and a few years saw a new family, which was also a new church, gathered at Menilmontant. On its banner was inscribed, " To each, according to his capacity, and to each capacity, according to its work ;" its government took the form of a religious hierarchy, and its main political principle was the abolition of inheritance.

It was evident that a society so constituted could not long be held together. Made up of enthusiasts, without definite principles of organization—trusting to feeling and not to science—its members soon began to quarrel, and the latter days of its existence were stained by disgusting license. St. Simon was one of the noblest spirits, but an unfit leader of any enterprise. He saw all things. says a friendly critic, through his heart. In this was his weakness ; he wanted head ; he wanted precise notions ; he vainly hoped to reconstruct society by a sentiment ; he laid the foundations of his house on sand.

But it must be said to his credit that he began an able and brilliant school of criticism, and that among his disciples have been found many of the most clear-headed and benevolent of modern thinkers. No previous school have done one fiftieth part as much as these men to direct the attention of Europe to the awful condition of the laboring classes of civilization.

(2.) *Robert Owen.* He was born at Newton, Montgomeryshire, in the year 1771, and appears to have had little education, except what he acquired by his own industry. His industry and economy were such, however, as to enable him, in the various capacities of clerk and cotton-spinner, to lay up a comfortable fortune in a few years. About the year 1784, he became associated with his father-in-law, Robert Dale, in the manufacturing establishments of New Lanark, a rude district in Scotland, on the romantic borders of the Clyde. When he joined the enterprise, it was in no sense a prosperous one; for the workmen engaged in it were composed of the refuse of the population, and crimes of every description were perpetrated. Mr. Owen's benevolent sympathies were touched by the sight of so much misery, and he instantly undertook vigorous measures for its relief. It was a long and painful task, to convert a society, in which masters and workmen were alike debased, into a family of brothers. He studied their vices one by one; he gradually introduced changes in their habits of cleanliness, of economy, of order, of intercourse; and a few years saw the almost miraculous transformation of an entire community. Dirt, theft, intemperance, were banished; neat cottages had taken the place of filthy hovels; the children were educated in beautiful school-houses; and New Lanark, spite of all natural drawbacks, became the home of happy and thriving families.

The moral change which Mr. Owen had effected by the mere change of outward circumstances, was a pregnant fact for his suggestive and benevolent mind. In 1812 he published an account of his experiment, and proposed its extension to other districts, in a work called "New Views of Society," which attracted almost universal attention. Travellers to New Lanark returned in raptures with the orderly and beautiful results of its arrangements. His name became a theme of newspaper praise; his system a subject of debate in the cabinets of kings. The Dukes of Kent and Sussex presided at his meetings; Lord Liverpool, the premier of England, aided by Lord Sidmouth, in their official capacities, sent his speeches and plans to every prominent man in Great Britain. Even the clergy, generally the last to sustain any scheme of well-doing which does not emanate from themselves, took part in the organization of new industrial colonies. Mr. Owen was, beyond all question, the most conspicuous and influential man in the kingdom, if not in the world.

But while his popularity was at its flood, he ran foul of the breakers. Before this, he had not developed his opinions on the subject of religion and politics, satisfying himself with a negative toleration of creeds and parties. His business had been to organize labor; he now undertook the criticism of church and state. He openly accused all existing religions of falsehood and impotence; he denied the personal responsibility of the individual, whose destiny, he said, was controlled exclusively by society; and he argued that all systems of reform, other than those which looked to a reform of outward circumstances, must inevitably lead to injustice, oppression, and misery.

Such sentiments were sufficient to startle the Church. Yet Mr. Owen proceeded to show also that the plans of radical politicians were alike futile and absurd. He attacked the most famous leaders of the people; he proved the yearly increase of pauperism, in the face of all their supposed ameliorations; he denounced their superficial notions; and he was never forgiven. From that moment, he fell in public esteem.

Religion was regarded as too sacred an element of society to be rudely handled by any man, however great and good, and therefore his Noble and newspaper patrons withdrew their countenance. His persistence in his course soon rendered him as odious to public sentiment as he had before been agreeable. Mr. Owen's views, by this time, had settled into the permanent convictions, that man is utterly irresponsible for his character, and that society is best constituted on the principle of community of interests. These views he unfolded for many years, with an energy and enthusiasm which have seldom been equalled. He has taught them personally in several of the continental nations, and in North and South America; he has spent millions of dollars in the publication of tracts; newspapers have been founded to propagate his doctrines; communities, more or less prosperous, have been started in many parts of the globe; and his disciples, in England alone, are numbered at five hundred thousand.

His character and merits may be summed up in a few words.

Mr. Owen is one of the most extraordinary men that ever lived, whether we regard either his errors or his truths. The former are few, but are fundamental; the latter are many, and also important.

His errors are the denial of personal responsibility, and the doctrine of common property, which we hold to be utterly untenable in argument, radically defective in morals, and of course, extremely pernicious to society. But our limits will not allow us to discuss the matter.

His truths are, or rather his services have been, that he has taught moralists and the world the important, almost vital, influence of outward circumstances upon inward well-being and happiness. He may be called the Apostle of Circumstances, and his experiments and arguments in this respect have done indescribable good in meliorating prevalent views as to the effects of social institutions. Those beautiful treatises on the laws of diet, cleanliness, the physical results of different kinds of employment, &c., on health, which have illustrated the latter days of benevolent exertion, may mostly be traced to the efforts of the despised and abused Robert Owen.

No one can regret more strongly than we do the moral and religious delusions into which Mr. Owen has fallen; but we trust we shall never allow any amount of error to blind our eyes to the positive and surpassing excellences of any individual or system. It is so rare that men of immense wealth devote their energies to enterprises of even mistaken benevolence, that we are disposed to forgive the mistake, for the benefit of the example.

We here close our review of the Social Architects of all ages, by a few remarks intended to characterize respectively their merits and defects.

(1.) Their defects have arisen either from ignorance or excess. Deeply penetrated with the evils of our present societies, conscious that there must be some better form of society, they have rushed into new organizations before they had scientifically understood the real wants of the old, or the principles required for the right constitution of the new. They have failed, therefore, because they were ignorant of the true science of social organization; or, driven to madness by the pressing necessities and grinding wickedness of existing arrangements, they have run into the opposite extreme, and rejecting all the institutions of the Past, instituted social forms that were wholly at war with the instincts and habits of the race. Thus, the doctrine of a community of property, we have no doubt, is a reaction from the flagrant injustice and intense suffering produced by the present unequal division of property.

(2.) Their merits have been, that they have been a living and perpetual protest against the disorders of prevailing institutions; that they have pointed public attention to the enormity of social abuses; that they have called in question those taken-for-granted sentiments, which hang like an incubus over the human mind; that they have kept alive and stimulated the hope of social perfectability, and, from time to time, from the storm-clouds of their tempestuous restlessness and discontent, have shot those thunderbolts of wrath, which have shocked and overturned the rotten and perishable structures of the state.

But their chief value, to our mind, is the testimony which they bear to the fact, that in all ages of the world there has been a lurking faith that God had prepared a better social system for the adoption of man. They have been groping their way after this system, in the midst of much darkness and many entanglements of error; and while their want of success proves that they have been deficient in head, their continued energy and enthusiasm show that they were not wanting in heart. Their instincts led them in the right direction, but there was not enough of practical skill among them to teach them when and where to stop. In this respect, they may be compared to the early alchymists, who went in pursuit of the Philosopher's Stone, which was to transmute all the baser metals into gold, and of the Elixir of Life, destined to confer wealth and happiness upon all mankind. In the course of their inquiries, they departed on some fool's-errands, they turned out much dross, they spent valuable days and nights in many a silly, many a dangerous experiment; but they were animated by a sublime Hope, and prepared the materials which a future Man of Genius (Lavoisier) was destined to construct into the orderly forms and proportions of a beautiful and useful science.

Has there yet been a Lavoisier, to gather the scattered observations of Social Alchymists, and, out of the rude mass, build up a True Social Science? We shall see!

CHAPTER II.

CHARLES FOURIER.

"We must not speak lightly of Fourier. A man who could devote his whole life to the worship of such an Idea, who wished to turn the Passions of man in a good direction, who undertook to associate all families and interests, and who labored with such unprecedented energy for the extinction of social evil, was no vulgar dreamer, however Utopian the character of his projects. And after all, Utopianism is often only a more advanced opinion, proclaimed in the face of a generation which does not yet understand it, and destined to become a standard of faith in the generation that follows."—BLANQUI.*

OUR object in the last chapter, in showing that Man in all ages had been groping after a more perfect and agreeable social state, was to prepare the reader to perceive how all the advantages of former undertakings have been combined, and all their difficulties and errors avoided, in the discoveries of Charles Fourier. We consider him the flower and consummation of all these rude and fragmentary efforts—the true Teacher whose system fulfils all the aspirations of the past, and is also adequate to the demands of Humanity for many years to come.

He was born at Besançon, in Franche Compte, on the 7th of April, 1772. From his earliest infancy he was remarkable for the avidity with which he sought knowledge and the tenacity with which he maintained his opinions when he conceived himself in the right. An incident which occurred when he was only five years of age seems to have produced that implacable hatred of falsehood which was ever afterward one of his most marked characteristics. He was punished for telling the truth in the shop of his father, who was a woollen-draper, and he never forgot the injustice. It was the first hint his mind had received of the necessary dishonesty of commercial dealing, as it is now conducted.

At school he was remarkable for his diligence, and generally took the prizes for French themes and Latin verses, although the favorite study of his youth was geography, for the prosecution of which he was accustomed to spend all his pocket-money in the purchase of charts and globes. He had also an exquisite taste in cultivating flowers, and his sister relates that when he was a boy he had his room so lumbered with plants that a narrow passage from the door to the windows was the only space left unoccupied. His great pleasure consisted in cultivating all the varieties of any favorite species of flower. But his passion for music was even more intense, the theory of which he understood perfectly, so that among other indications of reform in arbitrary methods, he has given a plan of musical notation, "by which all the different voices and instruments may give the same name to the same note, instead of employing seven or eight different keys or particular scales."†

---

* M. Blanqui, the able and distinguished Professor of Political Economy in the University of Paris, is one of the few men, not professed disciples, who have given anything approaching a fair statement of Fourier's doctrines.
† See Mr. Doherty's fuller explanation in the London Phalanx.

Another striking trait of his childhood was his kindness and generosity, of many of the manifestations of which he never spoke himself, his family having learned them subsequently from other persons. A particular instance, related by Mr. Doherty, may serve as a specimen of his modes of charity. As the college which he attended was not far from the residence of his father, he slept at home, returning every morning to his studies. His habits had always been considered somewhat eccentric, and it was not therefore remarked as extraordinary that he breakfasted earlier than everybody else, and after breakfast, always filled his pouch with bread, fruit, viands, &c., which were intended apparently for a lunch. One day, after he had departed from home to begin his commercial life at Lyons, an old cripple hobbled to the door and asked if the young gentleman was ill, and on being informed that he had left Besançon, the poor man burst into tears, and said he had lost his guardian angel, who used every morning to feed and comfort him. The first time Fourier wrote to his friends, he begged of them to protect the old man, whom he had forgotten in the hurry of departure, and his request was complied with; but the helpless creature lost his all when he lost his comforter, and though still protected by his absent benefactor, he pined away and died, as much from grief, it is supposed, as from infirmity.

At Lyons Fourier entered as a clerk in a commercial house, being then about eighteen years of age. He soon after, in the capacity of agent, travelled over the greater part of France, Germany, Belgium, Holland, and Switzerland. Wherever he went, the chief objects of his attention were the physical features of the country, the nature and processes of the industry of the people, and particularly the arrangements and architecture of the towns. His memory of details of this kind was prodigious. His walking-stick was regularly notched off in feet and inches, and he never passed or entered a building that struck him, without taking its dimensions, &c. He was also profoundly acquainted with every branch of science, particularly of the exact sciences, which he studied passionately, while he cared very little for the more uncertain and arbitrary speculations of the moral departments.

In 1793 Fourier's father died, and left him about sixteen thousand dollars, as his share of the family property ; but before the close of the year, having embarked it in commercial undertakings, he lost the whole of it, by the sudden seige and ransacking of Lyons, where it was stored. During the same fearful and revolutionary disturbance he was several times in danger of losing his life. On the 9th of October the city surrendered, many of its inhabitants were slaughtered, and others, among them Fourier, thrown into prison. He was condemned, by the blood-thirsty tools of the National Convention, to perish on the scaffold, but he made his escape in about five days and fled to Besançon. In a state of complete destitution, and worn down by fatigue and sickness, he was there again incarcerated, and only saved his life by conforming to the general requisition, which forced all ranks, sexes, and ages, into the national service. His only offence, in all these trials, was that he would not join the different parties of revolutionists who were successively in the ascendant.

He served two years in the army of the Rhine, when he procured his discharge on account of ill health.

" On obtaining his liberty, he entered again as a clerk in a commercial house, pursuing his studies with perseverance whenever he had leisure. In 1799 he was employed at Marseilles, in a wholesale warehouse, and in the early part of the year was charged with a commission which gave a powerful stimulus to his favorite speculation, of introducing the practice of truth and honesty in commercial dealings. He was chosen to superintend a body of men while they secretly cast an immense quantity of rice into the sea. (In the hope of realizing a great profit, this rice had been kept till it was completely spoiled.) France had been suffering from exceeding scarcity during the past year; and notwithstanding the risk of famine among the people, these secret monopolizers of corn had allowed their stores to rot, rather than sell them at a reasonable profit. These abuses of monopoly, and many other fraudulent operations of commerce, with which Fourier was well acquainted, appeared to him in the light of real crimes against humanity, and he thenceforth resolved upon studying incessantly until he had discovered, not the means of detecting and punishing, but of permanently and effectually preventing them. This holy resolution, if we may be allowed the expression, was crowned with success before the end of the year.

"In 1799, Fourier discovered the laws of universal unity, and the essential destiny of humanity upon earth.

"From his earliest youth, the great object of his ambition had been to discover the means of introducing truth, honesty, and economy, in commercial operations. Being himself engaged in mercantile pursuits, his natural love of truth, and obstinate adherence to equity, were daily and hourly thwarted by the common practices of his profession. His predominant passion being constantly irritated, left him no respite from the task he had undertaken, notwithstanding the endless difficulties he encountered. Something or other constantly occurred to give him new courage in continuing the arduous task, which had been several times well-nigh abandoned, in the despondency of impossibility. Besides the every-day practice of lying and cheating in trade, there were certain anomalies which made an indelible impression on his memory. We have already mentioned the impression left on his mind by the injustice of being punished for speaking the truth in his father's shop, when he was only an infant. Another fact which had a powerful influence in directing his thoughts, happened when he was about eighteen years of age. Shortly after leaving school, he was allowed to visit Paris : it was in the year 1790, and his first visit to the capital. The things which attracted his attention most were the Boulevards, the public monuments, the general style of building, and the excessive dearness of all the necessaries of life. One circumstance in particular seemed a most revolting instance of mercantile extortion : being exceedingly fond of fruit, he was obliged to pay sevenpence for one apple, of a particular sort, which he had often purchased at the rate of three farthings a dozen in the country. This instance of a simple commodity like fruit, being augmented to one hundred and twelve times its original value, seemed to him an almost incredible anomaly. It is true that the year 1790 was an exceptional period in France ; but the circumstance of the apple was not the less remarkable for its influence on Fourier's mind. From that period to 1799, a lapse of nine years, he labored incessantly to accomplish his favorite project, but all his efforts were inadequate to the task : the more he advanced in science and a true knowledge of the world, the more his hopes were chilled by the deep shadow of impossibility. Despair of success, however, did not quench his thirst for science in general; and, as we have already stated, he was again induced to resume his favorite meditation, by the painful idea of monopoly forcing the people to starve while an abundance of provision was exposed to rot in the sordid clutch of private speculation.

"His first inquiries concerning commerce, led him to discover the evils of incoherence and jarring individual interests. He perceived that the only possible mode of introducing truth, equity, and economy in productive and distributive industry, was by means of agricultural association and wholesale trade. This discovery only increased the difficulty of realising his favorite project—commercial honesty. He was under the necessity of discovering the practical means of associating human beings, with their natural instincts and tastes, diversity of character and conflicting opinions, before he could proceed; but he was encouraged in his task, by a firm conviction of such a practical science existing in principle, and only remaining to be discovered in order to be applied. The immense advantages of economy, rapidity, equity, education, and science, which he saw might be realised by association, thoroughly convinced him that Providence had pre-ordained society as the natural destiny of man, and he believed that these pre-ordained laws of association were permanently revealed in the general laws of Nature. He found that attraction and repulsion were the two principal laws by which the Creator governs the world; and in order to obtain a complete knowledge of these laws, he resolved to study simultaneously the highest and lowest orders of creation in the universe. He considered the stars as the highest order of creation, mankind as the middle term, and the inferior orders of creation as the lowest step in the scale. He supposed that there must be certain general laws of unity common to these three orders of existence, or it would be impossible for them to compose one harmonious whole; and he hoped that by studying all that was known in the positive sciences concerning them, he might discover the natural laws of correlativeness, which bind them together in unity and eternity. His principal lever in the work of discovery was a sort of algebraical calculation, by which he supposed every law that was common to any two of these general terms, must be common to the third; and he never abandoned any branch of study until he had discovered those principles of nature which were common to the medium and the two extremes.

"His first discovery was the universality of distribution, according to a law of ascending and descending progression, in every order of the creation, from the highest to the lowest degree of animate and inanimate beings. This law of progressive distribution he termed series: accordingly, the first grand axiom which he established was this—'All the harmonies of the universe are distributed in progressive series.'

"Having observed a perfect correspondency between the various orders of creation in the universe, he was led to infer, that, as the Creator was one and the same being, infinite and eternal in his attributes, there must necessarily be a principle of unity in all his works: that the creation must necessarily be a reflection of the attributes of the Creator; that the Creator being all in all, it was impossible for him to paint or represent anything but himself in the creation. If he had represented anything foreign to his own attributes, that something must exist independently; and, in that case, the Deity would not be infinite. Such an hypothesis being perfectly absurd, we must admit that the Creator is infinite, and that it would be impossible for him to create anything which was not analogous to some of his own attributes. From these considerations, Fourier derived his second axiom—' The Creator being one infinite harmonious being, everything in nature must be an imitation of his attributes, and therefore there exists in every order of creation, similarity or universal analogy.'

"Considering attraction and repulsion as the universal laws of nature, and God as the original distributor of all sorts of attraction, it is perfectly rational to infer, that the respective faculties or impulses of attraction and repulsion in all orders of beings, are distributed exactly in proportion to their respective functions in the general harmony of the universe: the affinity which binds the atom to the atom, the attractive power which rules the movement of the planets, the affections which bind human beings to each other in society, are only so many different modes of the one universal law of attraction and repulsion; and from this self-evident induction, Fourier derived his third general axiom—' The permanent attractions and repulsions of every being in creation, are exactly in proportion to their respective functions and their final destinies in the universe.'

"With these three axioms for guides, he set out in quest of the grand principle of associative unity. The first thing to be discovered was, an exact knowledge of the nature of man; his natural impulses, attractions, and repulsions. The second object for consideration was, the progressive distribution of these faculties according to the general laws of series which regulate the harmony of the universe: the third fact to be ascertained was, the analogy between the newly-discovered principles, and the other known laws of nature, as a confirmation or refutation of the discovery.

"It would be superfluous to enter further into these details at present; they will be fully developed in the following treatise: but we may observe here, that Fourier does not speak of 'Revelation' as a guide to him, in his first work, published in 1808, though he never fails to appeal to it for authority in his subsequent publications. He mentions one fact, however, in his last work, which proves that he never was indifferent to religion. In refuting a newspaper allegation of 'materialism,' he states that he was imprisoned at Besançon in 1793, for refusing to renounce his faith in the Gospel, and in 1835 he was falsely accused of materialism; and in both cases by what he terms the dupes of false philosophy in different characters of corporate duplicity.

"By 'false philosophy,' Fourier alludes to both theology and arbitrary science, as erroneous and one-sided interpretations of Scriptural and Natural Revelation, though he seldom alludes to errors in theology, otherwise than by observing that 'neither philosophers nor their rivals (divines) have had sufficient faith in Providence to discover a remedy for social misery;' and that their views of permanent subversion are equally fallacious. He objected strongly to a republication of his first work, on account of some considerable errors it contained, and which were rectified by subsequent discoveries he made in 1814 and 1819.

"About the time of his discovery, Fourier returned to Lyons; and as he was not able to devote the whole of his time to study, he endeavored to combine his favorite pursuits with an easy occupation, which would procure him the common necessaries of life. To be constantly confined in a warehouse or countinghouse would have occupied too much of his time; he preferred being free, and gaining less; he became what in France is termed a 'Courtier Marron,' an unlicensed commercial agent. This function, occupying very little of his time, formed a valuable link between practical application to business and theoretical speculations concerning society. It is probable that this every-day recurrence to the actual practices of the world, formed a very wholesome check to the illusions of theory; for no philosopher ever wandered so little from the confines of reality, or advanced so far in the intricate mazes of actuality, as Fourier: his most transcendent speculations are traced through analogy, down to the lowest orders of creation, the insect, and the atom; his critical analysis of history and existing society proceeds from the most minute details of every-day life to the highest considerations of national policy. His favorite method of demonstration consisted in contrasting the infinitely small with the infinitely great, according to that universal law of nature, the contact of extremes, in every branch of the creation, in every series of natural classification.

"In 1808 Fourier published his first work, under the title of 'Théorie des quatre Mouvemens,'—the theory of universal attraction and repulsion. The first volume was merely a prospectus of the work, intended to procure the means of publishing the rest by subscription; but little or no notice being taken of the prospectus, the publication was suspended. He had bestowed eight years' labor in working out the principles of his discovery before he attempted to publish them; and having discovered that certain parts of his theory were still incomplete when he published the first volume, he resolved to withdraw it from circulation, and continue his studies. After seven years' additional elaboration, he was preparing to go to press, when Napoleon returned from the island of Elba, in 1815, and France was again thrown into a state of agitation. During the short reign from the time of his return from Elba until the battle of Waterloo, the Emperor Napoleon named the Count Fourier prefect of the department of the Rhone, and the count placed his namesake, Charles Fourier, at the head of the statistical department of that provincial government. On the return of the Bourbons, Fourier retired to his sister's, at Tallissieu, that he might quietly continue the preparation of his manuscripts. This sister was a widow, living in a country village near Belley, where her husband had been sub-prefect, a function similar to that of county-sheriff in England. Fourier had another sister living at Belley, where he resided chiefly from 1816 to 1821. Two of his nephews are now residing in that neighborhood. One is a barrister, the other a notary.

"As he always led a very quiet and studious life, little is known of his particular habits and private transactions during his residence at Lyons from 1799 to 1816; but it is probable that they were in every way similar to his general bearing from that time to his death. He was thoughtful and reserved; more studious of comforting and assisting the poor who surrounded him, than desirous of flattering the rich, or courting their acquaintance. Indeed, he had an absolute dislike to the falsehood and dissimulation which pass for politeness. Morality, justice, and the love of truth, were the principal features of his private character. He was very moderate in his eating and drinking; but particularly desirous of obtaining the best quality of everything, free from adulteration. He used to say that half the things we eat and drink are poisoned by adulteration, which is only one of the many evils of false competition and monopoly. From a continual habit of study, he had acquired the habits and manners of a hermit, lived almost entirely alone, and appeared to avoid long conversations with strangers. He lived and died a bachelor, almost as great a stranger to his own family as to the rest of society. This taciturnity increased as he advanced in years; for those who knew him when young, say that he was very lively and witty. General Pajol relates that he was in the habit of dining with him every day for several years, at a table d'hôte in Lyons, while Fourier resided in that city; and that his wit and gayety rendered him the admiration of all who knew him. Even in later years, particularly during the last two years of his life, he was cheerful and communicative with those persons whom he knew intimately, and who had the good fortune to possess his confidence.

"Having withdrawn his first work from circulation, a few copies only were in the hands of the public, and no notice had been taken publicly either of him or his system. In 1814, however, one of those copies which were in circulation fell by chance in the way of an inquiring mind at Besançon, Fourier's native city; and the gentleman, M. Just Muiron, who had accidentally come in possession of the book, was so much struck with its originality, the sublime simplicity of the theory it announced, the immense importance of the discovery, if it were practicable, that he immediately resolved to find out the author, and learn more of the subject. This was no easy matter, as the book had been printed at Leipsic, without indicating either the name or address of the author: the only clue to his residence was contained in a paragraph relative to the subscription for publishing the rest of the work. Those who were desirous of subscribing were referred to M. Charles at Lyons. It was not until the beginning of the year 1816 that Muiron succeeded in discovering the retreat of Fourier at Belley. When informed of his real residence, he wrote to Fourier, to inquire about the rest of the publication, and received a very simple, polite, and friendly answer. The correspondence was continued for some time; and Muiron, more and more convinced of the truth and importance of the discovery, became the intimate friend and the first disciple of Fourier.

"Muiron soon became as anxious as Fourier himself concerning the publication of the system, now almost complete in every detail, and he offered to advance money for the necessary expenses. As Fourier had saved a little money, and had inherited about forty pounds a-year from his mother, he lived very economically, and labored incessantly to prepare his manuscript for the press; but the materials were so immense, that nearly four years were occupied in the laborious undertaking. The publication was again purposely delayed by a new discovery which Fourier made in 1819; and though this discovery related principally to cosmogony, he deemed it prudent to delay publishing until he had thoroughly verified the unity and universality of his whole discovery. Having fully satisfied himself of the correctness of every part, he removed to Besançon in 1821, where the first two volumes of his great work were printed. In 1822 they were published, under the modest title of 'A Treatise on Domestic and Agricultural Association;' and he went to Paris in the hope of having them favorably reviewed, as a means of obtaining the necessary funds for realizing the practical part of his system. After remaining more than twelve months in vain, he found that money was the only means of obtaining notice in journals and reviews; and his funds being exhausted, his book was left unnoticed. In this position he had no resource but that of patience. Not being able to live on forty pounds a-year in Paris, he was obliged to employ a part of his time in procuring the necessary means of subsistence. He returned to Lyons, where he remained about a year; but finding it inconvenient to be absent from the capital, he became corresponding clerk to a commercial house in the Rue du Mail in Paris, and remained five years without obtaining any serious review of his work, or making himself known to any influential person. At the end of that time, his friends in the country advised him to publish an abridgment of his work, which would be cheaper and more simple. In accordance with this advice, he published a methodical elementary treatise in 1829. This volume met with the same reception as the others—absolute silence on the part of journalists and reviewers. Fourier still remained in Paris, sending his book to everybody he thought likely to understand it, and take an interest in the realization of his theory. Silence and indifference, however, were still the only result of his efforts to obtain publicity, until a lucky occurrence brought him into notice in 1832.

"In the beginning of that year, the St. Simonians made a stir in Paris by their preachings and writings. Fourier had sent his works to the teachers of these new doctrines as early as the year 1830, informing them of the possibility of realizing that social regeneration for which they appeared so anxious in their predications. Instead of listening to the simplicity of Fourier's advice, they deemed themselves vastly superior to everybody else, and gave him to understand they were perfectly competent to the task which they had undertaken. They did not, however, neglect to read his works privately, adopting many of his principles without acknowledging the source from which they had drawn them, until at length several of their proselytes, who were really serious in their convictions, abandoned the defective theories of St. Simonism, and publicly professed the principles of Fourier. It may not be improper to observe here, that these principles are directly opposed to all systems of community, and that it is quite erroneous to confound Fourier with Owen. Soon after the desertion of Transon, Le Chevalier, Paget, Lemoyne, and several other learned and influential men, the St. Simonians were dispersed, and a weekly journal was commenced for the diffusion of Fourier's principles of association and progressive policy. This journal, called 'La Reforme Industrielle,' was conducted with spirit, and obtained many adherents to its principles. A joint-stock company was formed to realize the new theory of association; and one gentleman, M. Baudet Dulary, member of parliament for the county of Seine and Oise, bought an estate, which cost him five hundred thousand francs (one hundred thousand dollars), for the express purpose of putting the theory into practice. Operations were actually commenced; but for want of sufficient capital to erect buildings and stock the farm, the whole operation was paralyzed; and notwithstanding the natural cause of cessation, the simple fact of stopping short, after having commenced operations, made a very unfavorable impression upon the public mind. Success is the only criterion with the indolent and indifferent, who do not take the trouble to reason on circumstances and accidental difficulties.

"Fourier was very much vexed at the precipitation of his partisans, who were too impatient to wait until sufficient means had been obtained. They argued, that the fact of having commenced operations would attract the attention of capitalists, and insure the necessary funds: he begged them to beware of precipitation; told them how he had been deceived himself in having to wait more than twenty years for a simple hearing, which, from the importance of his discovery, he had fully expected to obtain immediately. All his entreaties were in vain: they told him he had not obtained a hearing sooner because he was not accustomed to the duplicity of the world; and, confident in their own judgment, commenced without hesitation, and were taught, at the expense of their own imprudence, to appreciate more correctly the sluggish indifference of an ignorant public.

"Since that time, numerous partisans have been recruited among the learned and influential classes in France; many elementary works have been written on social science, and the epoch of a successful realization is probably near at hand; but Fourier himself has descended into the tomb, as a martyr to the skeptical indifference of the age in which he lived. Sent by Providence to deliver humanity from the bondage of duplicity, to discover the promised land of peace and happiness, and bid the suffering multitude to enter and be glad, his body, worn with years and exhausted with fatigue, yielded the spirit on the eve of success, that his soul might be crowned with a glory in heaven worthy of its more than terrestrial perseverance in the cause of truth and justice upon earth.

"In 1835 he published the first part of another volume, entitled 'False Industry.' There is little in this work which had not been given in his earlier publications, if we except the spirited criticisms which it contains on general duplicity. He was on the eve of publishing the second part, when he was cut short in his career by the unsparing hand of death. There remained but one chapter to write, which he was obliged to defer on account of the rapidly-declining state of his health. As those chapters which were written had been printed, he was asked, as an especial favor, to have a copy stitched before the work was complete. In compliance with this request, four copies were prepared in an incomplete state; and, as he did not live to finish the work, it is worthy of remark that the last words he wrote were—

"'Exegi monumentum ære perennius.'

"In the early part of 1837 he met with a very serious accident, from which he never thoroughly recovered. On returning home, rather later than usual, one dark night, he missed his footing on the staircase, and in falling down the stairs, his head was cut and bruised considerably. The wound was healed in the course of a few months, but he never recovered his health. His strength failed him, his features became totally changed, his stomach refused the functions of digestion, and his whole frame was evidently hurrying on to dissolution.

"Having no confidence in medical science, he constantly refused all medical aid. Though two of his intimate friends were physicians, he neglected their prescriptions, and confided in his own judgment. He had a particular dislike to being surrounded by servants and friends during his illness: accustomed to being alone, he preferred solitude to the tiresome assiduities of officious persons. He would not allow any one to attend him during his illness but the old woman who was in the habit of serving him on ordinary occasions. Many of his friends offered to sit up with him, and remain in the adjoining room, that he might not be disturbed by their presence, but he refused peremptorily. He would not even allow the nurse to remain with him after midnight. He must have been sensible to the last moment. On the eve of his death, he sent the servant to bed about twelve o'clock, requesting her to be up at five the next morning. When she went to see how he was at the appointed hour, she found him out of bed. He had had the energy to get up, and go to the night-table; and as he was making an effort to return, his spirit fled, and the dead body was left kneeling at the bed-side. He could not have been long dead, as his corpse was warm two hours afterward.

"His body was embalmed, his head and bust were moulded, and the conformation of his brain was minutely analyzed. He was buried on the 11th of October, in the cemetery of Montmartre; and on his tomb are engraved the three fundamental axioms of his doctrine:—

"1. 'La Serie distribue les Harmonies.'

"2. 'Les Attractions sont proportionnelles aux Destinees.'

"3. 'Analogie Universelle.'

"The third axiom is represented by mathematical symbols, instead of being expressed in words."*

Now this life, we conceive, is not the life of a quack, nor indeed of an ordinary man. Such life-long devotion to an object of inferior magnitude would indicate more than ordinary greatness. What shall we say of it, then, when we consider that it was devotion to the grandest and most sacred interests of man? Is an intellect which can thus slowly, painfully, patiently, evolve and elaborate its conclusions, to be despised? Is not the whole air and manner of the Man, the air and manner of one who looks earnestly into the facts of existence, and who wrestles sincerely to find the key of this mysterious and terrible life of suffering, and struggle, and despair, and darkness?

It does seem to us that no one can read the simple details of this life—so quiet, yet so intense—so scholar-like, yet so mingled with the sternest realities of every day—so impassive in its intellectual dignity and strength—so high in its moral aims—so rigid, direct, full of the consciousness of a mighty mission, but all the while so child-like, modest, without pretension or uneasiness—without feeling that it approaches the morally sublime. That lone man—friendless, companionless, poor—sitting there for forty years, in his scant garret, while the

* Doherty.

splendor and bustle of busy Paris rolled at his feet, working out his dark problem of the Destiny of Humanity on Earth, forging link by link in the chain of a complete science, as year after year came around, furnishes me with a conception of human grandeur and power, far more exalted than any that I ever derived from contemplating the debates of the Senate-house or the shock of armies. There, with his bread and water, while thousands of his fellow-mortals lay simmering and fretting in their petty cares, above even the fringes of lamplight that struggled upward through the dense cloud of dust and smoke of the great city, alone with Midnight and the Stars, with Thought and God!

As it is the object of this work to describe Fourier's principles, we shall not point out their peculiarities here, deeming it best to allow the reader to decide for himself; nor shall we dwell upon what we consider the defects of his method and of his discoveries, for there are plenty who would be right glad to do that, if they only knew what they were: but we must make a few remarks, in conclusion, upon the character of his writings and of his mind.

Fourier has left the impress of two periods of his life on his works: the first, of his earlier years, when his nature was lively and gay, and his head full of the glow of his fresh discoveries; the second, of his later years, when repeated disappointments and protracted neglect had soured his heart to many of the better phases of existing arrangements. The works undertaken under the former influence, flash and glitter with the exaggerated brilliancy which his exalted hopes lent to his warm imagination; those published during the second, teem with fierce and contemptuous denunciations, not of men, but of things, which show that he was poignantly alive to the stupid ridicule and more stupid indifference of the world. At no period, however, did he betray either the bitterness of selfishness or the meanness of personal malignity. He lived in his Great Thought, and with that alone he rose or sunk.

His books are by no means easy reading; not simply because their language is sometimes crabbed and harsh, for these traits are redeemed by a lucid directness and vigor of style, but because he has left numerous gaps and chasms in the train of his reasonings. He is like the Chamois guide, of which we somewhere read, who is perfectly familiar with the most inaccessible regions—so long as you are in his hands, you feel that you are held up and directed by a mighty arm, and you pass confidently along fearful precipices and over bottomless gulfs, knowing that your guide is there; but the moment you seek the way for yourself, your brains reel with amazement at the height to which you have reached, and the enormous abysses over which you have been carried. The glories unfolded on the journey, however, are a sufficient inducement to cause you to turn back to your place of departure, and to trace out the whole distance for your own delight and satisfaction.

As a thinker, he is equally remarkable for his critical and constructive faculties. Had he done no more than furnish the world with his exhausting analysis of the present relations of society, he would have been entitled to rank as one of its greatest men. His power of dissecting any method of business or social institution is so delicate, that he lays bare the minutest nerve and fibre, and yet it is so comprehensive, that it takes in the "thick rotundity of the earth;" nay, the complicated movements of the entire series of worlds in space. He is both microscopic and telescopic, permitting no object to escape his gaze, either small or large, and discerning the atom and the mountain with equal facility. It is for this reason that his criticism of existing society is so sharp, unsparing, and thoroughly unanswerable.

But his *constructive* power was much more remarkable than his *critical* power, because the sharpness and force of the latter were mostly derived from the former; we mean, that he had rare penetration in discovering the wrong, because he carried with him the touchstone of the right. Truth is your most biting and implacable critic. No man sees or feels so quickly or keenly even the slightest aberrations as he who possesses a universal standard of correctness. When Fourier, then, lashes with such vehement and caustic eloquence, the waste, the absurdity, the injustice, the iniquity of the present forms of society, we are to look for the cause of it in the fact, that he carried in his mind the mature conception of the right form. He had already worked out for himself, in all its details and in all its breadth, the structure of a perfect society. It is here, in the art of construction, of building up, that his mind shows itself in its noblest proportions. No poet, in the amplest circuit of his imaginings, has bodied forth such a magnificent ideal of the future life of Humanity on Earth as Fourier presents us, in rigid and mathematical outline, as the strict scientific development of his theory. He opens up to us views of Destiny, in the regular course of his moral reasoning, no less brilliant, grand, kindling, solemn, than those which colored the rapt vision of the stern but gorgeous old Hebrew prophets. And here let us observe, that it is for this reason that many of his more enthusiastic disciples think they will see, in the prevalence of his system, the realization of those bright Hopes of the Better Future, early ushered and long continued by the Seers of God, which have cheered the drooping heart of Humanity in her long pilgrimage through the valley and shadow of this living Death.

Fourier's Doctrine possesses a particular value to our minds because it seems to us to be Universal and consequently Reconciling and Pacific. It is both conservative and radical, Protestant and Catholic. It has resolved more difficulties for us, both in Politics and Religion, both as to the organization of the Church and the organization of the State, than any other doctrine that we have happened to fall in with in the works of uninspired man. We see by means of it, more of the bearings and tendencies of prevailing controversies, both in Church and State, than we ever did before, and we are better able to estimate, as well the excellences as the defects, of all creeds and parties. A brilliant light has been shed for us over many of the darkest and abstrusest questions that concern man's life on earth, in the Past, the Present, and the Future. Many too, are the secrets which it has revealed to us in Science—many the mysteries it has unlocked in Scripture. If, therefore, we were to attempt to assign Fourier his place among modern thinkers, we should cut him a niche higher than Bacon in Method, and higher than Newton in the importance of Discovery.

But this, we are aware, will appear to the uninitiated as an exaggeration, and we do not *now* insist upon his claims. One thing, however, we shall insist upon —that Fourier is at least one of the leading minds of the last century, destined to mould the thought and action of his fellows for some centuries to come. He has announced two truths, not to mention others, the bare announcement of which would have distinguished him, but the successful development of which has rendered him immortal. We refer, first, to the principle that *Industry can be so organized as to be rendered* ATTRACTIVE ; and second, to the momentous fact of the SOLIDARITY OF THE HUMAN RACE.* These truths, simple as they appear, are enough to give a turn and color to the destiny of the coming era.

By the former, Attractive and Organized Industry, the most inspiring and consolatory word that was ever spoken to them, has been spoken to the trodden and worn millions of the laboring classes, who in all ages and nations, and more in civilized nations than in others,† have cried to Man in vain for relief in the agonies of their distress. After centuries of hopeless degradation, of remedi-

---

* It is to be regretted that there is no word in English to answer to the uncouth French word. *Solidarité*, now coming into such use. For the meaning of it, metaphysically, we must refer to the works of the school of Fourier, to Mr. Leroux's *Humanité*, to the Abbe De Lamennais, and to some of Mr. Brownson's writings,—who as a metaphysician is superior to any man we know just now. The term expresses generally that the life of a man is not exlcusively the life of an individual, but a life which he possesses *jointly* with his race, that men live in *solido*, soldered together in one, if we may say so, that each man is an indivisible and indissoluble part of the life of all men, and all men are indivisible parts of each man. Fourier's writings imply what is meant by the term throughout all his speculations. St. Paul gives it in this shape,—" For as we have many members *in one body*, so we being many are one body in Christ, and *every one members one of another*." Rom. xii. 4, 5 ; also see in 1 Chron. xii. 12, Ephes. iv. 25, and other places. Those moralists and philosophers who hope to reform the world through *individuals alone*, may have their eyes opened by studying this subject of Solidarity. They will not, thereafter, seek to restore a dead body to life, by acting upon one of its limbs.

† See a pamphlet by the author on Constructive and Pacific Democracy, printed in this city.

less wrongs and sufferings, they have at last received the assurance that their destiny is not for ever to a debasing, monotonous, repugnant, ill-paid, painful, and disease-producing Toil; in filthy and pestilent shops; under cruel taskmasters; from night to morning, without relief or change; at cut-throat competition each man with his fellow; and all for a niggardly stipend, never enough to secure a man, much less his family, against sickness and old age, and always keeping him hovering in poignant anxiety on the brink of starvation and death. No: thank God, a way of escape has been found for the poor from the hovels of nastiness, the regions of darkness, in which they abide—a hand has been lifted to stay the wild deluge of ignorance, carelessness, and crime, which is sweeping their Manhood into Savagery and Brutedom. The fiat has gone forth that Industry—ever honorable, nay, noble and divine Industry,—must be organized, and already the Purveyor* to this glorious host of disciplined and valorous Workers and Doers has gone before to provide its food and habitations. Let a seven-fold chorus of rejoicing go up from the myriads whose emancipation is at hand.

By the second truth, to which we referred above, we learn, that each man of us is deeply and vitally concerned in the weal and wo of every other individual of the race. Never shall we obtain true happiness, never shall we gain true Liberty, until we shall have elevated all men to Happiness and Liberty. We are members one of another, parts of one great whole, living links in the great living organism of Humanity. The neighbor is most truly our brother,—nay, more than brother,—he is our other self; his crimes, our diseases; his sufferings, our curse. A nerve of the same Life runs through the whole human kind, and it can not be tormented in one, without sending its shock of pain to others, as the wounding of the remotest limb quivers throughout the frame. The pulse of moral life in society must beat irregularly, fitfully, feverishly, while the circulation is obstructed or vitiated in the least portion of its structure. Surely, those old dogmas of the Church heretofore so mysterious, relating to the *federal* headship of Adam, to the imputation of sin, to the Eucharist and communion of saints, may have a profound significance!

The superiority of this view of the relations of mankind is that it is the only one which affords a good ground for the conviction of perfectability in individuals and the race. It is a lamentably low and inadequate view which our preachers and moralists take of the whole subject of human improvement. Only reform the individual, they say, and you have reformed society! Most impotent and imperfect conclusion! Not to speak of the impossibility of reaching individuals at all, the utter hopelessness of giving a scientific and religious development to all the powers of the human soul, as society is now constituted, let us ask if mere *reform* is all we are to hope for, if there is to be no progressive refinement, no gradual perfecting and development of each sense and faculty? Conceive then, that you have reformed and perfected the individual, that his natural senses have received an increased sensitiveness and his moral perceptions, increased acuteness, and sensibility, both of which are implied in the word progress, and place him in the social medium in which he now is—why, you have only made him more miserable! The medium must be perfected along with him, to say the least, before you can more than begin his individual perfection.

To Fourier, therefore, we give our warmest gratitude for having, under God, taught us the true method of *Societary* Progress, including both social and individual advancement. He has been the instrument of discovering to us the true principles of social organization. It may be that we estimate him too highly in other respects; it may be that, misled by the enthusiasm of system-making, he has erred in his higher speculations, but the honor of being the first to propose the ORGANIZATION OF THE TOWNSHIP, on the basis of Human Nature and Christianity, is his forever. He has introduced a new Truth to the human race; he has given a new direction to human thought; he has turned the current of human opinions; he has evoked the spirit of a new era; in short, he is what his French name indicates, FOURIER—THE HARBINGER.

* Fourier's name in French means a *Harbinger*; also a *Purveyor*, or Quarter-Master to an army

BOOK SECOND.

GENERAL PRINCIPLES.

CHAPTER III.

OF GOD AND OF EVIL.

Q. For what were you created?
A. To know God, to love him and to serve him, and thereby obtain eternal life.—CATECHISM.

IT is not presumptuous in Man to inquire into the character of God, nor to ask what He requires of Man and in what mode He governs his creations. On the other hand, it is one of the highest duties of the creature to find out the ways of his Creator, that he may have the true and proper grounds for worship and love. If we have faith in Him, we shall be certain, by sounding his decrees, to admire his wisdom and goodness the more we are familiar with his operations. Timidity in this respect would indicate that we either distrusted Providence, or our own Reason, which is the image of God.

This reason teaches us, that if we have duties to fulfil towards God, he has duties to fulfil towards us, or in other words, that he would not have conferred existence upon any being for evil, inasmuch as he is infinitely intelligent and merciful. It is no hardihood, therefore, to inquire how far the works of the Deity bear the impress of these essential attributes.

Infinite wisdom. Consequently the laws of God are immutable; for if they could be modified or deranged in their action under any circumstances, we could conceive that they would have been more wise if they had foreseen and resolved these particular cases of exception. They must produce the greatest effect from the smallest means, or otherwise we could imagine the same results to be brought about by more simple, economical, and better methods. They must work together in perfect harmony, and for a single end, lest otherwise there should be contradiction, and loss of power through the effect of opposing forces.

Infinite Goodness. Consequently, every law or force of nature must tend to the greatest good of the whole Universe. We can only conceive of creation, then, as governed by laws, at once unchangeable and essentially good, for all ranks of creatures.

But here the first objection arises: Evil exists! How can you reconcile Evil with the paternal character of Deity?

This difficulty, never resolved or only half-resolved, has led men to doubt and scepticism, and produced those unfortunate atheists and infidels that are "without God and without Hope in the world."

At the first blush of the question it would seem as though we had undertaken to defend a contradiction or sustain a paradox; we are to show that Evil can exist in a kingdom governed by laws which only bring forth Good! Yet the reply is at hand, the solution is simple, since it suffices to observe a fact which takes place every day under our own eyes.

An engineer has constructed a machine wisely contrived for the production of its results. But an ignorant person, not understanding the mechanism of the machine, very foolishly charges himself with its management. Now, if he can not use it rightly, if he gets embarrassed in the wheelwork, if he wounds himself, if he kills himself, do you hold the Engineer responsible for the accident?

Is it possible to construct a machine, working well when rightly managed, which would not give bad results, when mismanaged?

Does not this impossibility exist for God himself, the great Engineer of the Universe?

He has made all things for good, but we must study the mechanism of his admirable work, before it can be used.

If man, refusing to make use of the Intellect with which he has been endowed, comes in conflict with the various forces of creation and is wounded in the conflict, the fault is entirely his own. For he may understand, if he will but only observe, and when he shall understand, will cease to suffer. Evil is ignorance. With the advent of Science it disappears.

Thus, a natural law presides over the movement of Heat, in the combustion of bodies. This law is altogether favorable to Man, who profits by it in a hundred ways, in his houses and in his shops, to supply his domestic wants, and to aid in his industrial labors. Yet, at the outset, the first person who came in contact with a burning body, was burned, and in his suffering cursed the new element, because he was ignorant of the art of controlling it, and of transforming it into a faithful servant.

It is necessary to understand that the moral world is directed by laws as positive as the laws of the material world. Thus, social movement takes place, because there are impulses in the heart of man, and the law of social movement, a consequence of those impulses, emanates directly from God, who has made man just what he is.

The inclinations of man, like natural forces, can produce good only in so far as they act in their fitting sphere. Out of that sphere, those inclinations are as destructive as the fire employed out of the legitimate bounds indicated by Science. To attempt to modify those inclinations because they produce evil, is to resist a natural law and strive after an impossibility. To urge man to suppress them, is to renounce the use of fire, because it may be the cause of disasters. No; the duty of man is to study his inclinations in order to arrive at a social form in which they will yield good results. This social form is what the Deity had in view when he made Man; for we can not admit that God, in making man, acted at random, and gave him inclinations and faculties of which he did not foresee the use. Still less can we admit that God has purposely organized Man for evil, by giving him inclinations that can not be applied to Good.

But might not God have prevented Evil in an absolute manner? Was it not required by his goodness, to reveal to Man, from the beginning, all those sciences which might have conducted him to Happiness, without the intermediate experience of pain?

Let us remark, first, that all human sciences are connected and must advance in parallel lines, and that if one of them precede the other beyond a certain limit, that excess will be without utility. Thus if God had revealed to man the art of Association, and had not given him the secrets of Nature which industry employs to create wealth, it would have been of no use to him, for Harmony can not exist without riches and luxury.

In order to prevent evil, God would have been compelled to reveal to Man all the sciences, and even with these sciences Man would have been obliged to pass through a period of suffering more or less long, to fabricate the instruments, buildings, &c., that were necessary to him; otherwise God would have had to make all these instruments, and commit them to man, and teach him the use of them. Having done thus much, and given us all that we strictly needed to keep us from suffering, it would have been pretended that he would have done better still, if he had discovered to us a greater number of things, to assure us a still greater happiness.

Thus the objection followed out into all its consequences, amounts to this:

Why has not God taught us all things, why has he not created us in the very plenitude of wealth, knowledge, and happiness? Let us see.

What we thus ask for ourselves, God has done for other creatures, yet they are far from being privileged beings.

These creatures, which know at birth nearly all they ever know—which have no collective infancy—who receive directly from God all the knowledge of which they stand in need—who advance, in their sphere, without ever deceiving themselves—furnished by nature with the instruments which are necessary to them, instructed by her to make a perfect use of them—these creatures are living around us in the form of animals, and especially such animals as the bee, beaver, &c., which live in society.

Thus, what God is reproached for not having done for Man, would have reduced man to the condition of an animal. If man knew all things at birth—if he could not err—he would have but one guide, *instinct*; but he would not have Reason, which in such a case would be useless! There would be nothing to be learned by him; nothing to be inferred; nothing to be decided: and why then should God, who is an economist of means, endow us with a faculty that would have no object? Men, then, would be happy as animals are, living under the most favorable circumstances, and their generations would pass away in a state of enjoyment always uniform, and always equal, but without either progress or decline.

But is such a happiness comparable to that to which Man lays claim, because he is, *in the image of God*, endued with Reason?

The labors of his mind, repaid by the satisfaction of his self-love and the consciousness of his worth; the varied enjoyments derived from differences of character; the desire of triumph, which in the future will be a noble emulation; that love of glory, which, during subversive epochs, he does not hesitate to gratify, by toils the most foreign to his nature, by war, carnage, and devastation; all these enjoyments, and a thousand others to be ascribed to Reason, he would no longer possess.

Surely, if Men were to select between a mediocre happiness, indefinitely uniform, and a high, varied, intense happiness, though bought at the price of some pain, they could not hesitate in the choice. Man is, therefore, a privileged being, in being obliged to labor for himself to render himself happy.

And, again, should any one ask for Man the possession of a Reason having the infallibility of instinct, let him reflect upon the differences of the two faculties, and he will see that he desires an impossibility. Or, if it be said that the epochs of ignorance and misery on earth have been very long in duration, we reply, that the word *duration* is relative, so that if the periods of rectitude are prolonged in proportion, Man, whose felicity depends upon the relation of the two periods, will still have abundant cause to felicitate himself, and render devout thanks to his Maker.

Three principles are embraced in this brief argument, which play an important part in Fourier's theory, and which, we think, throw a vivid light on questions relating to our social destiny and the nature of evil.

1st. *The law of exception.*—As a result of his investigations into all the branches of universal action and reaction, Fourier announces that they are all subjected to a law of exception, that may be generally estimated at *one-eighth*. By this he means, that when a positive law or proceeding is affirmed of any branch of movement, he wishes to be understood that an exception of one-eighth is always implied. In the social sphere, for instance, when he says that all the individuals of civilization are very miserable, it is intended to express that seven-eighths are in a state of great suffering, while only one-eighth are in a condition to be envied. The law of exception, however, is not invariably limited to one-eighth or one-ninth part, but varies from one-third to one-hundredth, and in some cases to one-thousandth part; but one-eighth part is the general proportion of exception.

Fourier's practical inference from this law of exception is, that if philosophers had applied it to the progressive transformations of society, they would have seen that its state of discord was only an exception to its general destiny, and that consequently social evil would only exist during the period of its infancy, while gathering the materials for its future growth and manhood. They would have discovered that Evil is not the eternal lot of mankind, but an accidental deviation from a general rule, which is Harmony and Happiness.

2d. *Theory of Transitions.*—Connected with this law, almost identical with it, is what is termed the theory of transitions. It is a principle of Fourier that there are no breaks in the chain of universal movement—no sudden leaps or voids—but that Nature everywhere observes regular and successive degrees or gradations of development. He supposes that everything in the Universe is a SERIES, which follows a regular scale of ascending and descending movement, which may be illustrated by the following simple formula of the life of a man:

Ascending Transition,	or	Birth.
First Phasis,	or	Infancy.
Second Phasis,	or	Youth.
Apogee,	or	Maturity.
Third Phasis,	or	Decline.
Fourth Phasis,	or	Decrepitude.
Descending Transition,	or	Death.

It will be seen that the *Transitions* here are placed at the extremes of the series, and being the mere beginning and ending of that Organic Movement called Life, differ from the usual course of its action, and are consequently periods of suffering, because, as happiness and harmony are connected with its regular organic action, they can not be connected with a state which is the opposite. Now this is equally true of all Series, of the life of Humanity on Earth, of the career of the Planet, of the declining of the Solar system; in short, of all manifestations of existence. Transitions are the links which connect one series with another, in all departments of universal movement. They are the ties between one general law and another, that preserve the unity of all in the midst of variety. Twilight, for instance, is a transitional state between day and night; amphibious animals are exceptionably organized, and form a link between fish and quadrupeds: the polypus is a link between the animal and vegetable; the bat, between birds and mice; the nervous fluid is a transitional element between soul and body; the quince forms a link between the apple and pear; birth is a transition from embryo life to atmospheric; and many other things belong to the transitional classes, which have never been explored methodically by our men of science. Transitions also exist in passions and characters, enabling us to connect different bodies of people into a whole.

These transitions are placed between two orders of existence, partaking of the features of both, without being either; thus giving unity to the countless variety in the forms and proceedings of Creation.

It is a singular fact that the larger number of these transitions are disagreeable, either physically ugly or morally painful.

Applying these principles, then, to social movement, we are led to believe that the career of Humanity is subject to Transitions, and that the periods of its sufferings are the links in the chain of its progress to organic harmony. It is clear, from the testimony of the geologist, as well as from other sources of evidence, that Man has not been upon the earth more than six or seven thousand years; so that the race may still be in the very infancy of its existence, and have before it a long future of happiness.

3d. *Duality of Movement.*—This is the phrase which Fourier has chosen to express the two-fold or two-sided development of which everything in the universe is susceptible. A machine perfectly constructed will either go right or go wrong: if the former, it produces harmony, and if the latter, duplicity, which is the counterpart or obverse of Harmony. An organism of any kind, from the very nature of it as an organism, must have a *true* action and a *false* action.

The consequences of the true action must be Harmony,—as health, in a vigorous and wholesome body, is the harmony of all its members; while the consequences of false action must be, just as inevitably, disease, discord, suffering, duplicity.

Now, Fourier says that human passions or impulses, the springs of action, are subject to this Duality: they have a right development and a perverted development; they are either harmonic or subversive. Consequently, we infer that hatred, jealousy, selfishness, are but the inversion of qualities that are capable of an opposite direction: *i. e.*, to love, generosity, and benevolence. In a right social medium, therefore, the very impulses which now lead to the most frightful and disastrous crimes, are those which would confer the most of general benefit; and the old adage, that extremes meet, is in one sense true.

For the social movement partakes of this Dual character, and its states of suffering and general depravity proceed from the false or subversive action of the social mechanism. This subversive action, however, being only exceptional and transitional, as we have seen above, taking place at the beginning and the ending of the series, we have a right to infer that a long career of social harmony must succeed its present state of incoherence and false development. In the following chapter, we shall undertake to give an illustration of the three principles thus described, or rather of one principle, with a threefold aspect, by showing the progress of society in the Past, and its probable transformations in the Future.

CHAPTER IV.

GENERAL FORMULA OF SOCIAL MOVEMENT.

"Many of the celestial bodies have disappeared, others present unequivocal evidences of decrepitude, while others again are increasing in magnitude and splendor."—ARAGO.

THE present form of society, not being the first form in which Humanity has existed upon the earth, is not likely to be the last, and it is therefore worth while to inquire into the history of the forms that have preceded it, and deduce from this, if we can, some probable opinions of the nature of the changes that may follow.

Everything that exists—vegetables, animals, man, the globe, the constellations—are subjected to a general law of life and death. Nearly forty years ago, Fourier announced this law as a universal law, and it has since been confirmed by the researches of modern astronomers, who tell us that the stars, like other existences, are the subjects of birth and decay. Indeed, it would be wonderful if it were not so, since we can not conceive how there could be creation without destruction, birth without death, or life without both birth and death.

Whatever may be the nature of a being, and with whatever forces it may be endowed, vegetable or animal, its vital power varies incessantly; it has a beginning, and if it be in the process of growth, it attains a term which it can not pass, it then gradually decreases, and is at last of necessity brought to an end.

Now, if we consider the Universe as a great Whole, we shall see that the amount of increase in beings which goes to augment the vital power, must balance the amount of decrease in those which are in the process of diminution. Nothing springs from nothing; nothing returns to nothing; the great Whole, finite or infinite, neither augments nor diminishes; the amount of universal force, like the amount of universal matter, remains constant. This force, individualized in myriads of different Beings, increases with some, decreases with others. Youth takes, old age restores; birth balances death; death permits of birth; birth and death are only extreme transitions from one existence to another existence.

Each living being incessantly changes its form and condition; it follows, departing from the period of birth, an *ascending* movement, which is relaxed as it approaches its apogee or plenitude; then, after a time of equilibrium, which corresponds to the *maximum* of its faculties, begins a *descent*, symmetrically opposed to its ascending movement, till it falls into decrepitude, and finally death. Thus, the greatest amount of forces is found in the middle of its career, which diminishes insensibly on each side till it becomes *null* in birth and death.

This regular and normal law, in all-developments, may be expressed in a general formula: for instance,

Ascending Transition,	or	Birth.
First Phase,	or	INFANCY.
Second Phase,	or	YOUTH.
Apogee and Plenitude,	or	MATURITY.
Third Phase,	or	DECLINE.
Fourth Phase,	or	DECREPITUDE.
Descending Transition,	or	*Death.*

Note that this table is not arranged by caprice; the swelling of the white intermediate surface, appropriately represents to the eyes the nature of that regular development which it characterizes.

The generality of this law is by no means altered, as we readily perceive, by diseases, accidents, *exceptions*, which cause a premature death.

If we apply to the social career of Humanity these principles, demonstrated by reason and proved by universal experience, we shall see that this career can not be indefinitely and incessantly progressive, as many suppose, contrary to the more vulgar faith; but that, as the telescope shows that the Suns are born and die, so this planet will die, and the Humanity which belongs to it will share its fate.

The globe is confided to Humanity as a domain, over the administration of which it is set. This is its terrestrial destiny.

But it can not accomplish this administration during its infancy, for we can readily conceive how it must acquire virility and force to be equal to such a task; how it must create instruments, the means of power, which can only come as a consequence of the development of arts, sciences, and industry.

Then, during its infancy, its first stages of weakness, Humanity is not in its true destiny; it can not then have *combination* of individuals, nations, or races; and man, *out of his destiny*, can not find happiness in the incoherence of his first societies. It is during the continuance of these first societies, designated by Fourier as *lymbic* or *subversive*, that the Earth is truly "a valley of tears and suffering."

It is not difficult to imagine a thousand circumstances that may either accelerate or retard the ascending movement. A discovery in the arts, or in the sciences, may quicken, as a war or catastrophe may delay or ruin, the most advanced people: for the same reason that a good or bad hygienic treatment of a child may help or prevent its growth.

But Humanity, when it has undergone its successive initiations, and passed through its painful epochs, attains its true and normal state, which must be, from the necessity of the case, a state of healthful and harmonious action. Yet it still follows the regular law of movement, which is ascensional, until the globe on which it is placed, having attained the plenitude of its life, comes gradually to lose its productive and vegetative forces. Then, the old age of the globe, and its impoverishment, draws with it a social decline,—very gentle, it is true, and insensible in respect to the life of a man—but none the less a decline, the destruction of Harmony, and a Fall into final incoherence and subversion. The human race, gradually losing its forces and its traditions, goes out, like an old Man stricken in years, from whom life departs after the departure, one by one, of all his faculties. This end is the beginning of a new order of existences, for the planet and for its Humanity.

Fourier, in order to illustrate this last idea, has published a conjectural table of the life of Humanity on this Earth, which is too long to be inserted here, but which may be consulted with advantage.

The extreme phases, the ages of weakness and suffering, are for Humanity as well as for other beings, of a short duration, compared with the true and harmonic epochs. They form an exception to the rule, and are reckoned by Fourier at one-eighth for our planet.

The four principal ages, and the Apogee of social movement, are differenced by successive characters.

This law is conformed, in all respects, to universal analogy and to pure reason; it is verified by the highest data of zoology, astronomy, and the natural sciences, as well as by history; by the traditions of Nature, no less than by the traditions of Man.

The four great phases are divided each, into a certain number of periods or particular societies. The phase of Infancy comprises seven, of which Civilization is the fifth, as follows :—

First Phase of Movement.		Five Periods organized into isolated households.	
	1st. Edenism,		Twilight of happiness.
	2d. Savageism,		
	3d. Patriarchalism,		Ages of perfidy,
	4th. Barbarism,		injustice, constraint,
	5th. Civilization,		indigence, revolutions,
	6th. Guarantyism,		and corporeal weakness.
	7th. SIMPLE ASSOCIATION,		Aurora of Happiness.

All the societies which have been, or still are upon the Earth, are related to some of the first five types, having their peculiar spirit and customs, in a greater or less degree. Incoherence, which is the prevailing character of Social Infancy, not allowing the law of movement a regular application, often forms *mixed* societies, which amalgamate characters, belonging really to different periods.

These exceptional cases are particularly found, while different societies exist simultaneously upon the globe, before they have been resolved, by a general fusion, into one great human Unity.

Let us give a brief examination of these first periods of Infancy.

§ I. *First Period, or Edenism.*

The state of Science at this day, no longer admits a doubt, that the creations of the three Kingdoms of Nature, were made at successive epochs, more or less distant. Man arrived on the Earth, and in fact could only arrive, after the mineral, vegetable, and animal creations, which compose the first furniture of his domain.

The human race, placed in the temperate zones, found an abundance of the best vegetables and animals. In the midst of this wealth, which Nature furnished them, as a fruitful and provident nurse, they formed a primitive Society, the remembrances of which are preserved among all the people of the temperate latitudes, under the names of, The Age of Gold, Paradise Lost, The Garden of Eden, &c., &c.

In this period, individual property in the soil did not exist, love was not restrained by conventional laws and prejudices, and the superabundance of wealth, above all wants, prevented contests of interest, and introduced mildness of manners. Oppression and war were unknown, and all the members of society, men, women, and children, lived in the greatest independence, exempt from pain and care. That such must have been the character of this period, we may infer even from the accounts which very many travellers have given us of the innocence, freedom, and general happiness of the inhabitants of the more genial and prolific latitudes. In this period, men enjoyed happiness : but it was a happiness not of a refined and intense kind. It was derived principally from the tranquil enjoyment of the senses, unaided by the delights of intelligence.

Those who think that the first men lived a wandering and isolated life in the woods, can not have reflected that under such circumstances the race must inevitably have perished.

The first period has a limit, since it is necessary that Man should acquire force and power. When milk ceases to be agreeable to the child, when its growing wants demand a more substantial nourishment, a painful crisis, DENTITION or Teething, furnishes it with the *instruments* for grinding and assimilating the stronger kinds of food. In the same way, the creation of the instruments of power and force is a painful crisis for Humanity; for the production of Science, Art, and Industry, is effected during the incoherent periods which can produce neither happiness nor harmony, since their mission is to create that industry and those sciences, which are the means and materials of Harmony.

Many natural causes brought about a rupture of the first society, the principal of which was the increase of population, which gradually reduced the primitive abundance and changed it into scarcity. So soon as that result was felt, the harmonious tie was broken, the feeling of individual selfishness began to control men, and the Primitive Association was dissolved!

(Here we have the great social fact which Moses has impressed upon his *Sepher*. *Eve*, the Will of Man, corrupted by the *Serpent*, an emblem of cunning, cupidity, and selfishness, seduces *Adam*, the universal Man. The *tree*, covered with fruits, symbol of material wealth, is the determining cause; and the Serpent is the potential cause of the Introduction of Evil.

The tree, which was the source of life, was also the source of good and evil. It was only by eating of its fruits that man lost his primitive ignorance, and that he will begin, through a life of sorrows, to learn, to know, to discover.

After the *Fall*, Adam, the Universal man, driven from Paradise, was deprived of the blessings of the first society, the elements of which are dissolved at his death. The *death* of Adam, the Universal Man, is the dissolution of the primitive humanitary Unity, and different people cover the earth under the name of his children. Humanity is no longer one Man, but many Men.

Man is condemned *to earn his bread in the sweat of his brow*, until the time of his social redemption, when *the head of the serpent* will be bruised by the annihilation of selfishness. The seed of the woman, or the volitive faculty of Man, restored to its true passional destiny, will bruise the head of the Serpent under its feet.*)

But whatever we may make of the cosmogony and symbols of Moses, it is certain that a state of Harmony among men is not consistent with a state of poverty. The former can only be maintained in the midst of an abundance of wealth. Thus, when penury and want began to make themselves felt among the primitive people, selfishness and individuality arose; society was dissolved; and only the affection which is necessary for the preservation of the species, Family Affection, survived the shipwreck of all other affections, to become the narrow and exclusive basis of subsequent societies.

§ II. *Second Period, or Savageism.*

The invasion of ferocious beasts, and the necessity of seeking subsistence in the chase, caused the invention of arms, which, now that Harmony was destroyed and the system of separate and incoherent households instituted, were soon employed by men in despoiling each other. War begun; and families uniting to increase their power of resistance, the Horde was formed.

Industry was then confined to the chase, to fishing, and to the fabrication of arms. Woman was reduced to servitude; men enjoyed a complete independence; and all took part in the councils of the Horde, and deliberated on questions of peace or war. Each man fully enjoyed many of the natural rights of Man, which are all more or less invaded in our civilized societies. They were these:—

---

* See the proofs of these news in the interesting work of Just Muiron, called, "*Les Transactions, religieuses et sociale de Virtomious,*" and in the *Hebrew Grammar*, and *Translation of the Sepher* by **Fabre** d'Olivet, both in French.

1st. Harvest,—or the right to gather the fruits of the fields and forests.
2d. Pasture, or the right to feed his cattle where he pleases.
3d. The Chase, or the right to take wild animals.
4th. Fishery, or the right to fish in all streams.
5th. Internal Federation, for mutual defence.
6th. External Appropriation of the goods of other hordes.
7th. Freedom from depressing anxiety as to the future.

These are evidently the rights which Nature concedes to Man, and which are more or less preserved by every horde of savages; they belong to all, and are a consequence of the fact that the earth belongs to the human race. The savage enjoys personal and corporal liberty to its fullest extent; he has the right to fish, to hunt, to gather the wild fruits, and to pasture his cattle where he pleases; he is protected by his fellows from the incursions of his neighbors; and he is exempted from anxiety in general, as to his future lot and that of his family. In many respects, therefore, his condition is to be preferred to that of the civilized laborer, whose natural rights are taken away from him, without the return of a guarantee of the right to labor, which is their equivalent. For this reason, several authors, at the head of whom stands Rousseau, have pretended to admire this form of social existence, and have advised a return to it from the present false and artificial customs of civilization. But, as great as may be the personal freedom of the savage, his state is not one that is to be on the whole desired. Its leading characteristic is an aversion to industry, without which Man is a degraded, ignorant, and undeveloped being. His mind is stricken with a stupid inactivity; the higher faculties of his nature slumber; he comprehends little of the glory and magnificence of the universe of which he forms a part, and a knowledge of which is absolutely necessary to his elevation in the scale of existence. If to this we add that the warfare of savage tribes is frequent, relentless, and cruel, that the condition of woman is that of the brute, and that the weak and infirm are not always secure against oppression, we shall see that it is among the least happy and harmonious of social states.

§ III. *Third Period, or Patriarchalism.*

"This form of society, circumscribed to a very few countries, is without importance or influence among the nations of the earth. The first step, however, in social progress, takes place in this period: industry begins to be developed; flocks are reared; a few branches of manufactures are undertaken, and some other of the elements of society are called into existence. Man becomes attached to the soil, and commences its cultivation; he looks to his own industry for subsistence, and does not trust to the precarious modes of savage life alone—hunting and fishing.

Some authors have praised Patriarchal life for its simplicity and virtue. With less ferocity than the savage state, but with more perfidiousness and petty tyranny, it is on a small scale as oppressive and as false a society as any other.

"It could be proved beyond denial," observes Fourier, "that all the abuses of governments are but imitations on an extended scale of those of the Domestic system, of that government, which, under the name of Patriarchal, superficial minds extol without having analyzed.

"Facts without number show that with a population in their infancy, in a savage and barbarian state, the father, or the head of the family, is a cruel and insolent despot. His wife is his slave, his children are his servants. While this king sleeps or smokes his pipe, his wife and his daughters perform all the household work, and even that of the fields, as far as it is pursued in that state of society. The boys when grown up, ill-treat and abuse them, and are waited upon in turn like their fathers."

It is a false one-sided system of society, as far from happiness and purity as any other, though it has its own peculiar advantages in rustic simplicity.

§ IV. *Fourth Period, or Barbarism.*

A rapid stride in social progress characterizes the third or barbarian period. Industry receives an important, and in some respects a brilliant development:

agriculture and manufactures become the occupation of the mass, and the arts and sciences are called into existence. Man commences in the outward or material world a manifestation of his higher faculties, and stamps upon nature the impress of his intelligence. We have only to examine the perfection to which art and industry were carried under the Caliphs of Bagdad, and the Moors in Spain, to comprehend how immensely superior in development is this society to the Savage and Patriarchal, and how closely allied it is to what we now call falsely, civilization. This period must consequently be considered as an important social progress, although accomplished at the expense of the liberty of the mass, and accompanied by the most oppressive tyranny—the corporeal slavery of the producing classes.

War, the main occupation of savage hordes, still remains the leading interest of barbarian rulers. The necessity of defence against the attacks of neighboring powers, or the enticement to invasions for the purpose of conquest or plunder, concentrates all political authority and power in the sword. War in this period is the all-absorbing object of human activity. Military despotism wielded by a single chief, who sways alone the destinies of millions, replaces the patriarchal and individual tyranny of the second period, and the action of the savage horde.

The injustice of the barbarian system is revolting, because it is open, direct, and based upon brutal force:—the injustice of false civilization is glossed over by an appearance of equity and justice; but the same enormous iniquity characterizes both societies. The producing multitude toil and drudge to create the means of sustaining in ease and idleness a favored minority.

"The pivotal character of the barbarian mechanism," observes Fourier,—"the character which distinguishes it from false industrial civilization—is simplism of action, the action of the civilized system being always compound. A Pacha levies a tax because it pleases him to extort and pillage; he does not search in the constitution of Greece and Rome for theories of right and duty: he merely informs you, that if you do not pay, you will lose your head. The Pacha employs consequently but one single means: violence or simple action.

A civilized monarch makes use of the double means: first of bailiffs, fines, and prisons, which are the true pillars of civilized law; to which are added moral subtilties on the sacred duty of paying taxes for the maintenance of the constitution and the enjoyment of our imprescriptible rights. They are levied, because the representatives of the people have voted them; it is consequently the people themselves who wish to pay. The mode of operation is here double; it is based upon two heterogeneous principles—violence and cunning. In the barbarian system the mode of operation is simple, being founded upon violence alone. This fundamental difference is found in all the operations of the two societies; both arrive at the same result; but civilization adds cunning to violence. The wily caution of the Tiger in addition to its power. The Lion and the Fox united.

We will enumerate a few of the permanent characters of the barbarian period, in contrast with those of civilization:—

1. Stationary Spirit.
2. Fatalism.
3. Prompt Justice.
4. Simple Monopoly.
   Simple Action.
5. Simple Dignity of Man.
6. Frank Action of the Passions.
7. Fanatical Theocracy.
8. Faith in Immortality.
   Direction by Instinct.

"How has it happened that men of science have given us no analysis of the three societies which precede Civilization, and which embrace so large a majority of the human race? Had they made such an analysis, it would have shown the turpitude, hypocrisy, and perversity of False Civilization, characters, which, more disguised than in the anterior social periods, are not the less real.

"Another leading character of Barbarianism is the enslaved condition o women. If Barbarians were to give liberty to women, throw open their seraglios and adopt our system of exclusive marriage, they would become civilized by this single innovation. If, on the other hand, industrial nations were to adopt the sale of women, their seclusion in seraglios, they would in time become barbarians."

A study of the characters which civilization has borrowed from the three other societies, such, for example, as—

The military code from the Barbarian nation;
The privilege of primogeniture, from the Patriarchal tribe;
The abandonment of the weak and feeble, from the savage horde;

Would have been important, as it would have led the scientific world to perceive that all four systems are links in a series of subversive societies, all of which are deviations of man from his social destiny.

§ V. *Fifth Period, or Civilization.*

In this society man accomplishes the task of his social infancy, the development of the elements of Industry, Art, and Science. which are necessary to the founding of Association. Their partial development takes place in Barbarian society, not only without the protection and encouragement of the political power, but in spite of the fluctuations and embarrassments caused by the wars in which that period is constantly engaged. Although this state of things continues more or less during the first ages of civilization, still Civilization is the true nurse of Industry. The two or three past centuries, particularly the present one, have wonderfully developed the positive sciences, and given all a rank which they never before held. Agriculture has been improved by a more scientific mode of cultivation, and by the introduction of more perfect implements; manufactures have received an immense extension; new branches have been discovered, and the genius of man has been actively employed in the invention of machinery, which, next to the spontaneous productiveness of the soil, is the greatest source of riches.

Experimental chemistry, one of the most important conquests of human intelligence in the material world, has also been called into existence, and is now assuming a high rank as the intellectual assistant of Industry. But with the present system of incoherent action and free competition, this noble science is often made the mere instrument of industrial and commercial fraud; for with the improvements in chemistry there has been a corresponding refinement in adulteration and deception in manufactures. This proves that false civilization, which opposes no checks to individual cupidity, turns the best of things to the worst of purposes. A second important achievement of the present age is the successful use and application of steam. It is an agent which has given man a new and mighty power, and which has become of the highest importance in navigation, manufactures, and internal communications: but more important application of the powers of nature remain still to be discovered.

To comprehend fully the progress which has been made, we must embrace at one view the two extremes; we must view man in the savage state, destitute upon the earth, without having taken one step toward its cultivation and improvement, or toward the development of industry; and then view him in the most advanced civilized nations; view the wonders in art and industry with which he has surrounded himself and we shall feel that an immense conquest has been made, and that a great preparatory labor has been accomplished.

In the first ages of false civilization, war is the leading occupation of society; in latter ages, commerce and industry take its place. In the first period the soil is held by military chiefs and feudal lords, and the laboring multitude are the slaves or serfs. Renown belongs to military exploits; honors and rewards to military services; history is a mere recital of violence and oppression, conquest, and spoliation. During this social chaos, industry receives a slow and gradual development, which is owing almost entirely to individual effort. It struggles against the oppression of the military power, and attains by slow degrees a permanent existence, and an influence in society. Its products become so important to the man of war himself, to enterprise and comfort, that he is forced gradually to respect it. The industrial or laboring classes increase in strength and intelligence, until they finally assume a position which enables them to demand and force a concession of their rights. A social transformation then commences, which increases until society completely changes its character, and becomes entirely commercial and industrial in its spirit.

If we pass rapidly over the period, during which this transformation takes place—bearing in mind how exclusively war and its interests once absorbed the attention of men—and then examine the present, in which commerce and its interests are the all-pervading objects of attention, we shall be struck with the extent of the change. The aristocracy of birth has given place to the aristocracy of wealth, and become a mere shadow in those countries where it has lost its possessions. The feudal baron with his dependants, who owe him allegiance, is replaced by the banker or capitalist, who is surrounded indirectly with a train equally dependant and servile. This is particularly the case in France and the United States of America.

If the pride and power of the baron were in his birth, his titles, and armorial bearings, the pride and the power of the man of our day are in his wealth and financial influence. If the skill of the former shone forth in military exploits, the skill of the latter is displayed in commercial and financial operations. Thus the spirit of society has changed from the military to the purely commercial and industrial. The feuds of powerful families, the exploits of war, glory, honors, no longer occupy the same importance with the heralds of publicity. The balance of trade, the state of exchange, commercial prosperity, and false credit, have taken their place, and become the great objects of public interest. Where commerce has not superseded birth and title, it has made itself their equal in wealth and influence.

The present epoch of civilization, then, has greatly developed the material elements of society, which are

Agriculture,   Education,
Manufactures,   Commerce,
Arts,   Navigation,
Sciences,   Internal Communications,

but it has not regulated and associated these elements, and established order and unity in their action. As civilization rests upon an infinite variety of isolated interests, conflicts and opposition exist in industry, as they exist in the political world. Strife is transported to this new field; for what else can we call the speculations, monopolies, and commercial and financial excesses which characterize the present day, than a war of industry and all its elements. In such a state of things, there must be anarchy, disorder, waste of efforts, and conflicts of opposing interests; there must be a miserable application of all the great sources and means of production, such as labor, capital, and natural advantages. To suppose that such a system is the best that can be devised to facilitate production, is an outrage upon common sense; yet the question of a reorganization of industry, which is of primary importance to society, is entirely overlooked for matters of minor interest and delusive controversy."*

Thus far, the forms of society which we have noticed have been those which are past or present;—the next step brings us to the future.

§ VI. *Sixth Period, or Guaranteeism.*

We have shown, in the last section, how Industry has been developed by what we call Civilization, but under circumstances of great incoherence and strife. This incoherence finally produces its effects; we see them already in all the more advanced nations, in the commercial feudalism to which it has led. The accumulation of money in the hands of the few; the competition between workmen; the invention of machinery which dispenses with human labor: all now tend to separate society into two classes—the rich and the poor. The suffering and degradation of the laboring people, in all the older nations, and even in the United States, already surpass conception, and writers on all sides concur in the belief that something must be done to put an end to the frightful

* See London Phalanx, page 74.

effects of competition and antagonism. Singular to say, their plans partake of the characteristics described by Fourier, many years ago, as Guaranteeism.

By this Fourier meant a general system of mutual insurance or guarantee, in which the separate interests of different classes might be combined, so that each would be directly interested in the general welfare of every other,—the application to society at large of the principles already applied to private companies for insuring life, property, &c. The safety-fund system in banking, applied to the general political relations of men, would be one form of guaranteeism. The savings banks and co-operative societies of England, the joint-farms of the rural districts of France, the benevolent societies among trades, as the Odd Fellows in this country, etc., are partial examples of the tendency of men at this day to escape from the uncertainty of existing civilization, and lay up for themselves a guarantee against disaster and fraud. Many of the professed Associations that are now forming, are only a method which certain individuals, feeling the pressure of social circumstances, have adopted, to secure, or, in other words, to guarantee themselves and families against misfortune and suffering.

The more general application of this principle would secure the most valuable results, especially to the laboring classes. It would protect them from the terrible effects of extreme competitive antagonism, tend materially to the augmentation of fortune, and diminish the fraud and injustice which is now the consequence of isolated interests. The more important feature of it, however, would be, that it would prepare many who are now unwilling to enter upon the higher degree of association, for that progressive step. But being of secondary importance, Guaranteeism may safely be left out of the account of the societary Reformer, who should labor for the direct introduction of what is strictly Association; as,

§ VII. *Simple Association;* or the complete association of domestic as well as industrial interests; but confined to distinct classes in society.

§ VIII. *Contrasted Association;* or the association of all classes or all interests, according to a graduated scale of inequality in rank and fortune.

These latter developments of the principle of association are the kind which it is the design of this book to describe.

Thus we have taken a bird's-eye glance at the various developments of history, to show the plans of Providence in educating man collectively for his ulterior destiny on earth. We have done so, not for the purpose of presenting a full view, for which we must refer to Fourier himself, but to enable us to deduce one or two conclusions that may be of service to the reader in the further perusal of our treatise.

1st. Each of these successive stages of society seems to have been ordained to prepare the materials of the form of society that immediately succeeded it, and, therefore, our present state of incoherent civilization, which accumulates Capital at the expense of Labor, is only accumulating it to be used hereafter by Labor in some better state.

2d. The progress of society, from one phase to another, has been distinguished particularly by these two marks: (1), the emancipation of woman to a condition of greater independence; (2), the elevation of laborers to a higher degree of knowledge and happiness. Whence we infer that the next steps in advance, from existing society, must be accompanied by the same characteristics, until Woman and the Laborer shall have attained their true position of Freedom, Independence, and Dignity.

3d. Societary growth is an approach from loose savage independence and individualism, through aggregations becoming more and more compact, to a state of more and more perfect organization. Thus, we ascend from the savage *Horde*, to the Patriarchal *Clan*, to the Barbaric *Nation*, to Civilization in an incoherent form, to Civilization in the form of Guaranteeism, or to Organic Association. No society that has yet existed has possessed a real organization; and since organization is the law of perfected existence, through the entire universe, we must look to the future for social periods of organic concentration and vitality.

BOOK THIRD.

UNITY OF MAN WITH HIMSELF.

CHAPTER V.

OF MAN, HIS FACULTIES AND DESIRES.

"We should learn to be cautious, lest we charge God foolishly, by ascribing that to Him, or the nature he has given us, which is owing wholly to our own abuse of it. Men may speak of the degeneracy and corruption of the world, according to the experience they have had of it; but Human Nature, considered as the Divine Workmanship, should, methinks, be treated as sacred; for in the image of God made he man."—BISHOP BUTLER.

THE truth that God, in organizing a being, foresees a useful employment for his powers and inclinations, is so clear, that it requires that whole atmosphere of prejudice which obscures the human intellect to prevent its being acknowledged *à priori.*

There must be, then, a social form possible, in which the impulses of Man will produce as much of good as they now produce of evil, in our present societies, so badly adapted to their play.

In the society to be discovered, Reason and Passion will be in perfect accord; duty and pleasure will have the same meaning; without inconvenience or calculation, man will follow his bent; hearing only of Attraction, he will never act from necessity and never curb himself by restraints; and, consequently, he will find a charm in all his functions.

Man, to accomplish his functions on Earth, must develop his physical and intellectual faculties by action or labor, to provide for the maintenance of his species and of his individual being. Is it not rational to suppose that the Deity, who is ONE, who has given Attraction as a guide to the animals, and who still employs attraction to lead man to many of the things which he ought to do, has not departed from so wise a law, to the detriment of our race, and in order to resort to coercive means to constrain us to labor?

Attraction is the general law. Written on the heart of all, it reveals perpetually and unitarily the Will of God; it acts at all times and in all places; and thus shows the constant solicitude of our Maker towards all his works. It impels each being on his way, it indicates to him his Destiny, and it remains for ever incompressible, in spite of prejudices and prescriptions, moral or legal.

In governing by Attraction, God was certain to be obeyed with gratitude and joyfulness If Humanity, in its earlier age, resists, through ignorance, this beneficent law, it is punished for its fault in the sufferings that spring from those injured attractions. It is a chastisement worthy of the greatness of God, who does not punish man, but allows him to punish himself, that he may find his pain a salutary admonition that he must return to Truth.

Now, Fourier promises to men a social system, in which Order will be produced by the free action of the passions. But let no one be so silly as to conclude from this that we ask men to abandon themselves to their inclinations in the actual condition of society. Constraint is indispensable in a false medium, liberty is foreign to it, and engenders when fully indulged only disorder and confusion. The reason of this will be seen in the sequel.

If there is a social form which is the best for man, it is evidently his highest duty and most pressing want to inquire what it is. Why has Humanity remained so long without finding it? Why has it never been sought?

Who, before Fourier, ever thought of a social system devised by God, and reserved for the discovery of Man! Those whose mission it has been to lead others, governors and politicians, wise men and philosophers, have all acted as if they supposed that God, having created man without any fixed plan, suddenly stopped, and left it to their wisdom to supply the deficiencies of His work. Everything in man, therefore, which deranges their arbitrary systems of law, they have pronounced bad. They proscribe his whole nature, as utterly depraved and corrupt. They attribute the evil to God, all the while making vain efforts to modify and correct human nature, in the hope of making it better than it came from the hands of its Creator.

Fourier alone has placed the question on its proper grounds. He alone has taken man for the *invariable term* of the social problem, and has alone found, because he has alone sought, the solution.

Seeking a social medium in perfect accord with the nature of Man, it was necessary for him to know strictly what Man and his passions were, and the inquiry into this fact, must precede all of our present investigations.

The Human Being is composed of three principles,

 1st. THE PASSIONS, *The Active or Moving Principle ;—Motor :*
 2d. THE BODY, *The Passive or Moved Principle ;—Movee :*
 3d. THE INTELLIGENCE, *The Neuter or Regulating Principle ;—Law.*

The body is moved according to laws dictated by the Intelligence or Mind, in obedience to the Will, whose springs of action must be in the Desires or Passions.

You write, for example ; that act can not be executed without the concurrence of your physical and intellectual faculties; but you write, not because you possess those faculties, but because you have some Desire to satisfy in writing. You write, perhaps in the hope of making yourself a name in literature or science, or to persuade your fellows to adopt some views which you think all-important to their welfare; and your body and mind are moved in obedience to your Ambition or your Benevolence. You write to the woman that you love, or to a friend whom you esteem, and your Love or Friendship is the passion which causes you to act.

Every free action of Man, every voluntary use of his body or intellect, is in the same way determined by some desire. This desire, whatever it may be called, either wish, impulse, affection, spring of action, &c., is what Fourier means by PASSION. The Soul, the Me, the Mover, manifesting itself thus only by its passions, may be regarded as their sum, or one grand Immortal Passion. If, therefore, we make an analysis of the Passions, we shall have analyzed the human soul, and shall know all about it which it is necessary to know, as to its application, as to its influence upon ourselves, upon others, and upon the medium in which we live.

Fourier thus gives to the word Passion, a new but well-defined sense, and he leaves no one in doubt as to what he means by Soul.

The meaning which he attaches to the word Passion must be kept in mind, throughout our whole controversy, because the objectors to Fourier's theory, on the ground of morals, have commonly substituted another meaning, as though they had a perfect right to do so, and then assailed Fourier for doctrines which were entirely of their own creation. Thus, when the Social school say, that by Passion they mean that which prompts men to act,—his Permanent Motives, many reply with the most imperturbable gravity, that there are in Man other motives beside the Passions!

The characters of men are so infinitely varied, that it would seem at first sight, as though there were too great a number of Passions to allow of the making of any satisfactory analysis. But colors present an illimitable number of shades; yet they all depend upon the seven primary colors of the prism. It is the same case with the passions, which may be reduced to a few elementary principles, which combined in different intensities, produce the whole infinite variety of character.

A. All the passions of Man are included in the Desire of Happiness, in the wish for a General Happiness in which the individual will take part.

This proposition will be in part contested, because we every day see Men seeking their own well-being, their own personal gratification, at the expense of others, profiting by the misfortunes of others, and striking down those who are obstacles in their way. But such facts do not give us a right to infer that the Evil of others is in itself or in an absolute manner a delight to us. All that is necessary to explain facts is to admit that while wishing the good of All, we yet chiefly prefer and will our own particular happiness. Thus, an enlightened and humane philanthropist may prefer his own nation to others, and rejoice in the triumphs which it achieves during a war, without our necessarily ascribing to him a love for the devastation and carnage of war.

If a man, having to choose between his own interest and that of others, attacks that opposed to his own, it is only by suppressing his natural sentiments of commiseration and sympathy that he can do it; the act which he commits is a pain which he imposes upon himself because it is less painful to him than the personal suffering which he would otherwise endure. If at the same time he sees the possibility of laboring efficiently and directly for his own well-being, by concurring in the general good, he will embrace the opportunity with the greatest ardor. We think, then, that we have a right to say what we have said; that Men would desire to advance all together in the road to Happiness, if the road were sufficiently large to enable them all to travel it, without fettering or incommoding each other.*

But Men can not see this desire satisfied, so long as they have interests in opposition. The Desire itself carries with it a need of accord and harmony among the desires of all.

Besides, if this Happiness were realized upon Earth, Men would feel the need of an assurance that they would never fall back into a state less happy. They would want the assurance of being called, after death, to a happiness at least equal to that which they had enjoyed here below. In a word, aspiring to a Happiness without end, they would wish that the fulfilment of their Desire were written in the divine laws regulative of their lot. It is therefore by the desire of Harmony between all beings, all creations, all worlds, and God, that this tendency to universal happiness is to be translated.

This tendency, the greatest which is in the heart of Man, since it contains all others, as white contains all colors, has been named by Fourier the TENDENCY TO UNITY, OR UNITYISM. Man's first immortal aspiration is toward God and Universal Unity—Justice—Truth. It constitutes his religious being. The perversion of this general and religious aspiration of the soul, is the desire of individual gratification, without regard to God and Humanity. The one, Fourier regards, in its perfect state, as religious holiness; the other diabolical selfishness. The one is light; the other darkness.

But if there were only this passion of Unity in man, we should derive from it

---

* There are many remarkable examples to prove that Devotedness to each other is natural to men when their interests are united. The French army, for instance, in the Russian campaign, was composed of men united by a common sentiment of glory. So strong was this feeling that when one of the most insignificant fractions of it was compromised, it was felt by the whole of the grand army, who were ready to avenge the disgrace by their lives. But on the retreat from Moscow, every general tendency disappeared, and the ties of the soldiery were completely disrupted. Each one thought only of himself, and looked upon his comrade as a rival for his poor pittance of bread or fire. Yet these were the same men that a few days before had so generously sacrificed themselves for each other! Nothing had been changed except the common feeling by which they had been animated, and which was now destroyed by their failure. They were no longer animated by the hope of conquest, which had before united them, but on the other hand they marched with the single object of reaching some less rigorous climate, where each one might be again comfortable.

only a sterile desire of harmony, without the means of its realization. This passion, therefore, may be decomposed into others, which we must seek by penetrating more profoundly into the human heart.

Man desires happiness and fears suffering; but he can enjoy or suffer only in three modes :—

  a. Independently of his relations to his fellows, either in himself or in contact with nature ;

  b. In his particular relations with those of his kind who are in more or less direct contact with him; and

  c. In his general relations with society.

Such are the three sources of good and evil; the three centres or focuses from which radiates all pleasure or pain.

  a. Man enjoys or suffers independently of his relations to his kind; 1st, in himself, according as his health is good or bad, his constitution robust or feeble ; 2d, in his contact with external agents, according to the degree of power which he possesses of bending them to his will, in order to procure the objects which he covets. Man therefore desires Health first, and then Riches, by which he can command the things which his constitution incites him to use. Wealth and Health are expressed by the word Luxury, in the language of Fourier ;—Internal Luxury, or Health; External Luxury, or Wealth. The TENDENCY TO LUXURY is the first of the sub-central or *sub-focal* passions, the first branch of Unityism.

  b. Man enjoys or suffers in his particular relations with those of his fellows whom he knows, according as he may or may not unite himself to those whom he affects, in order to engage with them in the objects of their common sympathy ; according to the facility with which he can put himself in relation with one or with another, in pursuance of the will, impulse, or caprice of the moment. Man has therefore the desire to mingle with his fellows and to form assemblages or *groups* with them, and the TENDENCY TO GROUPS is the second ramification of Unityism.

  c. Man enjoys or suffers in his general relations to society in the degree in which that Society favors or compresses his *tendency to luxury* and *to groups*, and directs, with more or less success the relations of those groups among themselves. The social form to be desired, ought then, accepting these groups freely formed as elements, to render them useful and productive, without depriving them of any of their powers of attraction, in such a way as to conduct to Health and Wealth, all the persons who are fully enrolled in them. It ought to determine the kind of relations to be established between the groups, to class them, to co-ordinate them, in a word, to organize them in *Series*—groups tending always to form series, as individuals tend to form groups. The TENDENCY TO SERIES is the third primordial subdivision of Unityism.

This second step in the study of Man, this analysis of the three sub-focal passions, teaches us that Harmony,—the gratification of Unityism, can only arise from the organization of men into *series of groups*, that society must present a vast social medium offering to each one the faculty of placing himself successively and fruitfully to him, in groups which are agreeable, near to those whom he loves, and in obedience to an actual need of exercising such or such a faculty.

But what will be the character of those groups and series ? On what condition can they be completed ? This is what must be found out in decomposing the sub-focal passions, as we have already decomposed Unityism.

  a. Tendency to Luxury. Remember that the word Luxury comprises two things which are necessary to each other, Health and Riches. Without health man is unable to enjoy the good things which he procures by riches ; and without riches he can not attain to the pleasures to which his health disposes him.

Man has five senses by which he can be affected in as many different ways. From these five sensuous appetites spring five branches of the passion *Tendency to Luxury.*

    a. Passion to satisfy—TASTE.
    b. Passion to satisfy—SMELL.
    c. Passion to satisfy—SIGHT.
    d. Passion to satisfy—HEARING.
    e. Passion to satisfy—TOUCH.

 These, the only passions of this order, we call the SENSITIVE PASSIONS.
 b. Tendency to Groups. An assemblage or group possesses a different quality, according to the cause which has determined its formation. This cause may vary because there are inequalities among men, and the inequalities to be considered, as to the formation of groups are only of three kinds :—
 1st. Men are unequal in the rank they hold—rank which is the consequence of their fortune, their talent, and their worth ;
 2d. They differ in sex;
 3d. They are of diverse families, and so differ by birth or blood.
   Hence, there are four kinds of groups :
 f. Group formed without taking into account any of the natural inequalities, and in which reigns an inequality and confusion of ranks,—called GROUP OF FRIENDSHIP.
 g. Group in which men, classed according to their rank, are conducted by superiors towards an end capable of satisfying their ambition—THE GROUP OF AMBITION.
 h. Group formed by the tendency of the sexes to love each other and to unite themselves together in marriage,—called THE GROUP OF LOVE.
 i. Group formed under the influence of the parental ties, being the family union of individuals, and called THE GROUP OF FAMILISM.
 Friendship, Ambition, Love, Familism, or the parental feeling, are the four passions comprised in the tendency to groups, the passions which tend to bring men together, and to unite them in the bonds of Affection. These are the AFFECTIVE PASSIONS.
 c. Tendency to Series.—The connection between groups must be formed by the social organization which brings them into relation. This relation of one group to another group can only be *hostile, friendly,* or *indifferent.* A man engaged with a particular group may desire the contact of another group for these reasons :
 j. He seeks the contact of *rival* groups, with which he desires to measure himself;
 k. He loves the presence of *friendly* groups, because they sustain his pretensions, and because he is pleased to sustain them in the same way;
 l. Then, the fatigue and ennui which he experiences, if he occupies himself without cessation in the same labors, in the presence of the same persons, cause him to feel the need of abandoning the group which he has chosen, to pass into a new group, *indifferent* to the pretensions of the first, but towards which he feels himself drawn by some *personal* attachment.
 Thus the *tendency to series* is decomposed into three passions : the passions of *Rivalry, Accord,* and *Diversity.*
 j. *Rivalry.*—This passion gives the love of intrigue, contention, cabals, so natural to man, that all his games, from infancy to old age, are only a contest between several parties. When this passion animates us, we forget all fatigue in our pleasure and ardor. It is an excitement, transport,—but a reflective transport; for he who is governed by it, calculates his acts in such a manner, that he loses no chance of success. Known already by many of its effects, this passion has received different names, according to the part which it has played in the circumstances in which it has appeared. It has been denominated generous emulation, the spirit of intrigue, management, diplomatic science, the passion of gaming, traffic, envy, etc., etc. Fourier having been the first to characterize the passion with precision, has given it the proper name which it required. He calls it CABALISM.
 k. *Accord.*—The need of accord produces a passion which is in every respect,

the opposite of the preceding. The friendly groups which pay attention to us, that vast assemblage of men who applaud our efforts, gives rise in us to a blind enthusiasm—an *irreflective transport*, which excludes reason, and carries us to feats of courage and devotedness, which would be impossible, if we were acting in cold blood. A simple pleasure is scarcely capable of developing this enthusiasm; it requires a *composite* pleasure, or one composed of several pleasures. This multiple satisfaction, which alone can engender the passion, has caused it to be called the COMPOSITE PASSION.

1. *Diversity.*—The last branch of the tendency to series, is the want which all men experience of varying their occupations. A pleasure even becomes in the long run monotonous and tiresome. This passion, under the name of inconstancy, is commonly regarded as a vice; we shall see that it is destined to play many important parts: among others, it is that which prevents excess by maintaining equilibrium among the various faculties of Man. It is called the PAPILLON, or ALTERNATING PASSION.

The Cabalist, Composite, and Alternating Passions, then, are those which distribute the groups according to their exigencies, and are called THE DISTRIBUTIVES.

The subdivision of the three sub-focal passions have thus furnished us with twelve *radical* passions, which may be divided in their turn in an analogous way; these subdivisions being continuous indefinitely.* But we have penetrated sufficiently into the study of human passions to enable us to determine the form that is to be given to the natural society which we wish to discover. The following table recapitulates what we have said:

Pivotal Passion.	Sub-focal Passions.	Radical Passions.
A. UNITYISM. *Harmony, Religion, Justice.*	*a.* TENDENCY TO LUXURY. *Relation to the external world.*	a. Passion answering to TASTE. b. ——————— SMELL. c. ——————— Sight. d. ——————— Hearing. e. ——————— Touch.
	b. TENDENCY TO GROUPS. *Connection with Humanity.*	f. AMBITION. g. FRIENDSHIP. h. LOVE. i. FAMILISM.
	c. TENDENCY TO SERIES. *Societary Connection.*	j. CABALIST. or *contrasting.* k. COMPOSITE, or *exalting.* l. PAPILLON, or *interlocking.*

Some developments are still necessary, in order that this table may be thoroughly understood.

a. The sensitive passions, being able to find some satisfaction in the isolated man, not tending directly to unite him with his fellows, are not *directly* social. Society ought to know how to render them social *indirectly*, by making them a stimulus to sociability.

b. The affective passions are *directly* social, man not being able to satisfy them out of contact with other men. In order to understand the passions of this order well, it must be remarked that each one of them has two springs, the one spiritual and the other material, which are indicated respectively in the following table by the letters S. and M.:

FRIENDSHIP,	S. Affinity of character.
Unisexual Affection,	M. Affinity of industrial tastes.
AMBITION,	S. League for benevolence and glory.
Corporate Affection,	M. League for interest.
LOVE,	M. Physical Love.
Bi-sexual Affection,	S. Platonic Love.
FAMILISM,	M. Ties of Consanguinity.
Consanguineous Affection,	S. Ties of Adoption.

* Thus, in the passion *Hearing,* is found the desire of music, which may again be divided into the desire of Harmony, the desire of melody, the desire of symphony, etc., etc.; and so with the others.

It is impossible to conceive an assemblage of men, freely formed, which has not for its impelling cause one or several of the four affectives, acting by the material or spiritual springs of passion, or by both at the same time.

A group formed under the sole influence of the material spring of action, will want nobleness; it will want utility, if the spiritual spring is alone in play; so that it is perfect, elevated, and useful at the same time, if it be formed by the two springs of the passion.

The first two affectives in which the spiritual springs are placed in the first line, because they are there dominant, are affections of the *major order*. The last two are of the *minor order*, the spiritual being subordinate to the material.

Fourier has investigated the natural properties of the groups, and has recapitulated them in several tables, which we shall give in succession.

The first table indicates the natural *tone* of each group; the second makes known whence the impulsion arises when the group must act; and the third table, upon which the attention of the reader must be principally fixed, has relation to criticism—to criticism which corrects and redresses—and is therefore one of the elements of education. Each group has a mode of criticism peculiar to itself, which does not occur in any other group:

1st.—TONE.

GROUP of FRIENDSHIP, or *Levelling:*
Cordiality and confusion of ranks;

GROUP of AMBITION, or *Ascendency:*
Deference of inferiors to superiors;

GROUP of LOVE, or *Inversion:*
Deference of the stronger sex to the weaker;

GROUP of FAMILY, or *Descendency:*
Deference of superiors to inferiors.

2d.—ATTRACTIVE POWER.

Group of FRIENDSHIP:
All attracted to each other in confusion.

Group of AMBITION:
Superiors attracting inferiors.

Group of LOVE:
Women attracting the Men.

Group of FAMILY:
Inferiors attracting superiors.

3d.—CRITICISM.

Group of FRIENDSHIP:
The Mass *playfully* criticises the individual.

Group of AMBITION:
The superior *gravely* criticises the inferior.

Group of LOVE:
The individual *blindly* EXCUSES the individual.

Group of FAMILY:
The Mass *indulgently* EXCUSES the individual.

On reflecting upon them, we shall see that these tables are a faithful expression of the impulsions which we receive from Nature, and that it is only by conforming to these impulsions that men can remain in contact without irritation or uneasiness; while, if they are departed from, there must be disorder and vexation. Thus, a superior can not facetiously criticise an inferior without losing his authority; and he who, in a friendly reunion, would joyfully undergo a facetious criticism, would be greatly offended by one gravely given.

Criticism, strictly, belongs only to the *major* groups; for in the family and love, where it would always be discordant, it must give place to blind and indulgent excuses. But our present society does not allow the different groups to take the tone which is proper to them; and the father, that his child may not want criticism, is obliged to criticise him himself, although his natural impulse would be to caress and even spoil the child. Thus the child revolts against the critique which would have had no improper offensiveness if he had received it in the groups of ambition or friendship.

The Affectives predominate successively at the different ages of life, thus:

Ages.	Dominant Passions.	Analogy.
Infancy;	Friendship;	Bud.
Adolescence;	Love;	Flower.
Virility;	Love and Ambition;	Flower and Fruit
Maturity;	Ambition;	Fruit.
Old Age.	Familism.	Grain.

The sexes are also peculiarly under the influence of some one of the affectives—the *major* affectives dominating in man and the *minor* in woman. As to the kind of equality existing between the affectives: in relations of friendship or ambition, man is the superior; but the woman is in relations of family and love.

These rules are subject to exceptions, of which we shall speak in the proper place.

e. If men had sensitive and affective passions only, they would unite to form groups, but those groups would be always strangers to each other. The connection between the groups is the work of the Distributive passions, which tend to unite men into a single body, and make of the whole of Humanity a vast living organism.

A. Each man carries in his heart all the twelve radical passions, and the absolute or relative energy of the passions in the individual determines his *character*, and, consequently, his natural position in society.

As Fourier's system mainly rests upon this doctrine of the Passions, the analysis of them is not to be lightly passed over; we must see if he has omitted any, if there be not some motives not included in those which he has given.

In the tables of the passions, we have not embraced those vicious habitudes to which the name of passion is commonly given, and which are not passions in the sense we ascribe to the word, but the *subversive* effects of the passions.

Thus Anger is not a passion, for it does not subsist *in itself*; it arises from a *wounded* passion, is the bad result of a betrayed love or disappointed ambition, etc. Love, ambition, &c., remain always in the heart of man, but Anger would show itself no more, if we could attain a state in which there would be no contrarieties and deceptions.

The workman chained from day to day to a monotonous and repugnant toil, lest his whole life should be a continuous punishment, from time to time, seeks relief and distraction. What pleasure is offered to him in our societies, unless it be the bar-room or the groggery? He drinks, therefore, because he finds in drunkenness an alleviation of his cares, and an agreeable excitement. But if his life was happy, if his future was certain, if every day he could chose between several pleasures, would he surrender himself to one? Do we not see that intoxication would disappear if we could elevate the working classes in the social scale?

Theft, or burglary, which ordinarily springs from the need of satisfying the sensuous appetites, the *tendency to luxury* is not found among the middling and higher classes, where this tendency is satisfied by the activity of genial labor and the spirit of order. Thus many who now figure at the Police Offices, placed in other circumstances, would become worthy citizens.

Inconstancy is a wise impulse of Nature which induces men to exercise alternately all their physical and intellectual faculties, and which could not have been given them to be allowed to rust in inactivity. It is because they do not obey this inclination, because the rich neglect to make a regular use of their physical force, and because the poor do not use it intelligently, that they are both so often diseased in body and mind. Inconstancy is an evil in present society, where each man having only one useful faculty, becomes idle when he leaves it; but it would be a good, if society offered to each one useful occupations, at the same time varied and adapted to all their faculties.

Idleness is the very natural desire of avoiding pain and ennui, but *not action;* the most indolent being is often the most ardent in pleasure. It would be an anomaly when labor shall be made attractive.

The cabalist, the love of intrigue, which frequently engenders discord, hatred, and war, is likewise the source of that noble emulation which leads men to distinguish themselves in learning, talent, and usefulness.

Avarice, disengaged from all fear of privation for itself or for others, is only an effect of Unityism. He who is habitually economical and saving, will render great service in the societies of the future. Then, such a character, consecrated to the service of all, will no longer prosecute an end exclusively selfish, and will be no longer contemptible; he will save from destruction and waste many things that others disdain, and from apparently small and worthless savings, will effect magnificent economies for the social Whole.

In passing in review, in this way, all the excesses and vices that now degrade the human species, we shall convince ourselves that if those vices are intimately connected with certain passions, they are not an essential part of it, but on the contrary, depend upon external circumstances, which may be removed. All that is necessary is to discover a society in which every bad route for the action of the passions will be closed, and in which the path of virtue will be strewn with flowers, and not be a by-way covered with thorns. This is what Fourier supposes he has done.

But we must leave the passions for a moment, to resume them again when it shall be time to decide upon the organization of society which we are about to propose and explain.*

CHAPTER VI.

ORGANIZATION OF THE TOWNSHIP.

" The beginnings of a right political reform are to be made in small districts."—JEFFERSON.

§ I. *Material Arrangements.*

THE reforms attempted in the Social System, till now, have always been of a general nature, setting out on a grand scale, and proposing to apply themselves to a whole nation. But this process is dangerous; for if the promises of the theory are not realized in practice, the whole of society will have been agitated and disturbed to no purpose, without being able, perhaps, to return to its point of departure.

In ordinary enterprises, in which private interest alone is concerned, men proceed with much more prudence; a discovery, however brilliant the hopes it excites, is never generally applied until it has been tried and verified on a small scale. Why should we not act with the same caution, when we experiment upon the more serious interests of society?

* The reader will bear in mind, that this chapter gives only a theory of *motives*, and not of *mind*. Besides these passions, which are the moving springs of the soul, the mind makes use of certain *instrumental* faculties, the best account of which, although that is very imperfect, is given by Phrenology.

Is not society composed of a certain number of aggregations of men united in a centre, where they live in daily relations with each other, and where they may, if they please, remain strangers to whatever is passing without their own borders? Should not every reform begin in the bosom of these elementary aggregations or townships, since the greater part of men are only acquainted with life as it exists in the townships? In that case, how much would the danger be diminished, in the case of a want of success?

But if the experiment succeeded, other townships would imitate the example, till it spread from one to another, and finally, according to the importance and evidence of the results obtained, the nation first, and then the globe, would present a series of reorganized townships.

This is the sure and progressive method of reform indicated by Fourier, who requests that his project may be tried, and if it is not sufficiently sustained by experience, can only temporarily injure a small corner of the earth. It is this project which we are going to make known, by sketching the principal features of a reorganized township, called a *Phalanx*.*

Let us suppose that in a township of about 400 families (from 1600 to 1800 souls), the inhabitants deliberate among themselves and adopt the following resolutions:—

1st. An association is formed among all the inhabitants, rich and poor, of this township; the social Capital to be composed of the fixed property of all, and of the moveables and floating capital which each one may see fit to put into the society.

2d. Each associate, in exchange for his quota, shall receive certificates representing the exact value of what he may have surrendered to the society.

3d. Each certificate shall be a mortgage upon the part of the fixed property which it represents and upon the general property of the society.

4th. Each associate, whether he shall have contributed real estate or not, is invited to assist in the productive employment of the common fund, by means of his labor and talent.

5th. Women and children enter the society on the same terms as men.

6th. The annual profit, the common expenses being first liquidated, shall be divided among the associates in the following manner:

a. A first part shall pay the interest on stock.

b. A second part shall be divided among laborers, according to the difficulties of their work, and the time which they are respectively engaged.

c. The third and last part shall be distributed among those who may be distinguished, in labor, either for intelligence, activity, or vigor.

Thus, each man, woman, and child, will touch a portion of each part proportioned to his or her concurrence in the production by means of his or her three productive faculties, *capital*, *labor*, or *talent*.

This question of the equitable distribution of profits, may seem at first insoluble; but we shall show in the sequel that it is very easily solved. For the present we must suppose the division made by common consent, and reserve the question for its proper place.

The basis which we have laid down for an Association being adopted, we shall have obtained, by a simple transformation of Property, important results, which may be briefly indicated:—

This transformation is not a dispossession; property in a mortgage is as well guarantied as the Property itself; for even in our societies the revenues of the richest men depend upon hypothecations and mortgages.

The first advantage of the reform is to *converge* the interests of the inhabitants of the township, until now more or less *divergent*. Each of them immediately understands that his part in the three distributions will augment or diminish with the general profits, and that he can not labor for the general benefit without laboring for his own, or *vice versa;* and each one feels that the fortune of one can no longer be the misfortune of another.

---

* Phalanx, is a word which expresses the idea of wholeness, accord, and unity of object. The *Phalanstery* is the dwelling-house and work-shop of the Phalanx. It is the opposite of *Monastery*.

The soil of the township is no longer to be worked in isolated farms, many of them hardly worth cultivation; the enclosures, fences, and many of the roads will disappear; and the whole territory be thrown into a single domain, for general cultivation. Thus, the advantages belonging to a large estate will be combined with those of a small estate; for the only salutary effect of a subdivision of land is that it permits a greater number of persons to become owners of property; while, in the associated township, the smallest saving may be converted into a coupon of stock, which makes one a co-proprietor of the domain of a phalanx.

In the isolated township, every head of a family, whatever may be his tastes and his aptitudes, must cultivate his own fields, vines, gardens, and orchards; he must preserve his own grains, vines, fodders, &c.; and it is clear that no one can be occupied with so many different tasks with success. In an associated township, among 1800 inhabitants, there will be a certainty of finding persons, capable of every particular kind of labor. These persons will take the direction of the labor in which they excel, and the whole will be executed with greater chances of success, because cultivation on a large scale allows of more beneficial and economical methods. The kind of soil, too, best adapted to each kind of cultivation, will be chosen, which can not always be done by isolated families.

A township thus organized will soon feel that it has gained immensely by replacing its 400 poor granaries and its 400 bad cellars, by a large central tenement, perfectly adapted to the reception and preservation of its harvests. It will soon understand that it must substitute for its 400 kitchens, occupying exclusively the time of 400 women, a common kitchen managed by a few persons, and in which the consumer will find, *in accordance with his fortune and his tastes*, repasts more varied, better prepared, and less costly than any he was able to procure in his isolation. The same would be true of the labor of taking care of children and other domestic occupations, which could easily be directed and controlled by a few women,—as we now see in Asylums, schools, &c., &c. Thus seven-eighths of the women, now absorbed in the details of housewifery, would be emancipated from their petty cares, and turn their energies to productive labor.

As these modifications would necessarily effect great economies in work and time, mere agricultural labors would be insufficient to employ all the moments of the population, and they would proceed to engage in other branches of industry. They would establish workshops, manufactories, &c., on the same unitary plan, adapted to the local circumstances, and in such a way that they might not lose a minute in passing from one occupation to another.

These changes being executed, each one would require only a small number of chambers for the accommodation of his family and friends, or for his own private labors, studies, and reflective retirement. These apartments, for the sake of simplification, would be found in the same edifice which contained the kitchen and dining-hall, the cellars, the granaries and the storehouses, the school-rooms, the work-shops, and the children's dormitories, &c. The rooms could be of all sizes and modes of finish, to suit the fortunes and tastes of the different members. Then, the 400 dwellings which composed the village, would disappear, or be converted into summer and out-houses, and all the people be established in the grand unitary edifice, called *The Phalanstery*.

Mark that we are not speaking of a convent, a barrack, or a community! The arrangements proposed are in every respect directly the reverse of those of a community. The whole population, it is true, will inhabit the same edifice; but each one may have a house or suite of rooms to himself to suit his fancy, and at just such a rent as he chooses to pay, separated entirely from others, as much as the houses in a city, and exempt from intrusion. Nor will all the associates take their repasts in common, seeing that while there will be common tables, those who choose may order their meals in their own rooms,—meals to consist of whatever they may select from the *carte* of the day, as it is the custom to do now, at hotels and restaurateurs.

Fourier gives many details in his works as to the construction of the Mansion. What especially establishes its unitary character, is a covered gallery running around the whole building at the first story, and forming a street of communication between all the different apartments, and the work-shops, the chambers, the school-rooms, &c., &c. It would be ventilated or warmed, according to the season, and prevent the necessity, at any time, of outward and dangerous exposures.

But the following cut will give a more complete idea of the general plan of the building, than any description in words :—

GROUND PLAN OF THE EDIFICE OF AN ASSOCIATED TOWNSHIP.

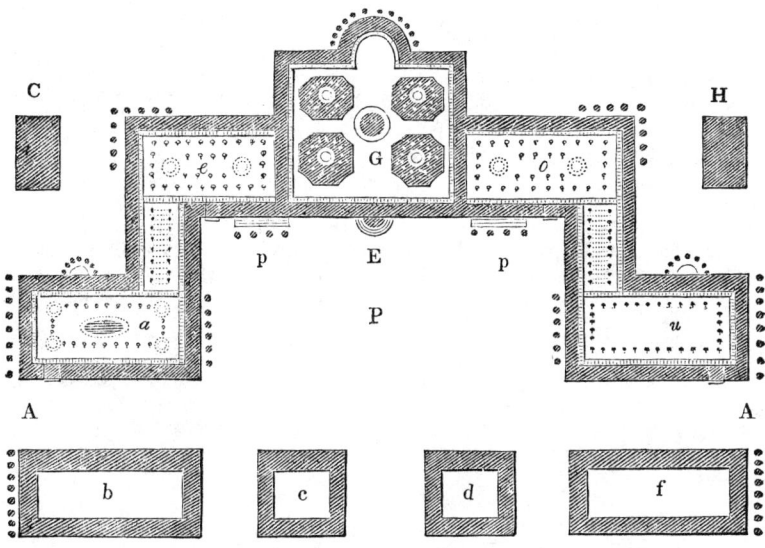

The following is the explanation of the letters on this map :—

A Avenue passing between the main Edifice and the store-houses, granaries, and other out houses.
P—Public Square, formed by the centre and projecting wings of the Edifice.
G—Garden enclosed within the central range of buildings; it would contain the green-houses and form a winter promenade.
 a, e, o, u—Court-yards between the different ranges of buildings; they are about a hundred feet wide, ornamented with trees and shrubbery, and crossed by Corridors.
E, p, p—Large portals or entrances to the Edifice.
C—The Church.
H—A large Hall for musical representations and festivities.
b, c, d, f—Granaries, store-houses, and other out-buildings.

To avoid giving too great a length to the Edifice, it must be composed of a double range or line of buildings, encircling the court-yards—*a, e, o, u,* and the garden—G. The broad dark line does not represent the foundation walls of the Edifice, but the entire width of a range of buildings; it is intended, together with the light dotted line around the inside, which is the Corridor, to represent a width of seventy-two feet.

Around the inside of the Edifice winds the spacious Corridor or enclosed Portico, which we have described; the reader will see that it forms a belt, encircling all parts of the building and uniting them in a whole.

The ranges of buildings which enclose the garden—G, will be reserved for public purposes. They will contain the Council-Rooms, Reading-Rooms, Library, Exchange, Public Halls, Banquet-Rooms, Saloons for parties, social unions and public assemblies, and some of the higher-priced Apartments.

The open spaces left between the parallel ranges of buildings should be from a hundred to a hundred and twenty feet wide; they would form elongated court-yards, traversed by corridors, and should be planted with ornamental trees and shrubbery; in Association the useful and the beautiful must be in every way combined.

The noisy workshops would be located in the basement of one of the extreme wings; their noise would be lost in this distant part of the Edifice, and would not incommode the inhabitants.

Play-grounds for children would occupy the court-yard of the same wing; such a place would be necessary, particularly in winter.

A portion of the wing opposite the one devoted to noisy occupations, would contain the suites of apartments reserved for travellers and visiters.

The Edifice of an Association of the largest description would be about twenty-two hundred feet in length; with these dimensions the grand square could be twelve, and the wings each five hundred feet long. As we descend to smaller Associations, the size of the Edifice could be much reduced, and for an Association of four hundred persons, a comparatively plain building would answer the purpose.

The gardens should, if practicable, be located behind the Edifice, and not behind the granaries and other out-houses, near which the fields of grain had better be placed. This distribution must, however, be regulated by localities.

The square or garden—G, would be planted with evergreens and would contain the greenhouses; it could in winter be enclosed, so as to form a beautiful promenade, where flowers and foliage could charm the eye and perfume the atmosphere. What a source of pleasure and health would a winter garden of this kind be!—and how many similar improvements over the present mode of living could be introduced into Association!*

These material arrangements would be insufficient for the great results we have announced; for in themselves, they would not, of a certainty, lead to a distribution of profits perfectly equitable and unanimously agreeable, to the accord of all interest and wills, and to attractiveness of Labor. But we have not yet spoken of the *passional* arrangements under which the laborers would be brought; we have not applied the results of that investigation of Man, which we presented as the base of every problem having relation to the organization of societies.

In order to facilitate the exposition of our ideas we have supposed the case of a township suddenly adopting the theory, and conforming itself to its conditions. This supposition, purely abstract, can not be realized, and the experiment, if made at all, must be made, to use a common phrase, out of whole cloth, by which we mean that existing townships will not adopt the theory until they see it exemplified, in some experimental association, instituted on purpose for that end.

§ II. *Passional Arrangements.*

One of the inherent characters of Civilization, is what Fourier calls *Simplism.* It consists, as to discussion, in the fault of considering only one of the aspects of a complex question, and, as to action, in losing on one side what is gained on the other, so that real Progress is after all only negative.

We have already given an example of simplism in speaking of great and small estates. These two methods of cultivating the soil present advantages which ought to be cumulated or combined, and the minds of agriculturists instead of devoting themselves exclusively to one, to the utter neglect of the other, should seek out some mode of reaping the benefits of both.

A no less remarkable example of *Simplism* is presented in the practice of manufacturing industry; where, it is stated, the *division of labor*—parcelled labor—contributes prodigiously both to the quantity and quality of its products. There is then progress in this respect; but, great God, on what conditions!

The workman devoted for life to the exclusive exercise of a single organ is stupified and imbruted, the human species is degraded by it, and in those countries where it has been carried to the greatest extent, instead of flourishing youth as formerly, you find only a degenerate race—only poor sickly and emasculated beings, that after a painful and short career, give place to a generation still more miserable and degraded!

Yet as the principle of division of labor is capable of producing the best results, it ought to be extended to all branches of human industry. Should we extend it at the awful moral risks by which it is usually accompanied? By no means. The only course, therefore, that is left to us is to discover some way of

* Social Destiny, by A. Brisbane.

avoiding the evil and still retaining the good, or in other words, to prevent the debasement of the workman, while reaping all the advantages of his work, and thus cause the progress of the individual and the increase of wealth to advance in parallel lines.

That's impossible! you will perhaps say; but it is an impossibility which the genius of Fourier has accomplished.

In all the labors of the Phalanstery, domestic, agricultural, and manufacturing, each person will be charged with a fragment or detail reduced as much as the nature of it will allow. The task will not be very difficult, the time of service will not be long, and the same man will be able to take part in thirty* different kinds of labor, so as to employ alternately all the physical and intellectual forces that he possesses.

Nature has too much foresight to have gifted us with even a single faculty that was designed never to be used. A great number of the maladies that attack us come from our not knowing how to develop and employ, integrally, with measure and equilibrium, all the springs of action that are in us.

Thus, we shall retain all the advantages of Division of Labor, without subjecting the laborer to suffering. Thus too, the laborer, passing successively from the workshop to the fields, from domestic cares to occupations of the laboratory, &c., will make progress on every side, will become all that it is possible for him to become, and will render to society and to himself all the services that are in his power.

In the phalanx, isolated labor does not exist. Every work is confided to a collection of individuals composing *a group*.

Each individual of the group is charged with some detail of the common work that pleases him, with some speciality in which he excels. In this way, all will have a sense of their personal worth, and of the necessity of their concurring with others in the production of the general result.

The group responsible for any labor, being directly interested in its perfect execution, calculates the time which shall be consecrated to it, and divides that time into sessions of two hours; it distributes these sessions among the days of the year, month, or week, etc.

Out of the hours thus fixed for the sessions of the group, its members betake themselves, as they see fit, to other groups, of which they make a part, in order to fulfil other vocations by a different employment of their activity.

It must not be thought, however, that any first comer may attach himself to a group, and, perhaps, compromise the success of it by his ignorance; he who feels a desire to engage in any labor, must first present himself as a novice, to the group which has the charge of that department. After having gone through an apprenticeship, more or less long, according to his capacity, he becomes entitled to a portion of the profits, if he is skilful; but he can prefer no claim until he shows himself decidedly useful.

Each one, having worked in thirty groups, becomes by his labor entitled at the end of the year to a thirtieth of the dividends, in addition to the interest on his original stock, and to such several sums as he may have earned, in the various groups, by his distinguishing talent.

We need hardly stop to answer the objection that a man engaged on a minute detail of work, to which he returns only periodically, will not do it as well as if he gave himself up to it all the time and without an alternative. A man whose faculties are developed in perfect equilibrium, is more intelligent and more adroit than he who develops only a single one, to the disuse and atrophy of the rest. Even now we see persons engaged in certain arts which they can only practise at intervals, which are more difficult than a majority of the details of industry, but which are executed with astonishing facility and success. A surgeon, for instance, may become an exceedingly skilful operator, although the opportunities for the exercise of his profession are very infrequent.

As to the labors of science, letters, and art,—the labors of him who observes,

---

* Thirty is only an approximation, as are all the figures that we use.

perfects, and invents,—they constitute an exception. But these exceptions are too rare, compared with the multitude of industrial processes, to invalidate the rule. Beside, the philosopher himself, when labor shall be attractive, when it shall be performed in assemblages always agreeable, will abandon willingly, and many times in a day, his high intellectual regions, to mingle in the more active groups, and strengthen his body, and quicken his intelligence, by the employment of his physical powers.

The whole number of groups practising the different branches of the same industry, form a *series of the first degree;* a certain number of a series of the first degree, working in analogous relations, form a *series of the second degree;* the series of the second degree is disposed in the same way into still higher series; and the union of the whole makes the Phalanx.

Thus, a series of orchardists may be divided into inferior series, some applied to the cultivation of stone-fruits, and others to that of seed-fruits, etc.; the series of seed-fruits will comprise the Apple series, the Pear series, etc.; each *species* of Pear will then have its particular series, and each *variety* of the same species will have its appropriate group.

We need not be astonished at the great number of series or groups that would be furnished by a single Phalanx; the more the number of series is multiplied, the more simplified the task of each would become, and the less time it would have to give to it. Each person taking part in thirty groups, in consequence of the different combinations that the laborers might form, there might be many more groups than there were individuals.

It would be necessary to observe with great care, a rule which insists upon subdividing each kind of Industry into as many branches as possible, in order to apply a group to each one of them. It is necessary also, among groups forming a series, that neighboring groups should approximate as near as possible, in their kinds of labor, and the nature of their products. This disposition of the series into *compact scales*, as they are called, aids essentially in rendering the labor attractive.

Minute division of labor—short and varied services or sessions*—and groups of laborers disposed in series of a compact scale, would be the mode of executing work in a Phalanx.

§ III. *Consequences of these Arrangements.*

We have now explained the principal arrangements upon which we rely to establish accord among the associates, and to transform all the occupations of men into pleasures.

Attractive Labor is something so foreign to our customary notions, that we are not surprised at the incredulity with which it is received, although there is no real reason why it may not be effected.

Whether a man amuses himself or labors, he equally employs his physical and intellectual faculties,—he is equally occupied. Why are certain occupations an amusement or pleasure, and why are others, labor or pain?

It is not simply because an occupation is fatiguing that it becomes a pain, since there are pleasures still more fatiguing, both to body and mind, than the most hard and complicated toil.

It is not (except in the direct gratification of the senses) in the action that one performs that the pleasure is found; for the action may be very insignificant in itself, so much so that a man alone would never look to it for a moment's

---

* *Short and varied occupation.* It has been objected that the frequent change of place which passing from one group to another would occasion, would lead to a loss of valuable time. Fourier meets the objection by stating that the times for engaging in any group will be known beforehand, so that it would not be difficult to find it; that all the workshops are near each other; that the whole domain of a Phalanx would not be a league square; and that there will be plenty of conveyances always ready to run to the more distant parts of the territory. The whole time lost in passing through thirty groups would not equal that frequently lost, under present arrangements, by a workman who is obliged to walk home for his dinner. In a Phalanx, too, the small loss of time occasioned by change of place, will be amply compensated by the new ardor imparted by engaging in a fresh pursuit.

diversion. One scarcely ever thinks, for instance, when he is alone, of dancing or playing billiards, yet these are exciting amusements in company.

The pleasure found in a pursuit then, is more or less independent of the fatigue and even of the nature of the act, and must be derived from certain external conditions and accompaniments. Let us see what these are, and whether it is impossible to apply them to Labor.

1st. Pleasure is found in freely-formed reunions or assemblages of persons who love to be together.

All Labor, then, ought to be executed by a group of which the members are chosen by each other. It is thus that men give satisfaction to their *affective passions*, or those spontaneous impulses by which they are drawn together into groups.

2d. Men united for purposes of pleasure like to separate as soon as they are weary of it.

Then, every group of laborers ought to be dissolved as soon as tedium has succeeded to attraction. Working thus in *short and varied sessions*, they would obey the impulse of one of the *distributive* passions, the Papillon or Alternating Passion.

3d. Men, in their games, where they are constantly contending with each other, seek to excel and conquer their rivals.

Rivalry must then exist among the groups of laborers, and for that purpose, several groups ought to be engaged on similar products, between which, on comparison, it would be difficult to decide. Thus, for the gratification of the cabalist, the groups ought to be distributed into a *compact scale*.

4th. Men are infatuated with pleasure, when their address or talent obtains them brilliant triumphs, in the presence of a numerous assembly.

The groups then, ought to be connected with each other by the serial organization, in order that the attention of the greatest number should be directed upon the acts of each; in order that there might be alliances among the groups whose designs accord, against groups of similar and therefore rival pretensions. In this manner, the laborer, feeling himself observed, sustained, applauded by the mass, knowing that his part of the work is rendered distinct and brought into relief by its *parcelled exercise*, will find himself in a condition for the most favorable development of his irreflective enthusiasm, or the *composite passion*.

5th. When men find pleasure in useful occupations, they necessarily abandon the mere purposeless amusements in which, until then, they had looked for it. When Labor shall be a fete, it is for that fete that men will reserve all the luxury and art with which it can be embellished. Thus, the passions of sense, *the tendency to luxury*, will be gratified at all the meetings of the laborers, by arrangements as comfortable as the nature of the work will admit of being made.

6th. After ranging himself under the great *Serial Law*, which shines throughout creation, Man beginning to understand that nothing in the universe is fatally hostile to him, that the happiness of others is the proper complement of his own happiness, will be filled with a high and exalted Love for his fellows, and with Gratitude to that Divine Being, who has arranged the entire mechanism of the world with such perfection of Art and Wisdom. He will experience a degree of Blessedness, by means of his lofty Sentiment of Harmony, through the gratification of the passion of passions, Unity, that none of the race have as yet felt in this Life. He will find, in truth, that *laborare est orare*, that work is worship.

Industry divided into parcels will offer parts agreeable to all ages and sexes, so that each group will generally be composed of men, women, and children. This union of the three sexes (Fourier calls infancy the *neuter* sex), is a powerful means of imparting attraction to labor. Nature, in order to insure this arrangement, has given to some men the most feminine tastes, and to some women tastes decidedly masculine. These *transitional* characters are ridiculed in our present societies, where they have no utility; but they will be appreciated in Association, where even the labors exclusively reserved to one sex will not be stripped of the charms of that kind of emulation which arises from the presence of the other.

"But Morals," interposes some grave guardian of his neighbor's conscience; "Morals will be corrupted by these frequent meetings of the two sexes." Verily, a society which sees nothing reprehensible in balls and parties, has no right to criticise such meetings of the sexes as we propose, because they will mostly take place in public and in the presence of children, nor to blame an arrangement which will spread a charm over fruitful labors, equal to that which it now lends to frivolous and often dangerous assemblies.

Labor being organized as we have explained, society will no longer be composed of men devoted to the exercise of a single function, as tailors, masons, shoemakers, etc., etc., but of men consecrating, to various labors respectively, only a part of their time and faculties.

There are certain kinds of labor, however, to be executed in series, which demand a more particular explanation.

The series having the management of domestic duties, for instance, will be a numerous one, and will daily furnish a detachment for the service of the day. When its functions shall be like other social functions, and be rewarded *in the mass*, when they shall have lost all character of personal servitude, they will be by no means repugnant, and many persons will delight to consecrate two or three hours per week to the object of rendering themselves useful to friends, who, in a thousand other respects, will return the kindness.

The ties of affection being many in a Phalanx, where the members are often in contact, and on points in which they sympathize, the labor of the domestic series will be distributed in such a way that each person will be charged with cares relating to those whom he or she loves. A new charm will thus be imparted to the task, which beside being paid for as other labor, will receive an additional reward in thanks and affection.

Thus is resolved a problem, which has often been started in the Christian world, but never settled, THE ABOLITION OF DOMESTIC SERVICE. There will be no more *servants*, yet everybody will be served with the utmost zeal, intelligence, and promptitude, by the groups which have undertaken that portion of the common duties, and who will be repaid by consideration and respect.

If, on one side, domestic service is a flagrant violation of the liberty and dignity of man, as seems to be universally demonstrated by the fact, that the force of circumstances—want and poverty—is the only power which can compel a person to engage in it; on the other side, man has an absolute need of personal services, in the cooking of his dinner, in the preservation of his clothes, and in the general care of his house. Now, here is a problem for those who are so fond of upholding the liberty, dignity, and rights of man, which they will find of singular difficulty in the solution! How are they going to reconcile the two facts? The truth is, that many of our would-be democrats have never thought of the matter in this light. They have accepted Domestic Service, as the ancient philosophers and modern clergymen do slavery, as an established and consequently eternal fact! Even those who have seen the evils of either kind of servitude, are apt to regard them as remediless. The atrocious injustice which Masters and Mistresses are almost everywhere guilty of towards their *helps*, is everywhere looked upon as something which *must* be, until at least the individuals are changed. *But it is a part of the system.* Individuals may be and are greatly to blame for the cruel and selfish modes in which they exact the time and disregard the rights and interests of their domestics; yet the system is more to blame. And Association is the only practicable reform of this abuse that has yet been suggested.

A series, principally composed of women and small children, is charged with the care of the younger children, which are reared in saloons perfectly appropriate to their destination. During the night, the different groups of this series will alternate in the discharge of the duties of that season, so that the work will not fall frequently or heavily upon any class of persons.

This series is in close relation with the series of physicians, who watch over the sickness of the younger children, and especially charge themselves with the arrangement of those parts of their clothing and rooms which have an influence upon health.

Every mother, undoubtedly, who might prefer it, would have her children near herself, and might nourish them herself, if she pleased, either in her own apartments, or at stated seasons in the general saloons. The practice, in this respect, would depend upon the peculiar feelings and position of each person, whether more or less opulent or more or less disposed to engage in the labors of different groups. In cases of sickness, and of very young children, mothers would perhaps choose to have the attendance of good and faithful assistants, in their own apartments; but, in general, we think it would be found that the group of nurses were so excellent, the public halls so well adapted to health and other purposes, and the advantages in every way so decided, that a larger part of the women would of choice leave their children to the education of the proper groups, in which, doubtless, the mother would be herself enrolled.

The number of women necessary to the care of young children being limited, Nature has given the inclination to that kind of occupation to only a few. It would be easy to assure ourselves that this was the case, if the spirit of our present society did not oblige women to dissimulate, and feign tastes that are often the opposite of their very organization. Yet, in spite of this hypocrisy, how often do we see mothers that are willing to yield the care of their offspring to mere mercenaries, and who are thankful when sleep relieves them from the fatigue and constant attention which a single child always demands. To give all the moments of one's life to the care of children, is often a punishment, instead of a pleasure; but Association reconciles the most perfect management of infants, with the continued, but not exhausting, devotedness of the mother.

Fourier indulges throughout his works in the most vehement denunciation of civilized commerce, which he justly characterizes as incoherent, anarchical, and false.

Commerce is designed to bring the producer and the consumer into relation: that is, if it has any object. But in itself it produces nothing; it adds nothing to the commodities which it circulates. It is obviously then for the general interest to reduce commercial agents to the smallest number, and to carry over the excess to some productive employment.

In our societies, precisely the contrary takes place; the agents of commerce are multiplied beyond measure; designed only to play a subordinate part, they have usurped the highest rank; they absorb the largest portion of the common dividend, out of all manner of proportion to the services they render; they hold the producer in a servile dependence; they reduce to its lowest terms the wages of workmen, and they extort from the consumer without mercy.

Blind Competition, so much boasted of by the political economists, has largely contributed to the evil. Traffickers, in consequence of it, give themselves up to a regular war against each other; and in order that they may not be beaten, they are ready to resort to any expedient. They lie, cheat, and falsify products; they alter grains, meats, wines, and sugars; they would poison the community, if they dared, as we have recently seen in one or two instances; and they spoliate the public in a thousand modes, by exchange, brokerage, usury, bankruptcy; in short, they deceive in every way, and defraud at all seasons; yet commerce, in our corrupted societies, is the most certain way of arriving at fortune, honor, and distinction.

We speak here only of intermediate commerce, by which we mean the commerce which consists in buying from one in order to sell to another. The manufacturer and mechanic belong to the class of productive laborers, although their functions are often complicated with the character and vices of Commerce, strictly speaking.

We know very well that Humanity must employ a portion of its force in the transportation of products, in order to bring them within reach of the consumer. But it is evident that it ought to devote to this task only the force that is rigorously necessary; every expenditure of time or money, beyond this minimum, being a real loss for society.

It does not enter our thought, in saying severe things of Commerce, to attack either classes or individuals. Our criticism relates to the system, which is guilty of placing men in a position exposed to so many debasing temptations and influences.

In a phalanx, the commercial mechanism is simplified as much as it can be; a series is charged with effecting exchanges, purchases, sales, storage, and distribution. This series, always divided into groups, applied to each part of the work, will devote to the service only as much time as is strictly necessary, and will never lose a moment waiting for the consumer. The days and hours of distribution will be regulated, and the series, paid by the phalanx, will have nothing to gain from the individual. It is this method which is generally observed in the magazines of armies.

Philosophers and artists will likewise form groups and series. The series in science and art, in all the phalanxes, will be classified, and attached to centres, which are again connected with a single centre, where all will converge, and which will radiate light in all directions.

This arrangement will yield immense advantages, and cause the sciences to advance with the steps of a giant. When a philosopher, in the silence of his cabinet, shall have discovered a principle, he will unfold it to his associates, to test it by discussion, and then communicate it to their particular hierarchical centre. The centre, if the principle requires the confirmation of experience, will communicate the suspected law to the three million Phalanxes that cover the earth, and the concurrent observation of such a multitude of series will throw a vivid light upon the subject, and in a little while either verify or reject the inference.

The mechanical part of science, calculations for example, which sometimes absorb the greater part of the life of a man of genius, will be executed with a wonderful promptitude, in a similar manner by special groups, taken from the phalanx, the province, the kingdom, &c., &c., according to the degree of importance attached to the work. Tables of logarithms, containing a million of numbers and calculated to thirty decimals, will be constructed in as short a time almost as it would take to establish a communication between the phalanx and the centre, since each phalanx would have only one logarithm to calculate, even by demanding, for its verification, each logarithm from three groups.

The series of physicians, divided into groups, of which each would apply itself to a special form of disease, as takes place already in large cities, would be connected with every other series exerting a direct influence upon health, and to the culinary series among others. The art of appropriating nourishment to temperaments, will enter into the duties of the physicians, who will be paid in proportion to their success, i. e., as there are fewer diseases, so that their interests will be brought into accord with the interests of the mass.

Thus, with all the labors of the series ; they will be performed in short and varied terms, and under conditions likely to transform what is now considered a burden into a pleasure.

There are nevertheless some works of such a nature, that it will never be possible to draw men to them by a direct attraction. These are few in number, and association, aided by the progress of mechanical invention, will reduce them still further, and render the execution of them less disagreeable. But while they continue disagreeable they must be provided for, and Fourier, with admirable ingenuity, has organized *little hordes*, composed of the most frank and decided children, whose business it will be, under many inducements, to undertake the removal of filth, and the purification of pools, &c., &c. We have not space enough at our command to go into details on this point, which is not of the highest importance.

§ IV. *Education.*

What will become of children in your society of laborers ? how will they be raised ? who will occupy themselves in their moral and intellectual development ? It is time to answer these significant questions.

ORGANIZATION OF THE TOWNSHIP. 61

In his inquiry after natural education, Fourier takes for his guide the attractions of childhood, and endeavors to act upon its mind in such a way as to give a charm to all its studies, and at the same time, to develop its faculties *integrally*, with a due attention to all parts of its nature.

As soon as children have some gleams of intelligence, and are capable of some address, from three to four years of age, corporations, devoted to the guardianship and guidance of children, have the care of conducting them in the different workshops of the Phalanstery, and in the gardens, orchards, fields, kitchen-gardens, stables, cow-houses, and poultry-yards, where they have constantly under their eyes the labors of organized groups and series. The superintendents will consist chiefly of old men and matrons, for old age sympathizes most with childhood. The various aptitudes and talents of these young children will be allowed freely to dawn, grow, and develop themselves; their instinct of imitation is such, that to attract them to industry, it would be sufficient to allow them the use of miniature tools of gardening, and general industry; they will immediately make use of them ardently and passionately as they are instructed. They will not seek to break and destroy; but, stimulated by the example of children a little older than themselves, already useful workers, who enjoy certain privileges, such as larger and more substantial instruments, agreeable uniforms, a regular organization in groups and series, the little children will strive to put all the address of which they are susceptible into their miniature labors. A certain pride innate in children will likewise be taken advantage of, a feeling which makes them aspire to participate in the labors of those a little older, to render themselves useful, to be of importance; this will be turned to account from the earliest infancy upward. In the gardens they will grub up noxious weeds; in the kitchen, they will turn little spits, shell peas, wash the vegetables, sort the fruit, wash the plates, etc.; in short, they will be employed in everything that does not require degrees of strength above their age; and all these little children, already stimulated by emulation, will apply themselves with pleasure and with ardor to the labors permitted. From the moment that they become useful they will be formed into choirs and corporations, groups and series. regularly disciplined in all their studies and their occupations. In each group are established different degrees of capacity, which is a means of emulation contained within the group itself, without reckoning the rivalries between contiguous groups. A means still more powerful, is the successive passage of childhood in different phases, corresponding to different ages. In proportion as he acquires vigor and intelligence, the child passes successively through different choirs and companies of youth, all of which enjoy the prerogatives and privileges conformable to their employments, which are successively more difficult and more elevated. So that each child has before him a group more advanced in strength and skill, into which he can not enter, without perfecting himself and passing the examinations necessary to prepare him for the labors and studies of the group above. He will thus pass through a successive number of groups and series, which mark the various phases of childhood and youth to manhood. Then only will he enjoy a complete independence, and be entirely free. Till then, he is never forced, never constrained, but he is guided. He has the choice of labors; but as they are divided into several degrees for children, it is necessary, in order to pass from a lower to a higher degree, to give proof of sufficient strength, and skill, and aptitude, in various branches of art, and science, and industry.

God himself is the type and source of order in the universe—the Trinity in unity, the universal Triune or series; and education in a Phalanstery has a triune basis—spiritual, social, and material. Domestic and industrial harmony and education centre in the Phalanstery proper; spiritual harmony and education in the church; artistic or material harmony and education, in the opera or theatre, a school of art and measured harmony for every age, from infancy to full maturity; for those who take an active part, as well as those who passively look on. Children from the age of three to four will there be organized in choirs, and exercise themselves in measured chants, in measured steps and movements, and in all the measured harmonies of sense so intimately linked with those of soul and mind. This diversion, under the control of higher principles of unity, will powerfully attract all the members of the Phalanx at every age, and each will find himself fit for some employment. This is an habitual pleasure for all, and at the same time the most useful instruction; for spiritual harmony, the harmony of the passions, the pledge of happiness and concord, intimately unites itself with measured or material harmony.

We see how many motives unite to excite children to useful labors from the earliest age. We know how powerful their faculty of imitation is. All that they see done, they will attempt. We also know their incessant activity, their turbulent and restless nature. This is the disturbance of individual households; the child would touch everything, and yet nothing is within his reach; continual chidings and scoldings are employed with the poor little one, who follows the impulse of his nature; a valuable impulse, inasmuch as when well directed, it impels the child to industry. It breaks and destroys, because it is not duly furnished with the means of employing its faculties. At present even, this may be observed; if a little girl can assist her mother in the household; if she can have the charge of her little brother, guard him and nurse him; if she is permitted to go into the kitchen and assist the cook, she will do her best, and delight in being useful. In the same manner, if a little boy can dig and rake the ground; if he is permitted to handle tools; if he is employed in some department of useful occupation, he will put forth all the care and all the skill of which he is capable; he will pass hours in patiently putting stone upon stone, in turning a wheel, in arranging a heap, through the mere sentiment of the importance of his labor. Children have all the useful passions and desires in germ; it is only necessary to know how to apply them, to render them capable of everything good, grand, useful, and generous. In the Phalanstery care is taken to inspire the children from the first dawnings of intelligence, with the feeling of their importance and utility. All their toys are tools, and have a useful end; all their plays are metamorphosed into labors, and become fruitful. With them it is a habit so native, that they can not understand how time can be ever sheerly wasted. Labors and pleasures are identical for the children of the Phalanx; they are ignorant that they can be disunited. Their labors and their tools being always proportionate to their strength and their skill, they feel neither pain nor fatigue. Laboring by groups in short and varied occupations, they know neither tedium nor disgust; but, quite the contrary, constantly stimulated by example, the expectation of examinations, the desire of advancing in grades, of passing from a lower to a higher corporation, in which they see children classed of a strength immediately above their own, they are full of zeal and ardor. They have motives yet more powerful: the affection of all that surround them; the desire of responding to it, of pleasing; love, enthusiasm, religion, the power of devotedness, of which children are eminently capable. The love of God, humanity, their country and their parents—all these impel them to duty, that is to say, to co-operation with the order and the harmony in their native Phalanx and the whole world.

By mere imitation and successive initiation, the children go through an apprenticeship to all the labors to which they are attracted by taste and inclination. But this is only one part of instruction properly so called. It is the imitative, mechanical, material part, that which develops the physical powers, the senses; it is by this that childhood must commence. The body acquires strength before the mind; but the mind has never been absolutely neglected: the child has acquired a thousand notions; he has divined in part the theory by the practice; he has seen much, heard much, felt much. His observation and his judgment can not be distorted; they have been developed spontaneously; they have been exercised on the truth, and on the reality of things. The heart can not be perverted, for these young children have constantly under their eyes examples of piety, goodness, concord, and harmony. Everything speaks to them of God, his justice, and his goodness. They see God in his works; they feel his presence in themselves—around themselves; in the peace of the society in which they live, in the harmony of their own feelings and desires, in their whole being. Their life is a perpetual feeling of love and gratitude towards God and their fellow-creatures. They are ignorant of the subversive passions—hatred, doubt, and incredulity. In the infant of harmony, love and faith will be spontaneously developed; he examines, he thinks, he reflects by himself; he abandons himself to his natural sentiments; he is susceptible neither of deceit, nor of concealment, nor of fear; he knows but truth—he seeks it, he speaks it as he feels it. It is thus that the development of the soul and of the spirit does not remain behind the strength and vigor of the body. Spiritual, social, and material education are continuous and simultaneous, though the last is most predominant in childhood.

With the natural development of the mind, and of the aptitude for various branches of industry, the child acquires science, properly so called; the complete theory of the arts and the various kinds of industry which he cultivates, the principal notions of the sciences which interest every thinking being; the description of the heavens and of the earth, the history of nations. The rules of grammar and literature are constantly developed by Professors for all ages and in every degree of instruction. The children and young people will attend to them according as their inclinations dispose them. In the Phalanx, who will be the professors? Generally, all those learned in science and theory; their mission is naturally to teach what they know. It is a natural desire for those who possess knowledge, to communicate it to others. In the Phalanx, learning is not confined to the closet: professors are at the same time workers, men versed in theory and practice, of art and science, and industrial activity. There are too many means of combining theory with practice in the Phalanstery for them ever to be separated. The savants do not form a class apart; all the laborers are more or less acquainted with both theory and practice, and most of them are professors. They will enrol themselves in the various groups of instruction; they will rival each other in the zeal and ardor with which they cultivate the kindly feelings and intelligence of the rising generation. The most learned will form, in their respective corporations, under-graduates and assistants, among the most apt and intelligent pupils, to distribute the instruction, according to their methods, to various groups and classes of students. Every branch of art and science is thus taught in many graduated groups, according to a method at once mutual and simultaneous. The practical lessons, whenever the season and the climate permit, will be given in the open air, among the very objects that serve as matter for instruction. If it be gardening, agriculture, and botany, in which the professor instructs his pupils, he takes the earth and its productions to demonstrate his discourse; if it be astronomy, the heavens; if it be painting, it is before the master-works of the great painters, and still more in the presence of Nature herself, that he will develop the beauties and magnificence of the art; if it be music, he will enchant the ear by harmony before developing the principles; if it be the mechanical arts, the trades, the various branches of industry, the professor conducts his pupils into the workshops, gives practical demonstration with precept, and in all cases gives a triune lesson—theory, practice, and variety of application.

The kitchen, the barn, the cellar, the cow-house, the stable, the poultry-yard, the garden, the orchards, the fields, serve at once as the scene and the text of instruction, which is, in some measure, perpetual.

We do not here speak of elementary instruction, of reading, writing, and arithmetic; because this first instruction is so simple, that it is an amusement, as well for the professors as for the pupils. Young girls from twelve to fifteen years of age will divide this professorship with grave old men, who will seek infancy from predilection; young girls are also fond of acting the mamma. The one and the other will enrol themselves in the groups of elementary instructers, and emulate each other in the invention of easy and attractive methods.

The aged are not a burden to the Phalanx, as they often are in civilization. Loved, honored, and respected, they labor and render themselves useful as much as their strength permits them, bringing to the office of instruction all the advantages they have derived from long experience and extensive practice; and when their strength declines, they link themselves with tender infancy and become their guides, protectors, guardians. Sublime harmony! the old man and the child mutually aid each other; the one to live, the other to die!

The children and the adolescent remain entirely free to follow the course that suits them. They instruct themselves or remain ignorant, according to their desires. But it is with studies as with labors; civilization alone renders them repugnant. Man at every age is anxious to instruct himself. With all, men, women, and children, it is a passion to know, to acquire knowledge. All instruct themselves spontaneously, and seek light on all that has been, on all that is. This passion or attraction is particularly active in the child. As soon as his intelligence is open, he begins to question and examine; if he finds instruction suited to him, he seizes it with ardor.

The passion for study will be excited in Harmony, where instruction, which will be free and spontaneous as well for the professors as the pupils, will have practice for its immediate object, and will link itself with daily labors, which already please and captivate the mass. In harmony, instruction will be one of the strongest passions, and among the most lively enjoyments of childhood, adolescence, and mature age, of young girls and women, as of men. The old man himself is still a disciple, and at the same time a professor. As long as he preserves his intelligence, he has the desire of instructing himself. The Phalanx forms a vast school of mutual instruction, where all are both disciples and professors, mutually enlightening each other on all branches of science, and ever pushing their investigations further, so that the human intellect, freed from all the cares and troubles of material existence, will enlarge in vast proportions; and by an even more extended application of the sciences, it will enlarge the field of industry beyond the limits of our actual imagination.

Every Phalanx will not contain within itself alone a full development of every branch of art, and science, and industrial perfection, but each will be renowned for some superior developments, and they will learn from one another their respective excellencies. Some will be more central and important than the rest, and higher branches of instruction will be found in these, as in our universities.

One of the advantages of the unitary system also, is that every one will be able to travel for instruction and delight—a taste at once so general and so powerful. Each individual will travel as his nature prompts him with a view to pleasure, want of motion, variety, or for instruction and utility.

If a traveller makes some stay in a Phalanx, he will either accept the minimum offered to all, or he will take part in the labors of the groups and the series, which, with regard to objects of necessity, are similar in all the Phalansteries; and he will thus defray his own expenses by the profits of his labor. Travelling, which will be a necessary part of education, will not be expensive, and young people may be allowed to travel everywhere, without fear of danger or corruption.

The labors of one Phalanx, however varied, would not suffice for the activity of man, especially during the first periods of life. Youth has need of seeing, of travelling, of undertaking extraordinary and marvellous things.

In the present day, travels have but a mean aim, which is known beforehand; armies and wars have lost all the magic, the grandeur, the chivalry, which formerly disguised their hideous atrocity. War is nothing but a common and a tedious trade, which offers but inferior chances of advancement, and has nothing that can satisfy an ardent mind. At the present day, when young people have finished what is called their education, their university studies, and would launch themselves into the world, even when they have fortune at command, what can they do, what brilliant career is open to them? At best, they travel monotonously, distastefully, to come back wearied with what they have seen, disgusted with what they find on their return.*

* Madam Gatti de Gammond.

ORGANIZATION OF THE TOWNSHIP. 65

§ V. *Distribution of Profits.*

We now reach the question as to the repartition of profits, and we have to show that the Reformed System, is so harmonic that it will produce accord upon a point on which our individuality and selfishness are apt to be the most discordant.

By the word *profit*, we mean benefits and gains of all kinds, whatever recompenses the services rendered, whether honors, ranks, titles, decorations, influence, or power, as well as money.

Justice demands that each laborer be consulted in this distribution ; for, whoever does anything for society ought to have an influence in the direction given to that society, proportional to the worth of his acts.

Thus, we are the friends of *universal suffrage!* But let no one fear that we are about to fall into that abyss of absurdity and confusion into which our political reformers have fallen—reformers who would give the right to vote to men who are not competent to read even the names of the candidates they are about to vote for, and to whom they deny at the same time the much more important and valuable right—the right to labor and subsistence. If equity demands that every member of society should be consulted in the management of it, Good Sense fixes the limit of the right, by prescribing that the opinion of each one should be asked only so far as he knows, both theoretically and practically, and that this opinion should only have the weight of the person from whom it comes.

We have to demonstrate, then, that in a Phalanx, *all* men exercising their rights in the sphere of their competency and capacity, *can* decide, if they will, with equity and right: we shall therefore establish that the laborer *who can be just, will be directly interested in being so, and that he will wish to be just.*

It is necessary to repeat : in the Phalanx, individuals form groups, groups form series of the first degree, the series of the first degree form series of the second degree, etc.

Thus, in an army, detachments or *groups* form companies, companies battalions, battalions regiments, regiments brigades, etc. ; only that in the Phalanx the same laborer makes part of many groups, and figures in several series.

Elections begin in the group. The members of the groups distribute their respective titles, honors, and grades, and name their chiefs, officers, and sub-officers.

The chiefs of all the groups of the same series of the first degree unite together in order to choose the chiefs of that series. The chiefs of the inferior series name, in the same way, the chiefs of the superior series, and then the chiefs of the highest series name the chiefs or regents of the Phalanx.*

This mode of election satisfies the first condition laid down—to consult each one, but only in things which he understands. The laborers of a group, working together under each other's eyes, will soon come to distinguish the comparative qualifications of each other in that particular work, and will select their chiefs with prudence and sagacity ; moreover, in proportion as they are elevated in the hierarchical scale, in proportion as they are engaged in more general interests, the chiefs, subjected to new trials, chosen by a mass more and more enlightened, offer every guarantee of fitness for the functions which are confided to them. By this election, in several degrees, too, the electors and the elected, are never more than a step apart from each other, and are easily, on both sides, understood and appreciated.

Every laborer having to vote in all the groups in which he takes part, sees his influence increase with the number of things that occupy him ; besides that in each of these things his influence is by right of his capacity, since, according to the degree of his merit, he is called to act either simply upon the interests of the groups, or upon the less limited interests of the series, or even upon the interests of the whole Phalanx.

The recompense of honors and ranks is distributed in the same manner : and the pecuniary profits will be divided by a similar process.

* The choice is ratified by a ballot in which all the individuals take part, when it is submitted to the phalanx. The modes of election in some cases vary, as will be hereinafter explained.

The regency of the Phalanx, constituted as we have just explained, will first subtract from the annual product the sum required to meet the common expenses; 1st, the taxes, which will be collected in the most simple manner without expenses of collection, and without bringing the tax-gatherers into immediate contact with individuals, which is often so irritating; 2d, all those things which the Phalanx derives from without, not from the labor of its groups, but from the world, as provisions, instruments, &c., &c., which it may not be in a state to create; 3d, a reservation for the current expenses and labors of the ensuing year.

This first sum subtracted, the remainder will be divided into three parts, destined to remunerate each of the productive faculties—Capital, Labor, and Talent.

These three parts will be divided among the series, the groups, and individuals, by descending the hierarchical scale, of which we have given the constitution. Each laborer, besides the interest on his stock, will be entitled in each of the groups in which he has been engaged, to a certain amount, in payment of his work, and to another amount, in payment of whatever superior talent he may have manifested.

The interest on Capital being determined by a fixed rate, there will be no difficulty in making a dividend among those who possess certificates of stock.

Labor being paid not only according to the time spent, but proportionably to the difficulty of the work, it will be necessary at first to fix the right of each group in respect to the second point. Each group having received the sum which is due, will distribute it among the laborers, in proportion to the time in which each one has worked in that group, which time will have been accurately entered upon its registers. If any one or more of the laborers should have clearly performed more work than the others, they will be entitled to a reward for it from the sum designated as the remuneration of talent.

This third part will be divided among those who are distinguished in any manner whatever, who have merited titles, ranks, honors, who have shone in the display of force, address, activity, or intelligence.

As to those who have invented or improved anything, as the result of their labor will be of use, not only to the Phalanx but to all humanity, it is from all the Phalanxes that they will receive their reward.

An engineer introduces an improvement in machinery. His Phalanx which profits the first by his invention, pays him by voting an inconsiderable sum, a minimum, say of one cent. The discovery spreads, all the phalanxes of the globe adopt it successively, if it is found to be decidedly useful, and all in the same way vote a recompense to the inventor. If there are 3,000,000 of Phalanxes on the globe, he will be entitled to 30,000 dollars at least. The works of art, poetry, literature, will be recompensed in the same way.

This mode has a thousand advantages over that of granting patents or commissions. Humanity profits with the utmost promptitude by the discovery, and the inventor obtains a reward proportioned to the merits of his invention.

The spirit of intrigue or a coterie will be ineffectual in giving vogue to a discovery that is valueless. If, for instance, a poet by means of his friends, obtains an unmerited success—if he succeeds in a few neighboring phalanxes, where he is known and loved, his work can not go much farther without sinking, and both he and his too friendly phalanxes will fall into confusion and shame.

If, on the contrary, the poet or inventor should be unjustly dealt with by a Phalanx, he would appeal to the judgment of others, and receive a speedy recognition.

Such is the mechanism of distribution; but it remains to be explained how the reciprocal rights of Capital, Talent, and Labor, and of each kind of labor in particular, would be guaranteed according to principles of equity and common accord.

In a Phalanx, the problem of distribution may take the form of an arithmetical problem, like this:—

What are the domestic, agricultural, and mechanical labors, which the Phalanx must undertake for the general interest, to which all particular interests are connected? What development must it give to each of them? How much, consequently, of strength, of intelligence, and of capital ought each to attract? In other words, what are the labors it requires, to what extent shall they be prosecuted, and what are the means necessary?

It is evident that all will be interested in the solution of this problem, and that the solution of it will be the solution of the problem of distribution.

But in effect, the laborers being free in their choice, will not group themselves in such a way as to conform absolutely with what the general interest had determined. In order to establish equilibrium, therefore, to recal laborers to the points where they are wanted, to separate them from groups in which they are superabundant, the Association must make use of the lever of Distribution. By diminishing the sum appropriated to a group, it will separate from it the most lukewarm and so reduce the number of laborers. By the contrary process it will recal laborers to a deserted group. It will thus arrive, after a few trials, perhaps some blunders, at that equilibrium of which it feels the necessity.

There is nothing arbitrary in the determination of the sum appropriated to each group, inasmuch as that sum will depend upon the number of laborers of which it has need. In the group itself, the amount will be divided justly according to the merits of individuals.

If the group is unjust toward one who has served it with the greatest effectiveness, he, perhaps, the most capable laborer will abandon the ungrateful group, and the whole group will suffer, for its injustice, more than he who has been wronged.

The phalansterian organization is the only one that permits the laborer to resist the injustice of the majority. Everywhere else men who know only one business, who exercise only a single function, must be maintained by it, or hazard their position in life. It is for this reason, among others, that the working-men in civilization are so generally the servile dependants of their employers. They know that they must do what their master (fitly characterized by the name), bids them, or suffer the loss of their place, which is now equivalent to the loss of their own subsistence and that of their families. But in the Phalanx, the laborer, may without suffering sensibly, abandon one or another of his thirty functions; and he would lose nothing at all, if he presented himself to a group whose occupations resembled those of the group he had just left. He would be received with joy, and soon assume the rank which was his due.

It is not to be feared that self-love would exaggerate the pretensions of certain laborers. He who should estimate himself for more than he was worth, and thinking himself neglected, retire in discontent, would speedily be brought to see, that while on one side there was no note taken of his absence, there would be no eagerness to receive him among others.

The interest on stock will be determined much in the same way; it will be augmented when it is necessary to call in capital, and it will be diminished when capital is superabundant.

Working in a great number of groups and series, a laborer can not hold the same rank in all. If he is a soldier here he will be a captain there, and will, at one time, be in subjection to those, that at another, he will command. He may have, then, a superiority over the most eminent men, which will not wound their pride, although it may be a decided satisfaction to his self-love, however insignificant the superiority may be in other respects. The reason of this is that we always attach the highest importance to the traits in which we excel, because the character of our ambition is necessarily related to the kind and degree of our intelligence.

Thus, all those laborers developed integrally, by a thorough education, will have claims upon the sum designed for the recompense of *Talent.*

Serial labor yielding great profits, the poorest man will gain something beyond his bare subsistence, and with the slightest economy will enable himself to purchase some shares in the capital stock. Many advantages, of which we can not here take notice, are accorded to small capitalists, in order to favor such a result. All the members of a Phalanx, then, will be, in different degrees, *capitalists*.

Labor being transformed into a pleasure, the rich as well as the poor will be drawn towards Industry. All will be *laborers*.

The profits of the individual will, accordingly, be divided into a great many portions, to which respectively he will be entitled in all the groups in which he takes part, and for each of his productive faculties. In the arbitrations which will fix the value of one of these portions, the laborer could not manifest as much of avidity and blindness as he would were his whole fortune concerned, because just to the extent in which he unjustly pressed his claims on one score, he would injure himself on all other scores. Besides, in almost all the series of the Phalanx, he would find people that he particularly loved,—a wife, or children, or parents, or friends; and he would have extreme difficulty in combining his votes in such a way as to satisfy, at the same time, his selfish interests and the interests of those who were dear to him.

Nor is it to be feared that the rivalry between the series and groups would engender hatred and the desire to injure. That rivalry would differ essentially from that which now divides people of the same profession. A group would be interested in surpassing its rivals by raising itself above them, and not depressing them below it. The triumph obtained by the latter means would be purchased too dearly; as by the abasement of any one of the groups, the whole series will have lost in worth, and the victorious group itself will have a smaller dividend to touch and less honor to receive. Thus, in an army, the only example that we have of a series even approaching regularity, the rivalries of the companies, are silenced when they are engaged in the interests of the regiment, the rivalries of the regiments are effaced when it becomes necessary to think of the army. But of the Phalanx, so much superior in its discipline, because not forced, but passional, we must remark, that by the constant alternations of labor, the men who were just now engaged in a warm contest, would, in an hour afterward, be working side by side for some common end, so that the corporative rivalries would not extend to individuals.

These explanations are required by those who, living in Civilization, are habituated to see interest predominant, everywhere and always, over the more generous and elevated sentiments. Here the voice of self-interest is ever consulted and ever heard; but will it be so in the Phalanx?

There, labor being attractive, it will no longer be necessary to constrain men, who, laboring from passion, will be emancipated from the yoke of necessity, by the certainty of constantly enjoying, whatever may happen, a decent *minimum* in clothing, lodging, food, public conveyances, etc., etc. This minimum will be assured, even in cases of a refusal to labor,—cases that can only be anomalies proceeding from some derangement of the faculties. The society will be at the expense, moreover, of those children who cannot labor, and of old men and infirm persons that are unable to do anything, so that they may not distress themselves about the future, either their own or their families'.

An absolute loss of fortune, which in Civilization is a stroke almost as cruel as death, can only be a temporary mortification and disappointment in the Phalanx, because he who experiences it would not be lowered in his social position, nor be compelled to change any of his relations. Thus, each one would find himself in the possession of an inappreciable good, totally unknown in our societies, in the absence of solicitude or care; the mind would no longer be distracted by anxieties, and Mankind united in all their interests, united by reciprocal services, meeting everywhere good will and affection, would give themselves up to noble and disinterested sentiments, such as are seen among us only in early youth, before they are suppressed by the cares, the selfishness, the distrust, and the jealousy of more advanced life.

Can we not see how easy it would be to resolve the problem of the distribution of profits, when all are directly interested in having it decided equitably?

§ VI. *Property.*

It is time to approach a question which Science must resolve, if it wishes to prevent the commotions with which nearly all civilized society is menaced—a question which, in Europe, and perhaps ere long in this country, will leave the studies of philosophers and the pages of essayists, to take up arms in the streets, to get itself decided by broadswords and muskets. It is the question of Property,—the question of the reciprocal rights of Labor and Capital—rights that we ought to respect in an equal degree, because they are both legitimate.

This question, we say, must be settled by Science, or it will be by revolution. No one who considers the circumstances under which the mass of the people everywhere exist; that while wealth is generally increasing, they are as rapidly deteriorating—a fact which puzzles all our political economists; that the many are growing poorer and the rich richer; that the very improvements of the age are still further depressing the working classes; no one can consider these, and a thousand kindred facts, without feeling that a great change, violent or peaceful, must be wrought in the condition of the masses. They feel that the adjustments of Property are wrong, and they demand the remedy.*

Our philosophers and statesmen, governed by that spirit of Simplism of which we have given several examples, occupy themselves with only one side of this question; and regarding the interests of property-holders exclusively, have overlooked the rights of the laborer. On the other hand, many persons, impressed only with the rights of the laborer, and feeling that no one ought to depend for his living upon the pleasure of others, have denied all rights of property. So long as both are lost in their exclusiveness; so long as they join to their affirmations, which are just, negations of the rights which seem opposed to them, they will be unable to terminate the dispute, except by violence: and violence, if it should lead, by the annihilation of one party, to a factitious and precarious equilibrium, is incompetent to establish stable order or definite agreement.

The Social School of Fourier, often the object of attack to both parties, whose attacks, by the way, neutralize each other, has discovered a theory which can reconcile these hostile camps, and relieve the controversy of every difficulty. We shall unfold their theory in a few words.

The Deity has made the human race a present worthy of his magnificence; he has given them the Earth. This Earth, so splendidly illuminated, so full of life, so fruitful, enclosing in its bosom all that Man can desire, all wealth, all blessings—this Earth has been given to Man.

This gift belongs to all; no man, no generation of men, can legitimately dispose of it, to the exclusion of other men or other generations. The rich and the poor, the proprietor and the proletaire, have only equal rights over the primitive soil, over the rude products of nature. This right is the right to live, which all have acquired by the single fact of their birth. "Men," says Mr. Carlyle, in Past and Present, "men talk of selling land! Who can or could sell it to us? Properly speaking, the Land belongs to these two: To the Almighty God and to all his children of Men that have ever worked well on it, or that shall ever work well on it. No generation of men can or could, with never such solemnity or effort, sell land on any other principle: it is not the property of any generation, we say, but of all the past generations that have worked on it, and of all the future ones that shall work on it."

Yet Man, made in the image of God, may, like him, transform and create. Out of an ungrateful soil, he makes a fertile field; from the rude mass of rock, he constructs a palace; worthless earthy matter, he converts into gems and precious metals; in a word, he centuples the value of everything that he has received. What man thus derives from his labor, may with peculiar propriety be said to be his: it is that which without him would not have existed; he may dispose of it as he pleases; it is his property, his goods, his *right to capital.*

---

* See an Essay of the author, called "Constructive Democracy," published in the Present for December, 1843; also, an article headed "One of the Problems of the Age," by some intelligent democrat, in the Dem. Review for February, 1844.

But each one may claim his share in every object which has received no improvement from the hand of man, and in the primitive and raw value of everything that has been transformed or created by labor. This is the right of all —it is *the right of the laborer.*

This right is broadly recognised in the Phalanx, where each one may lay hold of all raw material which he expects to use, by enrolling himself in the group charged with the preparation of that matter. The Phalanx goes further; although it is impossible to live at this day without industry, upon wild fruits and roots, it concedes the right of doing nothing to whoever will content himself upon a minimum sufficient to secure him against every painful privation.

The right of capital is equally respected. In the system we are sketching, is perfectly conciliated the rights of capital and labor; the two are associated and sustain each other, and move in parallel lines, by augmenting or diminishing in the same ratio.

If man is the legitimate owner of everything that he has created by his industry, he may dispose of it as he pleases,—give it away if that be his inclination. He who receives it, through the voluntary abandonment of it by the first owner, becomes its legitimate owner. And as there is nothing to limit this right, the possessor may still give it away, even when quitting this life. Thus Inheritance, so violently attacked by some reformers, is a just, a legitimate means of acquiring property.

The adversaries of the right of inheritance have attacked the principle, because in civilization, Property has shut out the Laborer from his Right, and because Inheritance has ever been accompanied by a great many abuses. But every evil of this kind, it is too obvious to be dwelt upon, must totally disappear from the Phalanx.

Among the adversaries of the right of property are found men who have gone so far as to include in their reprobation, the rights of Labor and Talent. They have wished an equal division of all goods, whatever may have been the concurrence of individuals in the production of them. But this is absurd.

The inequality of fortune is much less than the inequality in the degrees of esteem and affection that each one is entitled to receive. If the Levellers, therefore, are forced to accept these natural inequalities, if they can not make each one gather an equal harvest of love, friendship, consideration, etc., of what moment is a single inequality more?

On the other hand, the proprietors, when they are willing to acknowledge that this Distribution among Capital, Labor and Talent is not Community, still accuse us of taking away the great charm of property, by putting it in the form of a joint stock possession, which deprives the possessor, they say, of the pleasure of feeling that "this is mine, my gardens, my woods, my house," etc., etc.

On the contrary, we contend that the feeling of true Self-Love, which is gratified by the possession of a beautiful or fine thing, will be developed in the Phalanx to a much more intense degree that it can be anywhere else. If the orchards, for example, are well cultivated, if luxuriantly furnished with fruits and flowers, they win the admiration of the traveller, the series of orchardists, composed of men, whose labor and talent have produced this delightful result, shall they not say, with more right than an unworking owner,—*this is my orchard!* than an owner who glories only in the talent of his gardener, the sagacity of his farmer, and who is not entitled to a single plume which, like the jackdaw, he borrows from the peacock.

§ VII. *Order and Liberty.*

The conception of Fourier may be recapitulated in two great theorems; the first relating to general Order, the second, to the Liberty of all beings.

1st. THE SERIES DISTRIBUTES THE HARMONIES OF THE UNIVERSE.—*Order*
2d. ATTRACTIONS ARE PROPORTIONAL TO DESTINIES.—*Liberty.*

The great serial law, applied to the social organization, would be manifested by the most perfect order on earth, and that order would be reconcilable with the most absolute liberty; for, in order to organize themselves and work in a

Phalanx, men have only to follow one guide, Attraction, have only to yield to their tendencies, only to listen to their Affection.

Men, women, and children, independent of each other, as to the employment of their faculties, will follow their aptitudes, and will do good, without being impelled by precepts or constrained by law; and it is only from Attractive Labor that liberty can spring. What liberty can the workingman hope for in our societies? Is he not, under all governments, subjected to the most pitiless and despotic of tyrants, Necessity? Necessity which strikes whoever resists it, with the most horrible punishments, with misery and famine!

In the Phalanx, liberty will be, if we say so, unlimited. Although all things are classed and formed into hierarchy, although the conduct of the groups and series is confided to chiefs, those chiefs *counsel*, not *order*, and each one may act contrary to their advice. Because, in a society in which individual interests agree with the general interest, we can not bring ourselves to believe that many persons will resist an invitation made, for the common good, by those who have been acknowledged the most capable,—we can not believe that there would be found many, who would injure themselves, to show their disdain of advice in itself good. Revolt against authority would evidently be an anomaly, an exceptional case, like the refusal to labor. They would leave the refractory to pout their fill, as they would allow the indolent to fold their arms, convinced that they would have few occasions for the exercise of tolerance in either case, and that it would be accompanied by no danger.

Thus, there would be absolute liberty for all, even for children, of whose emancipation the wildest radical has not yet dreamed, notwithstanding their palpable and decided right to the free use of their faculties, now held in a complete, severe, and most disastrous bondage.

It is singular to observe, how the nations of this world in their struggles after more satisfactory forms of government, have been able to accomplish only a distant approximation to a true and perfect form. The difficulty has been, that not possessing the correct formula of social equilibrium, they have vibrated around the true point, without ever having attained to stability. They have either had too little of liberty on the one hand, or too little of law on the other; and thus failed through excess in the opposite quality in both cases.

In order to elucidate the various schemes of political constitution which divide the world, let us resort to a table, in which the different kinds may be seen together yet in contrast. The table we give is entirely incomplete, being designed merely for illustration in this elementary and hasty discussion. We could easily extend it, so as to embrace forty-eight modulations of doctrines, but that would defeat the purpose we have in view which is simple and popular instruction. The table is as follows:—

TABLE OF CONTRASTED HUMAN GOVERNMENTS.

		Transition.	1. Autocracy.
Order.	I. ABSOLUTISM.	{	1. Hereditary Monarchy.
			2. Elective Monarchy.
	III. FEUDALISM.	{	3. Hereditary Aristocracy.
			4. Elective Aristocracy.
Liberty and Order.	X. ASSOCIATION. X. Attractive Hierarchy.		
Liberty.	IV. GUARANTEEISM.	{	4. Guaranteeism.
			3. Republicanism.
	II. INDIVIDUALISM.	{	2. Constitutional Democracy.
			1. Simple Democracy.
		Transition.	No-governmentism.

We have not space enough to develop fully the meaning of this table; but our readers, on little reflection, will find it out for themselves. All the forms of government here enumerated, are founded upon a true sentiment: what is affirmative in them all, is good and true; only what is negative is wrong. It is right that there should be in society Absolutism, or Unity of Purpose; it is right that there should be Individualism, or popular freedom or independence; it is right that there should be Feudalism, or distinction of class; and it is right that there should be Guaranteeism, or constitutional safeguards and defences of the rights of the mass. So far, then, as any of these principles are adopted by a society, so far it is legitimate; its falsehood commences when it denies the other principles. Individualism denies the authority of any power but its own will, and therefore leads to Disorder; Absolutism denies the will of the individual, and therefore leads to Oppression and Tyranny; and so of the other forms. But in Association, which denies none and accepts all, the liberty of the individual is conciliated with the order of the state, distinctions of rank harmonized with the guarantied rights of the masses. There is *absolute* unity of purpose and movement; hierarchical or *feudal* gradations of honor; the *guarantied* minimum and freedom of all classes; and the utmost *individuality* allowed to every person.

It would be curious to trace out the path of thought here indicated, were it consistent with the design of this book.

END OF PART I.

INTERMEDIATE.

ESSENTIAL DISTINCTION BETWEEN THE TWO PARTS OF THIS WORK.

There are many persons in these times who feel that there is no salvation for modern society, except through the organization of industry, and who have therefore adopted the constructive principles of Fourier, as the most rational and practicable that have ever been proposed. These men are of all parties in politics and of all creeds in religion; and it is because Fourier's principles for township organization invade no private rights, and wound no peculiar sensibilities, that they are enabled to meet on a common ground of benevolent action. It is of such that the Societary or Phalansterian School is composed.

It is true that some persons, with a lightness that verges upon malignity or bad faith, obstinately accuse that school of a design to abolish property, the family relation, and religion: but can they, in the face of the sketch we have just given, hope to persuade the public of so barefaced a falsehood? Is the division of profits between Capital, Labor, and Talent, likely to lead to the abolition of property, or to a stagnant equality? Is the family likely to be injured, in a condition of society which will furnish new and strong guarantees for its independence, peace, and happiness?—where the interchange of family affections will not be interrupted by the influence of adverse interests? Is there no longer meaning in words? Are the most positive avowals of intention and principles not to be believed?

Whoever, then, undertakes to criticise or accuse the Phalansterian School, must, to be honest, do so on other grounds than these. He must take up directly and only the project they present, and prove that it is in itself worthless or impracticable. Random charges against opinions which we repel and plans we do not propose, can only expose the authors of them to the contempt of all fair-minded people.

The School of Fourier proposes but one thing: THE ORGANIZATION OF LABOR IN THE TOWNSHIP. It has no other object; no other faith, as a School. Individuals are, of course, always at liberty to promulgate whatever opinions they may see fit.

Let a township be once organized according to our principles, and the reform will soon spread over the whole nation.

Slavery, direct and indirect, will then be abolished, because labor will have become attractive; savages and barbarians will more readily adopt the manners of refined and cultivated life; science, art, and industry, will be largely developed, and the most perfect order will reign along with the most perfect liberty.

This is our conviction: this is all we teach.

But as it is obvious that Law, Government, Manners, and Religion, would all be more or less affected by a unitary *regime* of Industry, as they would all be influenced to bring themselves under the operation of some unitary law, Fourier has extended his researches, and uttered his thought, as to what would be the state of these Customs, Beliefs, etc., in the periods of social Harmony. These conjectures, in the domain of pure theory, and not followed by any proposition, are to be accepted or rejected by the generations of the future, according to the light which time and investigation may throw upon them.

It is from this point of view that the reader is requested to study the second part of this work, in which are elucidated those ideas only which Fourier himself has called his musings or fancies (*reveries*). These fancies, it is true, in the minds of many of us, possess a clear and signal truth; but it is only, we repeat, the practical side of Fourier's doctrine which is universally adopted and defended by the whole school of Societary Reformers.

Even if these ideas of the Future, which we are about to unfold, were as objectionable as some have represented, would that prove that the township need not be, or can not be, organized? May not the same man have suggested good and bad thoughts? Would it not be absurd to confound all in the same reprobation? If what we have already proposed is good, can the foolishness or the wickedness of what we are going to say, make it bad?

After this reservation, then, which all candid and honorable men will receive in good faith, we approach frankly and fearlessly all the questions that Fourier has raised, well-assured that he who understands them will confess,—not their truth in all cases,—but the magnificence of the intellect and the nobleness of the heart in which they were born.

It has not been the policy of the Societary School to refer to these questions at all, and their very reserve has brought suspicion upon their intentions, so that what was in the first place a judicious caution has been converted into a weapon of accusation. We trust that the reader will see, in the sequel, that the reserve and the suspicion are now alike unnecessary.

No one is asked to believe in this second part; we do not ourselves individually accept all of it; and it is given, *as an amusement*, solely to complete our plan.

BOOK FOURTH.

UNITY OF MAN WITH HIMSELF.

SECOND SECTION.

CHAPTER VII.

ORGANIZATION OF SOCIETY.

> "J'ai vu la Paix descendre sur la terre,
> Semant de l'or, des fleurs et des epis :
> L'air était calme, et du Dieu de la guerre
> Elle étouffait les foudres assoupis.
> Ah ! disait elle, egaux par la vaillance,
> Francaise, Anglais, Belge, Russe ou Germain,
> Peuples, former une sainte alliance.
>   Et donner vous la main,
> Pauves mortels, tant de haine, vous lasse,
> Vous ne goûter qu'un pénible sommeil.
> D'un globe étroit divisez mieux l'espace,
> Chacun de vous aura place au soleil."—DE BERANGER.

§ I. *Hierarchy.*

WE have said that after having laid down the fundamental principles of township reform, Fourier could not stop there; he had yet to discover how, during the epochs of Harmony, the phalanxes should be connected with each other, to determine what should be the hierarchical constitution of society. We have shown also that the ideas of Fourier on this point are not to be regarded as *propositions* as to what must be done, but simply as conjectures or *previsions* of what would probably take place in the course of time.

If his conceptions in this respect are just, they will possess that character of Universal Conciliation which necessarily belongs to Truth, and the social hierarchy, which he foresees will have the power of causing itself to be unanimously adopted. It is requisite, therefore, that it should embrace all interests, that it should recognise all rights, that it should accept all established verities; it is requisite that it should make amends for all injustices, without ceasing to guaranty to each the undisturbed possession of all its peculiar advantages.

Considered as a territorial division, the Phalanx is called by Fourier an *Unarchy* (corresponding perhaps to one of our counties or to a barony in Europe); three or four Unarchies united form a Du-archy (as two or three counties here form a school district, or as in Europe three or four baronies constitute the jurisdiction of a Viscount); three or four Du-archies form a Tri-archy, &c. (similar to a State here, composed of several counties, &c.), until the number reaches a Duo-decarchy, which will be three in number,* together making the Omni-archy which will include the entire surface of the earth.

The administrations or regencies (*gerances*), in thirteen degrees, of all these divisions and subdivisions of territory, formed according to the elective system

---

* The three duo-decarchies will be 1st, Europe—Africa ; 2d, Asia—Oceana ; 3d, North and South America. Fourier says that he uses this barbarous nomenclature of Un-archy, Du-archy, &c., for the want of a better, and not as one which is proposed for adoption.

adopted in the Phalanx, will be constituted in the same manner, and of the same number of persons, fulfilling analogous functions in a sphere more or less extended. What we shall state, therefore, of a single administration will apply to all, to the administration of a simple phalanx, as well as to the omniarchal administration or the government of the whole earth.

We have seen that the Passions are the single source of all the actions of men, and although an action may depend upon many passions, there will be one passion dominant over the others, so that each action may take its rank or place according to the passion which gives it its character.

The influence of government upon society being nothing but its influence upon the actions of the members composing that society, or rather upon the relations which those actions establish between the members, government may be divided into branches corresponding to each kind of action, *i. e.*, into ministries springing respectively from one of the Passions. In this way, the social hierarchy will conform to the actual organization of man, to the hierarchy of the passions.

The chiefs of these different branches of government are denominated Sovereigns. Each occupies his throne by right of some passion and of the rank pertaining to the territorial division which it embraces. In all cases, the sovereignty is exercised conjointly by a man and woman, who have no other relations than such as grow out of their common function.

The sexes are thus treated with equal favor; youth even not being forgotten, inasmuch as there is reserved to it, through all the degrees of the hierarchy, the throne held in right of the passion of Friendship.

All these thrones, with one exception, are held by election, the greater part for a few years only, with the incumbents always re-eligible. The principal throne, that by right of character (a branch of Unityism*), is given for life or that portion of life in which a man enjoys his faculties in the plenitude of their power. The choice will be easily made, inasmuch as there will be few candidates for the place, its duties being such that only a small number of men will be fitted by nature to discharge them, while any others would be totally out of their element should they in any way get elevated to the dignity.

In this we take for granted that there is between inclinations or characters and the things to be executed, a just equilibrium, without which every attempt at social amelioration would be essentially futile. Science can only put each one in presence of his work, and then the work will have found its workman. In every function Nature presents many soldiers and few chiefs, so that each may take the place which he is the best adapted to fill. Actual society offers only one function for the thirty inclinations of the Individual, without caring even whether the exercise of that single function is likely to develop any of his natural tendencies.

The equilibrium of which we speak between the inward vocation and the outward function will be admitted by all those, who having studied the great book of Nature, are accustomed to admire the supreme wisdom of her laws. We see already an equilibrium of this kind between the sexes; yet that class of thinkers which ascribes the fact to Chance, have never had sufficient confidence in their theory, to disquiet themselves as to what would happen, if the Chance which makes this equilibrium should be broken, and the numerical equality between men and women cease to exist. So great is the instinctive confidence of mankind in the certain and uniform operation of the laws of God!

We have said that one throne, forming an exception to the common rule, is not determined by election. This is the throne by right of Familism, which is hereditary and remains in the same family for ever.

This passion of Familism presents a character which separates it very decidedly from the other affectives; the ties formed by these are ties of choice,— one chooses his wife, his friends, her husband; we attach ourselves freely,

---

* Each degree of the hierarchy will contain 16 thrones, 12 by right of the 12 radical passions, and 4 by right of Unityism. For the details we must refer the reader to the works of Fourier.

though ambitious, to the companies employed about the objects towards which we are drawn; but we do not choose either our parents or our children; nature gives them to us, and we accept and love them (or should love them) whatever they may be, without having any connection with them but that simply of consanguinity.

It is easy to conceive of the great utility of this exceptional character of Familism. It is well for man that he is connected with his fellows at every instant of his life, which could not happen if all the passions depended upon choice, since the child would not then have any ties with his fellows before having received a development sufficient to make him known and appreciated. It is by Familism that the infant is cherished, even before he sees the light, that he is impatiently expected at his entrance into life, and that he lays hold of so many by affection, in the interval of his being able to attach a greater number by other passions.

If it is necessary that Familism should be, so to speak, an instinctive passion, acting without the intervention of free-will, is it not also necessary that the particular character of the passion should be reproduced in all that depends upon it, in everything that tends to regulate its exercise?

There is found, then, in each degree of the Hierarchy, an hereditary throne for the direction of whatever relates to the family, to its civil condition; for the preservation of the traces of the past, the archives, the genealogies, the traditions, the history; for keeping an account of the crossing of races and their effects, etc., etc. Hereditary descent is requisite in functions which demand minute care, exact researches, and labor continued with regularity during centuries: and these qualities can only be found in a family, traditional itself, so to speak, and in which is transmitted from generation to generation, a function to which it refers, from time immemorial, as the source of its greatness and fortunes.

All opinions, political as well as others, must necessarily have some reason for their existence; they belong to some natural tendency, to some true sentiment of the human heart; and parties are wrong, not so much in what they demand, as in what they deny. Their negations more than their affirmations lead them into error. Science, Social Truth must accept all wishes (*vœux*), by removing the obstacles to their reconciliation, and by offering a combination sufficiently large to contain and to satisfy all at the same time.

The Hierarchy which Fourier has conceived gives ample satisfaction to all the desires manifested in the heart of nations, to the desire for elective chiefs as well as to the desire for hereditary thrones, but it circumscribes Heredicy to its natural limits by confining it exclusively to the domain of the family.

In contrast with this hereditary throne determined by chance, the human will not being consulted, the Hierarchy comprises a throne, the authority of which rests upon mere caprice. It is the annual throne of Favoritism (a branch of Unityism). A man is elevated to it for no other reason than that it is agreeable to have him there; where he assumes the presidency of festivals, fêtes, pleasure parties, and receptions; and which belongs to him on no other ground than that he best knows how to enliven and charm. The blind enthusiasm of the masses for certain individuals is natural to man, and ought to be satisfied, but always within the limits in which it can most happily act.

When reform shall have been generally carried into effect, the first titularies of Familism will be designated, and hereditary sceptres, twenty times more numerous than the thrones occupied at this day, and of which many will have jurisdiction over territories much superior in extent to the vast empires of either the present or the past, will be distributed.

The Regency of the inferior territorial divisions may be established at one of the principal Phalansteries; but for the superior divisions, there will be necessary manor-houses or head-quarters distinct from the Phalansteries,—cities more and more important, thus raising by degrees until they reach the Omniarchal Head-Quarters or the capital city of the Globe.*

* Fourier designates Constantinople as the city whose geographical position destines it to become this great centre of the world.

These cities will be the centre of commercial movement, where the Industrial Armies, of which we shall speak hereafter, will concentrate. There they will join the learned, the artistic, the agricultural, the industrial societies, and persons eager for profound instruction; there they will find the libraries, the associations, the museums, the galleries, the collections of charts, of mineralogy, of geology, of natural history, the great theatres, etc., etc. ; and there eminent men of all kinds will gather for intellectual converse and profit.

Thus, the cities will be occupied by a floating population, composed of bodies and individuals coming periodically from different places. For their regular service, each phalanx designed for the supply of the city, will furnish successive detachments, relieved as often as it may be necessary, and which will form what may be called the garrison. In this way, residence in the city, for nearly all, will only be temporary.

The cities resemble the Phalansteries in their external arrangements. They will be composed as at present of blocks of houses surrounded by streets ; but every block will have but one range of apartments on each street, and the ground enclosed by the block, now occupied by miserable second and third rate tenements—often by the most noisome and filthy sinks and stables, will form a great central garden. These gardens and streets, adorned with trees, will embellish and purify every neighborhood.

A covered way, or gallery, overlooking the garden, will run along the first story of all the buildings, and the different blocks will be connected with each other by means of bridges under which the carriages and carts may freely pass. Thus, as in the Phalansteries, people will go from one part of the city to another, without exposure to humidity or the influence of the atmosphere.

The cultivation of the gardens, the promenades and public grounds of the city will require only a small portion of the time of so numerous a population. In this way, as an exception, the labors of science, art, manufacture, and commerce, will, in the cities, surpass in importance, labors purely agricultural ; *purely* agricultural, we say, because there will still be carried on in the cities, the theoretical parts of culture, botanical gardens, nurseries, seed-plots, experiments, etc., etc.

Cities now in existence will be gradually improved, by the re-building of such parts as require it, according as the increase of wealth will permit of increased expenditures, by razing to the ground the inferior tenements, for the establishment of gardens, by bringing the lower stories, looking upon the court-yards, into communication by means of doorways and staircases; and by throwing bridges over the streets, destroying unwholesome quarters, etc., etc.

The Industrial Armies will undertake the labors which are interesting to several phalanxes at the same time, such as causeways, bridges, railroads, canals, the embankment of streams, and the wooding of mountains; they will have to purify and fertilize all parts of the globe, such as deserts, savannas, steppes, swamps, marshes, etc., which it will be necessary to conquer foot by foot ; they must open isthmuses, such as those of Suez and Panama, and they must bring the great lakes of the interior into communication with the ocean, etc., etc.

An army will take rank according to the rank of the territorial division interested in its labors, and will be convoked and arranged by the regency of that division, which will raise a part of the whole force from the region which it governs, and demand the other parts from the regencies of other regions. A country which shall have received the aid of its allies, ought to lend these equivalent assistance, in similar circumstances.

The union of bodies, taken from different countries, and each executing its tasks according to the methods of its own engineers, will excite a powerful emulation. They will engage in veritable industrial battles, and their triumphs, celebrated with pomp, will resound over the whole earth. The labors of industrial armies will be accompanied by greater glory than ever attended the labors of warriors. When they shall undertake, for instance, to render fertile the burning sands of Africa, they will be called upon to brave fatigues and dangers, to exert an energy, and to manifest an intelligence that will justify a much nobler pride than that ever felt by the most resistless of conquerors. It is here, that the talents of an Alexander and Napoleon, will have a suitable sphere for the exercise of their indomitable energies, and those sublime forces of genius, now turned to works of destruction, will be absorbed in functions truly constructive and extensively useful. The money and muscles wasted in the madcap expedition to Russia, might have subdued some barren and noxious territory, till it should have been made the fitting residence for millions of people.

Industrial armies, composed of the two sexes, will unite whatever is brilliant in both youth and age. They will be visited by the caravanseras of artists who will travel the globe, as formerly did the troubadours and the trouvers.* They will draw men towards them by the grandeur and usefulness of their labors, and by the splendor of their festivals; and, so far from having occasion to recruit their numbers by constraint, they will find a difficulty in moderating the enthusiasm which will be everywhere felt to share in their perils and renown.

§ II. *Atmospheric Equilibrium.*

The intelligent and combined labor of the Phalanxes and Industrial Armies will render Humanity more and more the Master of the Globe. Fourier announces that one of the results of unitary culture will be the regulation of the seasons, the moderation of temperatures, and the control of climates, in such a way as to have them always the most favorable. He even goes further, and thinks that by persistence in this method man will succeed in reducing the ices which defend the polar regions, and conquer those extreme parts of his legitimate domain, inasmuch as the Deity could not have created them for the single and cruel purpose of causing disasters and shipwrecks.

These bold affirmations are those which have led many to believe that Fourier allowed himself to be deluded by his imagination. Let us examine his predictions, and see whether they merit the raillery and disdain with which they have been treated. Let us see if there are not some faint grounds, at least, for the hope that his speculations were not altogether whimsical and crazy.

It can be shown that there exists a close relation between three things: the cultivation of the globe on one side, and on the other, the movement of the atmosphere, and the circulation of the imponderable fluids through the earth,— a circulation abundantly demonstrated, among a thousand other phenomena, by the variations of the magnetic needle.

By the "cultivation of the globe," we mean, all that belongs to Life, properly speaking, and not merely Vegetation,—the animals of a country being the consequences of its agricultural condition.

How can man, who pretends to disarm the thunder-cloud by means of a few metallic points affixed to his houses, refuse to admit the influence exerted upon tempests by the myriad of points offered by the forests with which he covers his mountains and hills?

Without speaking of the enormous quantity of gases absorbed and decomposed by animal and vegetable respiration, does not everybody know that the state of cultivation in any country essentially modifies its temperature, and that that temperature reacts upon the atmospheric equilibrium? Or think, again, of the mechanical action of a forest upon the current of air which passes over it: how the trees are blown hither and thither; how branches and leaves are shaken and torn off, and that the whole force required to produce these motions is just so much force lost by the moving fluid; how the specific gravity of wood is six or seven hundred times greater than that of air, and that consequently the motion of a tree renders stationary six or seven hundred times its volume of air coming against it; and we shall understand what a powerful influence the wooding or unwooding of mountains will have upon the atmosphere; we shall understand why regular winds prevail only on the sea and arid plains, and why their

---

* Troubadours, trovers, artists in general, will not be artists merely, but will engage in other labors that will develop all their faculties. Each member of a travelling troupe, arriving at an Army or a Phalanx, will engage in the labors of the groups, will communicate whatever he knows that is new in relation to improved methods, quicker processes, etc., etc.

action is so soon disturbed and modified when they traverse countries covered with high vegetable products.

The mutual dependence between the state of cultivation of the globe and its electro-magnetic circulation, becomes equally apparent on reflection.

What is the action of a galvanic pile upon a liquid holding salts and other compounds in solution? Each molecule seems suddenly endowed with intelligence and life; it separates under this influence from the molecules which displease it, and joins itself to others for which it has more affinity; and always acts in definite proportions of number or measure. There is something perfectly similar in all the phenomena of life; the liquid sap or blood, which carries nourishment to every part of a living being, accepts or repels with sagacity the materials offered to it, and disperses or assimilates them with discernment and symmetry. Nor must we, then, overlook the galvanic action which is necessarily connected with the action of that enormous pile called the Earth, the influence of which is felt at all times and places.

And since every action produces an equal reaction, there is a powerful reaction of the phenomena of life and vegetation upon the great magnetic currents.

Thus, the action of the electro-magnetic fluids upon the movements of the atmosphere is so evident, that it here needs only to be indicated. Thus, too, we see that there is a strict dependence between the movements of the atmosphere, the electro-magnetic circulation, and the cultivation of the globe.

The reciprocal action of these three things is not, however, the only one which influences their equilibrium. There are causes exterior to the globe itself, which tend to their mutual derangement.

These exterior causes are the attractions of the celestial bodies, chiefly the Sun and Moon. This attraction produces an effect upon the atmosphere similar to that of marshes; the movement returns periodically, with an intensity varying according to the relative positions of the stars by which it is determined.

The rotary motion of the globe may also be ranked among these exterior causes, since it takes place by virtue of a primary impulsion given from without, and produces trade-winds and similar currents of air, which cause themselves to be felt periodically in the same places. The sun, as we know, by its calorific or heat-producing agency, concurs in the production of these phenomena.

Such are, in general, the causes which tend to derange the atmospheric and electro-magnetic equilibriums. But what is important in regard to them, is to determine which of these causes act irregularly upon the equilibriums.

The exterior causes produce regular movements which can be foreseen and announced, so that it is in the globe itself that we must look for the causes of irregular movements or perturbations.

Now, since in the globe, everything is marked by regularity of movement or condition, except the state of its surface, we are forced to acknowledge that every irregular movement of the atmosphere or of the electro-magnetic system, arises from the irregular action of man upon the surface of the earth.

Everything is regular in the globe, for the "secular perturbations" ought not to be taken into consideration in the question which now engages us; and among those perturbations, we reckon the cooling of the globe, which, in the epoch in which we find ourselves, scarcely makes itself sensible in a great number of centuries. The action of this cooling on volcanic eruptions and earthquakes can now only be secondary; a derangement of the electro-magnetic circulation is the principal cause of the phenomena.

Thus, on one side, we can not refer the irregularities of which we speak to any other cause than the state of cultivation on the globe; and on the other side, we see that this cause is sufficiently powerful to explain those irregularities. We are compelled, therefore, to allow that by the regular cultivation of the globe, man can restore all these phenomena to regularity. By acting upon it in a unitary manner, in perfect harmony with natural laws, man will prevent all excess, all intemperature, every atmospheric and electro-magnetic perturbation. Lord of the airs, he will direct them each year so as to supply abundant wealth as the just reward of his wisdom and intelligent labors.

How did Fourier come to believe that the new equilibrium would result in breaking the ices of the pole, in removing the obstructions from the seas and straits of those latitudes, and in extending the domain of man over so many countries now deserted, and about which Man has disquieted himself so many years, with so much fatigue and danger, and so little success ? This is the next question.

In studying the arrangement of the Earth's continents, it has often been remarked that they both present a point elongated toward the south, and that, in that direction, the land terminates at a great distance from the polar circle. To the North, on the contrary, the continents approach the poles, widening as they penetrate the icy zone, so that the Arctic ocean, if it were practicable, could soon be made, like the Mediterranean, a centre of activity and a place of intercourse for all nations.

But these lands and seas, so favorably situated for the general interests of Man, are useless to him in consequence of the ice and frosts which forbid all access.

Fourier did not believe in Chance ; he believed in a Great First Cause governing all creation by beneficent laws; and he boldly concluded from the disposition of the land that the globe having been providentially prepared for man, man must have been endowed with forces sufficient to remove every obstacle to the complete subjection of his domain. And since the obstacle here is the temperature of the poles, he thought that it was given to man to moderate that temperature.

Man, we have said, may, by his action upon the surface of the earth, render the circulation of both winds and electro-magnetic currents more regular.

The irregularity of the electro-magnetic currents is manifested in many ways; among others, by irregularities in the emission of fluid during the appearance of the Aurora Borealis. If, by unitary cultivation, the electro-magnetic movement should be regulated, the Auroras Borealis would appear regularly, and not by fits and starts as they now do. Fourier predicts that they would augment, in duration, in such a manner as to become permanent, and in intensity, so as by their calorific action to rescue the circumpolar regions from their graves of ice and warm them into life and vegetation.

Fourier does not doubt of this result, because only in this way is it possible to understand why the continents have received a form, which, without this new source of light and heat, without this BOREAL CROWN, would be useless and unworthy of the wisdom and goodness of Deity.

An atmospheric and electro-magnetic equilibrium must have existed before the creation of man, when the virgin earth had undergone no perturbations through his agency. Then, warmed by the Boreal Crown, the poles were peopled by animals and vegetables. The crown was extinguished, when man, abandoning himself to social incoherence, and taking counsel only of his selfish interests, raised the thoughtless axe to brand the earth with ignoble marks of isolated cultivation.* The Crown will be reproduced, more radiant than ever, when Humanity, having identified private interests with general interests, advancing like one man toward its object, embellishing the globe by regular and unitary culture, shall cause disorder to be followed, not by the primitive and simple equilibrium, but by an equilibrium composite and refined.

Such are the wonders which Fourier, enlightened by his daring and comprehensive synthesis, dares to announce to men, who receive them with the smile of incredulity. In the meantime, Science marching slowly from observation to observation, discerns some fragments of these great things, under the object-glasses of its analysis. Thus for instance, M. de Candolle, the learned naturalist of Geneva, has acknowledged that a Boreal Crown must have formerly exist-

* The cooling of the globe, at first rapid, has been one of the principal causes of those great revolutions and cataclysms which distinguish the geological epochs. The cooling became less sensible in the last formations, and upon the globe prepared for the superior animals and man, an atmospheric and electro-magnetic equilibrium was established. Man ought to refine this equilibrium by clearings, but by clearings to which tillage would succeed, and not by unwooding elevated places, by the destruction of forests. The action of man upon the vegetable creation has been almost always unintelligent and fatal.

ed. In the "*Dictionaire Pittoresque d'Histoire Naturelle,*" vol. 3d, page 405, we read : " The opinion of M. de Candolle in regard to those ancient vegetables whose fossils are found in every country of the globe, obliges us to admit that those vegetables, of which some distant resemblances, infinitely smaller, exist only in the tropics, could only have existed by supposing changes in the axis of the earth—a supposition which both geometricians and natural philosophers repel; or that those vegetables, which have need of the action of some Great Light, besides that of a strong heat, have been able to find these essential conditions of their existence, only in the fact of a central fire, joined to the fact of A LUMINOUS FLUID DIFFERENT FROM THE LIGHT OF THE SUN. Thus to explain the presence of these vegetables, we are forced to admit the presence of an agent *which no longer exists;* in a word, the presence of a light like that which the Genesis makes to appear before the star of day was created, becomes necessary here."

The Genesis, and M. De Candolle, admitting the anterior existence of the Crown!

§ III. *The Equilibrium of Population.*

We can not avoid saying a few words here on a question, on which the Political Economists have reasoned, or, to speak more exactly, have jargoned to their mutual confusion;—the question of Population.

Let no one be astonished that an obscure writer thus dares to accuse, both of stupidity and error, writers who have acquired a high place in public estimation. The Political Economists themselves have dared a hundred times more than this, inasmuch as they virtually contend, in their empty theories, that the laws of Providence are absurd, silly, and merciless! They have not hesitated to accuse the Deity of the grossest unskilfulness and the direst cruelty, and have often proved themselves as presumptuous as they were impious and stolid.*

These men appear to imagine that God has never taken care to regulate the movement of population. They seem to think that he has left it to them to prevent disastrous exuberance, by teaching *caution as to marriages,* while He holds in reserve, to re-establish an equilibrium when there shall be occasion for it, such intelligent and fatherly means as war, pestilence, and famine!!

Let us see, if, with more faith, we can not arrive at a knowledge of the law of the movement of population, and if that law, like every other providential law, is not good for the race, after the race shall have resolved to profit by it.

The tendency of Man is evidently to possess himself of all parts of the earth, to cultivate them, to purify them, to draw from the globe all the wealth that it encloses, to augment the sum of his enjoyments, and to complete his happiness.

It is good for man, then, that population should increase, until he shall have occupied all countries, the burning deserts no less than the deserts of ice, and until the surface of the earth shall be covered with laborers, in number sufficient for its perfect cultivation.

Consequently, it must be inferred that the law tending to this result, is really providential and worthy of God, since nothing, until now, has shown that it is otherwise. For, God never having traced the limits which separate people and confine them, each by itself, in unfriendly herds, can not be held responsible for any excess of population accumulating upon one point, while there are elsewhere whole countries entirely deserted, or run over only by a few savage tribes and adventurous travellers. Men do not spring up in the midst of wildernesses, and, as long as it is good for population to augment, must be born in countries already peopled. Instead of endeavoring so ridiculously to oppose themselves to a movement resulting from a natural law, the Economists ought to have sought how that law could be made advantageous, and shown the easy modes in which the surplus of a crowded population might be spread in swarms over regions in want of laborers. There is not, perhaps, in all history, more singular facts than those which detail the slip-shod, wasteful, incoherent manner in which the colonization of new countries has been effected. It has sometimes been the result of commercial enterprise on the part of a few; sometimes of

---

* We purpose in some future work to *show up* this class of bunglers and pedants.

religious persecution driving a feeble sect into exile ; never the result of a comprehensive and systematic attempt to benefit mankind.

The Law is good, if population tends to increase as much more rapidly as the number of men is below the complement necessary to a perfect cultivation of the globe ; if the movement relaxes in proportion as the number approaches that limit; and if it becomes null, i. e., if an equilibrium be established between births and deaths, when the limit is attained.

But the movement of population must depend upon the external and internal conditions of life in which men find themselves placed. Let us see what relations may exist between the power of Humanity over its globe, and the physiological state of individuals.

It is by the progress of science, art, and industry, that Man becomes more and more the Master of his domain ; and human powers will attain its highest term, when all these matters shall have reached their completest development.

This development will result in placing Man in circumstances more and more favorable to the equilibrated employment of all his faculties and all his forces, to his wealth, his happiness, and his physical and intellectual vigor.

All these things then,—the power of Man over his globe, the development of sciences and industry, the refinement of the species, ought to advance by parallel steps, and tend together to a common apogee.

By *the refinement of the species* we mean that condition of human beings which leads to the complete and equilibrated employment of all their faculties. Thus, a population of farmers may be composed of robust individuals; but vigor without grace, strength without address, health without intelligence, does not constitute the refinement to which Humanity must attain.

The law of population, then, must be such that reproduction will be less active, in proportion as the species becomes more refined.

Again : this law must be admitted *a priori*, since the contrary law, which supposes that population would increase the more rapidly as its conditions were improved, would lead to atrocious results, in plain contradiction to all that we know of Nature and its laws. We learn, moreover that man, making use of all his faculties, employing all his forces, leaving none of his muscles inactive, no part of his brain idle, doing in a word all that it is possible for him to do, must expend a large amount of v .al energy of which a part would have gone to the organs of generation, if it had not been otherwise absorbed.

But let us examine the hypothesis in itself, and we shall confess that it is verified in every particular case in which it can be applied.

The Vegetable Kingdom ; when a plant is cultivated with care, under skies and in a soil which are agreeable to it, when it is found in conditions most favorable to its development, it becomes beautiful and vigorous ; but if the flower is brilliant, it is because the number of petals has increased at the expense of the stamens and pistils, because the organs of reproduction have been lessened, because they are indeed almost entirely effaced. If from this bed, in which the plant is cultivated with so much care, a seed escapes and the wind carries it to some arid soil, that soil will send forth a plant feeble and sickly, but presenting in perfection all the organs of reproduction, by lessening the petals to their smallest number. It seems, say the naturalists, that the plant perceiving the danger of death to which it is exposed, summons whatever of energy remain in it to the sexual organs, so that the loss of the species will not be a consequence of the decay of the individual.

The Animal Kingdom : it is very well established among domestic animals, that the female conceives with less facility in proportion as its kind is handsomer and more refined. Thus, in England, racing mares are not brought to the male until after they have been predisposed to conception by the precaution of a favorable regimen. Those precautions are designed to derange the perfect equilibrium existing in the functions of the animal, by giving her only insubstantial nourishment and sometimes even exposing her to mal-treatment. We know that many English mares received at the cavalry school of Saumer, a few years since, were tried for foals many times without success, until they had replaced the extraordinary care which was lavished upon them, in order to prepare them for conception, by an anti-hygienic regimen.

The Human Kingdom.—In physiological respects, the passage from vegetables to animals, and from animals to man, is an insensible one, and we must believe that a law prevailing among the first two is still the law of the human species. Besides, it is possible to point out a great many facts in Humanity, which go to confirm this law. The poorer classes, miserable, broken, are they the least fruitful? Has it not passed into a proverb, that "the poor man's quiver is full of arrows?" The most delicate, refined, and uniformly cultivated women, are they the most apt in reproduction? Recent publications teach us that the population of Paraguay, which lives under circumstances very favorable for the satisfaction of its wants, increases so slowly that it quite surprises that class of thinkers who regard the rapid increase of population as one of the signs of national prosperity.

Thus, 1st, the law which we have stated is alone worthy of Providence; 2d, it is verified in every case in which it can be applied.

CHAPTER VIII.

MANNERS AND CUSTOMS.

"To the pure, all things are pure."—JOHN.

IN approaching the more delicate topics of our inquiry,—topics which can only be approached with an extreme reserve, we feel the necessity of repeating once more that the Social School, which professes to teach the positive doctrines of Fourier, have but a SINGLE AND EXCLUSIVE AIM—*the Organization of Labor*. With the mere conjectural opinions of their Master, or any of his disciples, they have nothing to do, except to consider them, and to adopt or reject them, as they appear to each one to be false or true. There are some of Fourier's notions which strike the warmest of his disciples as fanciful, and to these they ascribe no authority, leaving the decision of them to the developments of time. Some of these opinions will be referred to in this chapter; and we have thought fit to say what we have just said because we foresee that the small wits of the newspapers, and other ill-disposed persons, will take advantage of the frankness of our statements.

If the reform which we propose were adopted; if the DEMONSTRATED experimental effect of our Organization were to give Reason and Passion the same direction, to identify private interest with general interest, all restraint, both moral and legal—all repressive action—would be at an end, since there would be no occasion for its manifestation.

We pretend to nothing more; we are not so senseless as to desire the suppression of all coercive means, and the full play of the Passions, before a long and satisfactory experience of the reformed state of society shall have shown, *to future generations*, that it would be unattended with dangerous results.

But so long as the Passions may bring forth Disorder, so long as Inclination may be in opposition to Duty, we reprobate, as strongly as any class of men, all improper indulgence of the inclinations and feelings; and where Reason is unable to guide them, have no objection to a resort to other means.

With this preliminary caution, we enter upon our subject.

Law, morals, and religion, can have but one legitimate tendency—to teach man to avoid those excesses which are personally injurious to him; to prefer his permanent happiness to any transient gratification; and to sacrifice his private interest when it comes in conflict with the general good; or, in other words, to conform his life to the principles of universal Justice, Truth, and Unity. They can have no other end : for if they commanded what was hurtful either to individuals or the species, they would be odious and absurd; and if they forbid things that were innocent, they would be capricious and arbitrary.

The acts proscribed by Morals are—1st, acts *absolutely* bad in themselves, independent of the actual form of society; 2d, acts hurtful, *incidentally*, in consequence only of the organization of society.

Acts, bad *absolutely*, in that they injure others* or ourselves, are condemnable for ever, and will be condemned under all social forms. Science ought to furnish the means of preventing these acts by destroying the sources from which they are known to spring.

Acts which injure *incidentally* only, in consequence of the particular organization of the society in which they are manifested, may become innocent under another social form, and in that way escape the province and consequent condemnation of Morality.

In Harmony, morals will continue to interdict all that is now forbidden on the ground that it is bad in an absolute sense. To prevent the recurrence of crime, all the instituted means of restraint and punishment may be preserved,—the whole apparatus of existing laws, courts, prisons, constables, and houses of correction. They may be preserved until it shall appear that there is no longer need of them, and they are permitted to fall into complete inactivity, or are converted to nobler uses. It would not be long, we think, before that event would arrive, and as we now see the magnificent but almost useless castles of the feudal ages converted into public school-houses, we should then see our Penitentiaries and Egyptian Tombs† made mineralogical cabinets or rooms for the preservation of fossils.

Already, at this day, are not crimes less frequent among the classes which are said to be in easy circumstances? Do they not spring, for the most part, from the lower classes, whose sensibilities are blunted by ignorance, and whose passions are fretted by misery? And may we not conclude from these facts, that if the poorer classes were raised to the condition of the middling classes, the larger number of crimes—certainly of the more gross and revolting crimes—would be prevented?

How much more surely, then, would crimes be avoided in Harmonic Society, where every individual would be developed, physically, intellectually, and morally, in the completest manner, and where all would be assured, for themselves and for others, a future exempt from harassing cares and privations?

How could the Passions lead to crime, when every thing should be arranged to satisfy them in the most agreeable manner, and when their exercise would determine the lot of each one as to wealth, enjoyment, and pleasure? By what strange caprice, when every honorable way would be opened for the action of the passions, would a man set to work to seek out base methods, which could only conduct him to contempt and the ruin of all his affections! For crime could not be hidden in a society where every one would be seen for the greater part of the day, and where it would be known, from hour to hour, what each person did. For instance, how and when would anybody be able to use a stolen object? In what way could he turn it to his own advantage?

Yet, if Crime should show itself in Harmony, it would be so infrequent and solitary, that society, regarding the guilty one more as a fool than a knave, would seek only to preserve itself from a second attack, by rendering it impossible for him to repeat his folly.

The excesses which Morality justly condemns, because they injure the individual himself, would be avoided in a social medium where the attractive exercise of one faculty would be unceasingly followed by the attractive exercise of

---

* Acts which injure others may be ranged into two classes : 1st, material violence,—the abuse of our physical force, brutality, etc. ; 2d, moral violence,—the abuse of our intellectual powers, perfidy, etc.
† The New York City Prison.

another; as the sportsman, though he may be a decided amateur in the pleasures of the table, would sit long enough only to satisfy his hunger, if the chase called him to another place. Men commit excesses because no other pleasure tends to withdraw them from the pleasure of the moment, or because the Alternating Passion which solicits them to change their occupation offers them no more agreeable employment as a variety.

As to acts which morality forbids because they are accidentally hurtful under certain social forms, Fourier says that they must cease to be culpable in a medium in which they would be innocent.

Thus, in our present society, Fourier says that Freedom in matters of love, would lead to a frightful confusion—to the abandonment of children, to the degradation of women, and to the destruction of the family, which is the single base of civilized society. Morality has therefore, a thousand reasons for insisting upon exclusive marriages, and denouncing every violation of the law upon which social order reposes.

But if Men lived in a society where a larger liberty in marriage and divorce would be without danger, where it would tend to strengthen the reciprocal affection of both parents and children, where it would render all the relations of the sexes, frank, loyal, and truthful, then it would not be obnoxious to the peculiar condemnations with which it is now necessarily visited. Fourier, therefore, regarding the passion of Love as good, useful, and innocent in itself, has proceeded to describe its probable influence in future states of society with a boldness and freedom that have shocked the feelings and prejudices of many worthy people.

That there may be no mistake in this point, that the public may know the substance of what Fourier teaches, we shall give a brief statement of his speculations, wishing the reader to bear in mind that they are only speculations to which we attach no authority, and which he is at liberty to condemn with all his might, if they require such condemnation.

First, however, we must remark that Fourier dwells upon what the state of the sexual relations is under systems which render all marriages exclusive and permanent. We know that there are multitudes of unhappy families, where the husband and wife ought never to have been joined together, and that there are many too, in which duplicity, violence, and discord, reign; we know that adulteries, even in the most polished circles, are not of rare occurrence; we know that a majority of the young men of our cities and larger villages, are in the habit of visiting brothels; we are told by physicians that practices of secret vice are undermining the constitution of thousands upon thousands of females; we know that that most hideous and awful of all social results, Prostitution, prevails over the civilized world (in New York there are more than ten thousand public prostitutes, and a proportional number in all the cities and villages in the United States); and we know that such crimes as Infanticide, Seduction, the Desertion of Children, accompanied by circumstances of the most keen and poignant distress, often occupy our courts and fill the police reports of newspapers.

Then, the injustice with which society distinguishes between the offences of the sexes; how it assembles its judges and condemns the poor unfortunate woman to ignominy, stripes, and death, while the infamous seducer, free, honored, and even caressed, perhaps sits upon the bench or in the jury box, which condemns his victim to her living tomb!

Again, childhood, the hope of the future, the tender bud which must sooner or later become the brilliant flower and the precious fruit, which must be nourished with so much care, what becomes of it in our present society? Cain! where is thy brother?

What terrible examples are daily set before children, especially the children of the poor, at home and abroad! What scenes of domestic strife, of intemperance, of brutal passions, of oaths and violence, are many of them called upon to witness! Wherever they go, their eyes and their ears initiate them into the dangerous secrets of vice. The placards on our walls, the conversations of the market-place, the reports of the newspapers, the tattle of domestics, theatres, and books are filled with impure and disgusting details, the only effect of which can be to blast the young minds perpetually coming in contact with them, by filthy imaginings and destructive propensities.

Now, Fourier asks, since all these disorders and vices have been developed under a law of constraint, have co-existed with force, have never been suppressed by any device of coercion, may we not hope that Order and Virtue will spring from greater freedom in sexual relations established under quite different social circumstances?

In the Phalanx, for instance, he says that childhood, working under the eyes of all, would never be abandoned to itself, neither in the fields nor the workshop, nor even in the dormitories. Preoccupied by the various industrial employments, for which it would have a passion, it would not know that profound ennui to which existing methods of education so stupidly condemn it, and which so greatly promote the vagaries of the imagination. At the end of every day, the child fatigued would only think of repose to which it would go smiling over its hopes of new industrial triumphs on the morrow.

In the Phalanx, nothing could awaken dangerous ideas in the child. Engaged at its tasks, its libraries, its museums, it would no longer look upon a world made only for the eyes of adults. Men would be careful to abstain from all acts or words of gallantry in its presence—the more so as they would be free to speak on such matters at the meetings in the saloons in the evening, after the children had retired to bed.

That the curiosity of childhood might not be too suddenly awakened, in passing from its customs to those of youth, Fourier suggested a transition through what he calls the Corps of Vestals. The adolescents, of both sexes, emerging from childhood at the age of 18 or 19,* would enter this body, and pass a greater or less length of time, according to their characters and temperament. There are many reasons given why it would be desirable for the young to remain in this corps as long as they could be permitted; among others that they would thus be trained to the highest purity and most spiritual perceptions of Love. Their first impressions of the relations of sex would be those of its high and awful sacredness.

During the time of the Vestalate, the young woman and man would likely make their choice. This choice would be determined by no considerations of rank or fortune, and parents would not trouble themselves to interfere with the arrangements of persons whose fortune would be so well secured. Each party would consult the dictates of the heart, and, in this respect, conform to the will of God, who has not placed so divine and beautiful a passion as Love in the bosom, to have it blighted by indifference, or crushed and trampled by the oppression of either husbands or parents.

The choice thus made under such circumstances, would be declared a MARRIAGE, and would be in all likelihood the best that could be made, and permanent. The parties would then pass from the Vestalate to some other corporation composed exclusively of the Married.

But suppose that this arrangement should have been entered into unwisely, that the parties subsequently find that they are not fitted to each other, or that one or the other should be inconstant in passion, does Fourier regard the tie as indissoluble? He answers, No! and in this he agrees with a large number of our modern statesmen and moralists, while he stands on surer grounds than they.

He thinks that Love is too sacred a passion to be forced, except in those incoherent and imperfect societies, where the rights and liberty of the individual are of necessity sacrificed to the general order. His leading principle is that perfect Liberty is perfect Law in a perfect state of existence, and that liberty gives place to law and artificial discipline, more and more strictly, as we descend the scale of elevation and refinement, and that in proportion as liberty, unchecked by discipline, exceeds refinement in mankind, depravity and anarchy disor-

---

* The active life of Harmonic Childhood, it is quite probable for certain organic and physiological laws, would postpone the age of puberty to 17 or 18.

ganize society and render it infernal. On the other hand, in proportion as society ascends the scale of progressive refinement, the bands of liberty may be relaxed, since it becomes more and more one with Law. While, therefore, in the present state of society divorce would be inadmissible, except in extreme cases of unhappiness, he holds that it grows the less dangerous, as society institutes those guarantees, and advances in that purity of thought, which take away its pernicious qualities and effects.

Mr. Doherty, of London, who has studied Fourier's science, both in his printed works and his manuscripts, more profoundly, perhaps, than any other living man, says that his views of marriage are, "that the present system will prevail until the female sex are rendered independent in a worldly point of view, and generally enlightened, which he supposes will require three generations at least to effect; after which the laws of marriage and domestic order, will be almost exclusively under the jurisdiction of the female sex, who will legislate on general principles, uniting female liberty and independence with moral harmony and Christian purity. When that sex shall have been rendered independent, he maintains that they will force the male sex to be honorable, chaste, and moral, to obtain their approbation; for a man who had deceived a woman would be deemed a traitor to the sex and banished from society."

We should be unfaithful, however, to the task we have undertaken, were we to conceal that Fourier was decidedly of the conviction, that while a part of mankind were formed for constancy in Love, there are some who are formed for change. It is this portion of his theory, in which he sketches a plan for the organization of the latter class, which has produced so much confusion and opposition in the minds of superficial readers.

In a Phalanx, where both sexes will enjoy an independent social position, and the relations of Love will not be complicated with fastidious questions of interest and selfishness, all characters which are true and worthy of it, he says, will be honored, and falsehood alone will be branded.

The various relations of the sexes will lead, like all other passional relations, to an organization into groups and series, comprising only those who have arrived at puberty. Departing from the Vestalate, each one will enter some corporation having constancy for its rule; many will stop there; but others are so peculiarly formed that they will join themselves to other corporations, more or less severe, as may be agreeable to their inclinations and temperaments.

The statutes of the different corporations of this series will be sufficiently varied to allow each person to find congenial natures. In this way, no one will have any inducement to dissimulate, and all, making known what they are, will scrupulously obey the laws under which they are ranked, since in acting otherwise, they would dishonor themselves without motive, being always free to follow another rule, simply declaring it by joining another corporation.

It is by the detailed description of the arrangements of these Corporations of Love that Fourier has brought the greatest discredit on his whole system. Many good persons have supposed that he designed his sketches for instant adoption, even under existing circumstances, and have thus been led to believe that he favored PROMISCUITY. Nothing could be further from his thought. And that this may be seen, we will, at the hazard of some repetition, state what we believe to be the key to what are considered his wildest speculations.

The time must come, he says, in the flight of centuries, when every one of the radical passions of man, must receive its highest development, and when society must be adapted to that development.

In our present incoherent and infant societies, not one of the Passions has received such a development or any approach to it, unless we except the pleasure of Hearing, which is developed in the form of Music. The sight has been partially developed by Painting, Architecture, Statuary, &c., but is susceptible of a much higher education, so that the time will come when the colors of our dresses, our habitations, and our fields, will be arranged by true scientific principles of harmony. Taste has received a still more incomplete attention, and that only in France, but is destined hereafter to have its *composers* who will rank in their science, as Mozart, Handel, Auber, &c., &c., now do in Music, or as Raphael, Angelo, and Reynolds, now do in Coloring. In this way every other passion must receive its scientific development.

By scientific development is meant such an education and perfecting of the organs as will cause them to impart the highest degree of pleasure of which they are capable to their possessor and to society at large. This Fourier supposes can only be given in the Serial Organization.

Now, Fourier continues, the Affective Passions, as well as the Sensitive and Intellectual, are susceptible of this scientific education and progress. Ambition, for instance, must be gratified in a variety of modes, in order to develop all the intense pleasures of which it will be susceptible in Harmony. The serial organization of government is therefore designed to give full play to the passion of ambition in all its methods of action.

The passion of Love, he argues, before it can yield all the results of which it is capable, must undergo a similar organization by series, to meet all the wants of all the natures that God sends into existence. The first organization, therefore, is that of the Vestalic Corporation, devoted to the development of the most purely spiritual relations between the sexes, and which is surrounded by the most attractive charms and the most ennobling honors, to retain its members as long as possible within its instructions; another would be a corporation of Constancy, as we have said, at which the most part of men and women would stop; while others again, named Bacchantes, Bayaderes, &c., &c., would pass into other corporations, not so strict in their requirements. Such characters as Aspasia, Ninon De L'Enclos, &c., Fourier regards as essential parts in the variety of the human race, who will always exist, who must be allowed for in every scheme of philosophy, and whom society, instead of rudely thrusting from its charities, must turn to some good account. The most irregular natures must be made to co-operate in the production of Harmonic Results.

The Passions which, for many reasons, will be the last to receive their high scientific development will be those of Love and Paternity, because they imply a degree of individual purity and social refinement which can only be attained in the course of many centuries. Until the female sex and parents should decide that such a state of purity had come, they must remain under existing regulations.

Liberty of this kind, according to Fourier, would destroy Falsehood, and Truth preside over all the relations of Love; and each one, bringing his conduct into the full light of day, no one, in loving, would ever have occasion to fear deception and perfidy.

These, then, are the views of Fourier on the subject of Love,—a subject which is one of the profoundest that can engage the attention of man, and which will not be satisfactorily adjusted until after society shall have been brought into the state of organic unity and individual independence. At present, we regard many of the marriages that we hear of, as what Miss Martineau calls, legalized prostitution; and we believe that marriage can not now, in many cases, be anything else; that it can not rise into the mystic and divine union of soul and body, of which St. Paul speaks, until woman shall have been redeemed from the curse of pecuniary dependence, and the regulation of the Affections committed to her as their most brilliant depository and Representative. Fourier's scheme of industrial organization is the only reform which can lead to this desirable object, and the only part of his system to which his present disciples stand pledged.

As to the details which he has given, in conjecturing the peculiar customs of the higher degrees of Harmonic Life, we must say that many of them strike us as fanciful, and that others are highly repugnant and erroneous; but seeing that they are only conjectures, that his school does not pretend to understand them, nor put them forth as authoritative, that he requires a preparatory discipline and progressive refinement of some THREE CENTURIES or more for their adoption; that no connection of love he contemplates can be secret, but must be openly approved; we are disposed to leave them to the adjudications of time, holding ourselves ready, however, at all hazards, to prove that they are not purposely Immoral, although we believe them to be false.

It was impossible for Fourier, with his deep longings after Truth and Purity, to have intentionally conjectured anything immoral; he has erred, no doubt, but not with any corrupt purpose. He says himself expressly, in his later works, that he wishes no society to adopt his *conjectures* or truths until Parents and Women are fully prepared for them, and then only after it shall be found that they are "the best and only methods of promoting PUBLIC AND EFFECTIVE MORALITY."

BOOK FIFTH.

UNITY OF MAN WITH GOD AND THE UNIVERSE.

CHAPTER IX.

COSMOGONY.

> "Our birth is but a sleep and a forgetting;
> The soul that rises with us, our Life's star,
> Hath had elsewhere its setting,
> And cometh from afar,
> Not in entire forgetfulness,
> And not in utter nakedness,
> But trailing clouds of Glory do we come,
> From God, who is our Home."
> WORDSWORTH's *Ode on the Intimations of Immortality.*

"There are celestial bodies, and bodies terrestrial; but the glory of the celestial is one, and the glory of the terrestrial is another." "There is a natural body and there is a spiritual body." "We are sown in corruption, we are raised in incorruption."—ST. PAUL TO THE CORINTHIANS.

WE have shown that man is endowed with the ability to place himself in a medium where he would be in *unity with himself*, or, in other words, where there would be a perfect accord between his inclinations and his duties, between his passions and his reason. But the Unity of Man with Himself does not constitute UNIVERSAL UNITY, which is composed of—

1st, The Unity of Man with Himself;
2d, The Unity of Man with God;
3d, The Unity of Man with the Universe.

If our life terminated with the present life, Man would not be in unity, in many essential respects, with God, whom he might then accuse of partiality or injustice.

Men living in the same age may have many interests almost identical during the greater part of their existence, but there would be no ties between different generations. Thus, those who have lived during the subversive period of human life, subject to its duplicity and misery, working like slaves to accumulate labor, art, and science, and producing the materials for an Harmonic Organization, might reproach the Deity for having created them in ages of suffering, and reserved his privileges for epochs of happiness. In Harmony, even, evil will exist, although reduced from the law to the exception; and he who should, accidentally as it would be, suffer injury in his development, so as to feel that his life was a failure, might rightly complain, if there were no other life. Then, too, the old man or the sick person, on the borders of the tomb, would lose his interest in the things of Earth, and would no more trouble himself with thoughts of progress, melioration, and discovery. What *solidarity* would there be between him and those destined to survive him?

In order that our destiny may be *one*, the future life must be intimately connected with the present life, and the two must depend upon one another in such a way that ignorance only could lead an individual to seek his own happiness out of the general happiness. Individual existences must be compensated, so that no one can complain of having been treated with disfavor; and this equilibrium must spring naturally from the laws of creation, unless God intervenes at every instant to modify the order immutably established. The attributes of God demand distributive justice or universal equity in all spheres of his creation.

Let us see if the theory of Fourier fulfils these conditions, and resolves all difficulties, to the exclusion of every other cosmogonic theory.

Natural substances may be classed into two distinct categories, according to their properties and their mode of action upon our senses.

The first class comprises substances which we may handle, divide, carry, weigh, etc., and are called *ponderable bodies.*

The second is composed of certain agencies, so subtle that they escape our senses, although they manifest themselves, in certain cases, with striking and fearful energy. These substances, which we cannot master, and which the most delicate balances fail to weigh, are the *imponderable fluids*, which we shall call *aromas.*

The globe is, then, made up of ponderable substances, and of aromas.

The human soul, we have said, is an agent or mover: this agent has need of instruments for its manifestation.

In the present life, called to act mainly on ponderable matters, the soul takes a body of ponderable matter.

But if it is the destiny of man to govern the globe, or to govern it in all its relations, his soul, to act upon the aromal part of the planet, has need, in its second life, of a more subtle and refined instrument,—of an aromal body.

Thus, the present life is a *terrestrial* life, in which the soul acts mediately through a ponderable body, on the ponderable part of the globe.

The future life will be also a *terrestrial life*, during which the soul will act mediately through an aromal body, upon the aromal elements which enter into the composition of the planet.

In the two lives, therefore, the soul will be always united to *a substance;* indeed, it is difficult to conceive of the soul without some mode for its manifestation. Yet this belief does in no wise tend to materialism, for the soul will be immortal, although always united to a mortal body, which it abandons at death for a new body. This doctrine is admitted and taught by the Church universally, when it speaks of the resurrection of a "glorious body."

There is nothing repugnant to common sense in the thought that the molecules of aromal substance may unite to form a body directed by the soul, any more than there is in the thought that the molecules of ponderable substance do, as oxygen, hydrogen, azote, etc.

Our two existences take place upon this globe. In the present life, the *Mundane or Inferior Life*, we shall be (with exceptions) without communication with the aromal life, the ULTRA-MUNDANE OR SUPERIOR LIFE, because the things and beings of that life escape our gross senses by their subtlety.

In the aromal life, without entering into relation with the *Mundanes*, we shall see, understand, and watch them in all their actions.

Before pronouncing upon a conception so apparently new, it would be well to comprehend it fully, and attend to the developments which we are about to make.

An aromal life, *that is*, the time in which the Soul is in possession of the same aromal body (the same body with its growth, decay, and molecular modifications, etc., etc.), is, like the present life, made up of sleeping and waking.

An ultra-mundane will operate, among his aromal companions, during a state of wakefulness, which will have about twice the duration of a mundane life—say two centuries.

At the end of this waking state, of this day of the higher life, the aromal body will have need of repose—becoming dull, it will give itself over to sleep. During this sleep, the soul cannot use the aromal body, and must make another instrument, which it finds in a mundane life, in a ponderable body; the moment of sleep in the aromal life, is the moment of birth in the present life—the moment when the Soul arrives to take possession of its newly-formed body. The inferior life is the sleep, the night, the dream of the superior. In the language quoted from the magnificent ode of Wordsworth, at the head of this chapter,

> Our birth is but a sleep and a forgetting:
> The Soul that rises with us, our life's Star,
> Hath elsewhere had its setting.

The ponderable body, offering the soul only organs that are absolutely new—virgin in respect to all the impressions of the past—it seeks vainly in those organs for traces of its anterior existence. The education of the new body is a thing to be done; it is a book, of which the pages are white, and which must be written upon before they are of any value.

The ponderable body is developed under the influence of the soul; it gradually acquires force; and then after remaining almost stationary a little while at maturity, it declines, decays, and is abandoned by the Soul, as we abandon an old vestment which is no longer worth using.

This separation of the soul and ponderable body is the awakening of the aromal body. Its night is finished, the Soul takes possession of it and enters upon the higher life, where it recovers the reminiscences of its preceding ultra-mundane existences, which were actively impressed on the aromal organs, and the reminiscences of its mundane existences, which acted passively* upon the same organs during their sleep. Thus, there is a double memory in the higher world and a double want of memory in this.

The life of Man, then, is composed of three terms:—
1st. Simple life, or *sleep;*
2d. Composite life, or *waking;*
3d. Super-Composite, or *aromal* life.

Thus, the soul alternates between night and day, between the mundane and ultra-mundane life. In entering upon the higher life, it finds its affections, pleasures, and labors, only interrupted by the passage through the present life, as we find, on awakening, the friends and objects quitted the evening before, whatever may have been our dreams in the mean time. In descending to the inferior life, the Soul takes each time a new body, begins a new existence, always connected with the general life of the species, but without direct relations to its anterior states of existence. It is thus that dreams are independent of one another, not even forming a consecutive train.

The conception of Fourier is a *metempsychosis,* but essentially distinct from the *simplistic* metempsychoses of the ancients,—the Immortality which he has conceived being what he calls a BI-COMPOSITE IMMORTALITY.

To raise ourselves to this discovery of the ultra-mundane life, we must be guided by an unlimited faith in Providence—a faith which can spring only from a wise and liberal spirit, by a knowledge of the laws of movement, that they can only lead to happiness, and that God does not desire evil, since he has given Man the power of conquering it, whenever it is presented.

Man can understand and conquer his destiny in the higher life, only after having learned and determined his destiny in this lower life. It is greatly to his advantage, that the two states stand in this relation to each other. If, in the subversive periods of his life, he had been without uncertainty as to the lot that awaited him after death, how often would he not have sought relief in suicide for the sorrows by which he was overwhelmed?

For the same reason, the transition to the higher life, Death, must be a painful transition. Without the repugnance which it inspires, the chasm would have been too easily leaped over during the incoherent and miserable phases in the life of Humanity. But in Harmony, death may, without danger, inspire little

---

* The ponderable body receives the direct imprint of the events of the present life, and the aromal body, which sleeps while these events are taking place, receives a counter-imprint, which the soul consults on entering the higher state. Swedenborg says that all we now hear or do will be made to re-appear at will in the spiritual world.

terror. When, by the culture and purification of all parts of the Earth, and by the equable employment of all his faculties, man shall have triumphed over the many diseases by which he is punished for his mal-administration of the globe, almost everybody will arrive at an advanced age, and die a natural death, without convulsion or pains.* Death will have lost all its frightfulness, when we shall know that it is a transition that separates us only for an instant from those we hold dear, that the dead continue to follow us with their wishes, and to be interested in our acts, that they will stand ready to receive us when death has struck us in our turn, and that all may be certain that final happiness is reserved to them in the future state, more perfect and more blissful than any which we can imagine on Earth.

The transition called Death, moreover, is absolutely necessary, to movement and life. If a man were arrested, for many centuries, at the same point of his development, or progressive career, he would be soon saturated and disgusted with the enjoyments of his actual condition. There must be variety in all things, variety in labor and in pleasure, and variety, as well as alternation, in existences.

All natural laws have their reason for being what they are, their justification, which may be discovered, if we are faithful in the research. We have said that the anterior states are forgotten in the present life, and the reason is obvious, since otherwise, the pleasures of the inferior life would be so insipid in comparison as to lose their value. In the higher life, that danger does not exist, and to be without remembrance there, the continuity of existence would not be perceived, and Immortality would be nothing more than an unmeaning word.

Many moral proofs, nor these alone, concur in giving certainty to the peculiar mode of Immortality which Fourier has revealed. His conception, resting upon data the most simple, the most easy to admit, and the least mysterious, enjoys, to the exclusion of every other, the property of resolving all difficulties, and justifying the providence of God, without conflicting with scripture or demanding of Reason the abdication of any of its rights.

1st. Without deranging his established order, God is just toward every generation and all individuals. The men who formerly formed the population of the globe, form it at this day, and will form it in the future, and no generation is reserved for the happy epochs exclusively, and no one is a privileged generation. In that indefinite series of mundane and ultra-mundane existences, through which all are called to run, the chances are equal, and all will have an equivalent part in evil as well as in good. The happy periods of life being very long, compared with the subversive periods, each one, at the end of the career of the globe, will cast his eye upon the past, and will lose himself in overwhelming gratitude to God for the experience of so much good purchased at the cost of so little evil. "And they shall sing the song of Moses, the servant of God, and the song of the Lamb, saying, great and marvellous are thy works, Lord God Almighty; just and true are thy ways, thou King of Saints."

2d. Individual destiny is in perfect harmony with General Destiny, and we learn at last that there is a perfect and perpetual SOLIDARITY between all men; young and old, sick and well, mundane and ultra-mundane,† are equally interested in the things of the earth and in the fate of Humanity. What savage or barbarous nation, what class of civilized society, can be indifferent to him who knows that he and his may one day share the fate of those wretched outcasts from knowledge and virtue? What haughty baron, what noble prince, would

---

* This view may be ridiculed, but why? When man appeared, for the first time, upon the earth, was he already afflicted with phthises, rheumatisms, scrofulas, pestilences, and fevers? Or did these maladies invade him, because of his excesses or his indolence, because he failed to employ all his faculties regularly and in equilibrium, i. e., by the mal-administration of the globe, whose neglected parts gave forth miasms, fevers, &c., &c. Why then, in harmony, under circumstances directly the reverse, should not diseases disappear, one after another, with the causes that engender them? Some classes of the animals already enjoy certain advantages which we promise to men, as the dog, his magnificent teeth, &c., &c.

† The happiness of the ultra-mundanes is fettered so long as the mundanes have not caused Harmony to reign upon the earth. They are fettered physically, because the deranged administration of the ponderable part of the globe, rests upon the aromal administration; merely because the ultra-mundanes would fear to return to a region where they knew they would suffer.

trample upon the crowd which flows at his feet, when he knows that they are in so many intimate senses, his brothers, who are a part and parcel of his life, members of his own body, but perhaps hereafter, when he shall be what they are now, destined to shine as stars in the firmament?

Evidently no man in a position to prevent an evil, to eradicate a vice, or to introduce a good, would even in a selfish point of view, hesitate to do so, if he were fully impressed by the belief that he would return many times to enjoy the good he had done, or to suffer the evil which he had neglected. Such a faith, indeed, would reconcile selfishness and self-sacrifice; or, in other words, selfishness would be rendered impossible by the strict solidarity which connects all the members of the human family.

No one would think of his mere individual safety, or harden his heart by the cowardly hope that he would be saved at any rate, whatever might become of the rest of his brothers. He would find that it was necessary to save humanity, in order to save himself, and that the promotion of general blessedness was the only method of securing his own safety. Behold the elevated aim offered to each of us! an end grand enough to warm every heart, and enlarge and fecundate every soul with the most exalted and generous sentiments.

The solidarity of men is a holy tie which implicates the whole of humanity in the sins of any of its members. Yet it absolves no one from his individual responsibility. The mundane and ultra-mundane lives are connected like one asleep and waking, and he who has failed in this life, who has disfigured it by excesses, by crimes, by suicide, will suffer for his errors in the life which succeeds. To take an imperfect illustration, the slumber that is tormented by nightmares and dreams, indisposes us for the enjoyments and labors of the following day.

Mankind have always had a feeling more or less distinct of the reality of their mutual solidarity—they have inscribed it upon their creeds—it has been stirring in their consciences. The doctrine of original sin, so widely prevalent and so unaccountable upon any other supposition, is a proof as to how deep the vague sentiment of it has sunk into the human heart. But no one before Fourier has been enabled to explain its nature or its justice; it has been a subject of faith and not of science; and the bi-composite theory alone, demonstrates how the living have labored from the beginning to conduct Humanity on its ways of good or evil.

3d. In connecting thus strictly the happiness of the Individual with the happiness of the Species, God draws men toward the practice of virtue and all good, in a manner which is at the same time sure and worthy of his Greatness. Governing paternally, by means of attraction, and leading men to piety and joy through solidarity, is he less worthy of honor and love than if he governed by the scourge and fire? then, how could we respect a Being if, as he has too often been described to us, he designs to govern us solely by arbitrary decrees? Has not faith in such a government led to the most frightful exhibitions of human malice? Was it not this faith which misled the church with the spirit of persecution, which has given rise to malignant devotees, and which has taught men to think that they honored God by inflicting tortures upon all who were not of the elect.

But the Deity has never wished to reign over pale and trembling slaves, but over happy and free men, acknowledging and proud of the lofty mission which he had comitted to their charge.

4th. Bi-composite immortality agrees with all our desires. Each old man asks to begin life again with the experience which he has acquired; and this wish will be fully satisfied, since all will recommence life, and all will profit by the experience of the past.

Let us descend into our own hearts; do we not feel that we abandon with regret the earth which science can render so beautiful? Do we not feel happy that we are bound up with its fate, connected with the fate of all men, that we must suffer with our brothers, but like them, too, be called to the enjoyment of all bliss? Are not these the very conditions on which we should have requested our life, while we should have refused it on the slightest chance of an eternal damnation?

Thus, by the aid of this theory, everything is explained with simplicity and the laws of creation have nothing in them either arbitrary or grievous. Moral proofs, we have seen are in its favor.*

Upon this important question, however, we are referred to more than one kind of proof. Universal Analogy, of which we have yet to speak, will give us many confirmations. It was stated above, that in this life we had no communication with the aromal life, *with exceptions*, of which Fourier gives instances in both the material and spiritual spheres. He says that we have some relations with the ultra-mundane world, through persons gifted with faculties that are ultra-human; and he instances in the material sphere the touch of a class of beings called Sorcerers, and the sight of those who are mesmerized; and, in the spiritual sphere, providential men, as they are sometimes called, or Men of Genius, and Prophets. All these varieties of faculties are transitional participations in different degrees of ultra-mundane or celestial perfection.

Animal Magnetism is the influence which one man may exert upon another by the influence of his Will. It produces a sleep, more or less profound, which is distinguished from ordinary sleep by many very curious phenomena. The sleep in this case has received the name of somnambulism, or, as Mr. Townsend calls it, sleep-waking. The somnambulist enjoys the use of his sensitive faculties, without the aid of their habitual organs. He sees through opaque bodies, and sometimes at great distances; he catches thoughts which have never been expressed by sign or sound; he perceives odors which exist only in the mind of the magnetizer; he becomes insensible to blows and burns; in short, his intellectual faculties seem no longer those which he possessed in his waking state, and he finds himself suddenly endued with knowledge of things, of which he never before had a conception.

The first effect of Magnetism is to suspend the sensitive functions of the ponderable body, and its second will be to arouse the aromal body, *very imperfectly*, from its numbness, if we may so speak, by restoring to the soul the power of making use of it. The soul appears to employ the aromal body in somnambulism; for it sees, hears, tastes, and has knowledge of itself, by means of its aromal organs, whose perfection explains whatever is wonderful in the manifestations of Mesmerism. Sight can easily be effected through substances, which, however dense, are penetrable by aromal bodies. The soul recovers, in returning upon the impressions of its aromal body, with the reminiscences of its preceding states, ideas and knowledge which it can not retain when compelled to make use of its mundane body.

The fact is stated by those who are familiar with magnetism, that the somnambulist remembers all that he has seen during his ordinary life and during his anterior somnambulisms; but that on waking up he knows nothing of what has passed during his magnetic sleep. This remembrance in one case, and forgetfulness in another, is precisely similar to what Fourier states of our two lives —the aromal life with its double memory, and the mundane life, without any memory. The explanation is the same: in somnambulism, the ponderable body asleep receives no impressions from without, so that when the soul takes possession of it, there is nothing then to be read; for nothing was imprinted.

There is a state described by Magnetizers, and in many religious books, as *Ecstacy* or *Trance*, which the theory of Fourier explains with equal facility. After returning to himself, after the crisis during which life seems wholly to have abandoned his body, the Ecstatic relates that he has travelled in space, that he met living beings, with whom he could not enter into any communication, but that he could communicate freely with the dead, who inspired him with no terror. This voyage of the Ecstatic is only a voyage of the aromal body, by means of which he can enter into relations with the ultra-mundanes, although he can not communicate with mundanes, even while seeing them. It generally happens, moreover, that the aspect of the higher life inspires the Ec-

---

* This reasoning, it will be remembered, is given as from Fourier, and not by the author personally.—P. G.

static with a vivid desire of remaining there, so that he complains of having been brought back to this lower existence.

Those who deny the phenomena of Animal Magnetism will be embarrassed to explain the analogous, and *no less extraordinary* phenomena of natural somnambulism, which have been too often authenticated to admit of a doubt. Indeed, with the evidence now brought to bear, as to the existence of the magnetic phenomena, a man who could doubt it, would not believe Moses and the Prophets.

Somnambulism is a state of transition, as we have said, between our two lives, in which the soul employs simultaneously, but imperfectly, the two bodies of which, in ordinary cases, it makes use only in alternation. This kind of transition is not the only one, in the material sphere, which we can observe, for there are too many instances on record of men enjoying faculties truly aromal, in cases of divining, discovering secret springs, etc., sorcery, magic, etc., etc.

Magnetism, which would be of double utility in Harmony, can not be fully developed in our present societies, where isolated experiences are only possible, and where the influence of individualism is so strong, that it interferes with the perfect process of magnetising.

As higher evidences of the same terrestrial state, Fourier refers to those *progressive human instincts* which he divides into two distinct orders, commonly called *prophecy* and *genius*, or, as they may be otherwise denominated, *passive and active visionaries.* The instincts of both these orders are regularly contrasted *by series* with those of the other, in all their respective varieties, and the peculiar functions of both these orders of mind are, to reveal progressively and continuously to mankind, the secrets of nature and the laws of Providence.

There are three grand distinctions in each of these orders—the *sensuous*, the *mental*, and the *moral;* but we have no space to speak of these at length.

In the purely mental department of what is called genius, in the *active* order, we may class those minds which are commonly called "theoretical visionaries" before their discoveries are proved by practical observation, and "great geniuses" after death and success have demonstrated their rank; and in the mental department of the *passive* order, we find those minds which are commonly called prophets, because it generally happens that they are only passive instruments of Providence, without understanding their own mission.

The progress of human society depends entirely upon these Providential Men, who are visionaries, because they foresee and foretell results, before they are actually proved by experience. There are many pretenders to both characters, but we must " try every spirit, whether it be of God."

Almost everybody now-a-days believes in the mission of Genius, but few have faith in the mission of Prophets, and they will be still more incredulous when we tell them that Prophets, as well as Geniuses, exist in all ages, though the faculties of vision and discovery are often neutralized in these precious individuals by the stultifying effects of ignorance and privation.

All religious people profess a belief in the prophetic genius of former ages, and by acknowledging Christ as the greatest of all prophets, they acknowledge different degrees of prophetic inspiration. Now, when did the spirit of prophecy cease? Is there not as great occasion for it as ever, and have we not reason to believe, in the case of Swedenborg and others, that there are modern prophets, working together with modern genius, to lead Humanity through its accidental destiny of Discord to its essential destiny of Science and Harmony? The function of *passive* inspiration or prophecy being to support the mind in hope until it is fully corroborated by *active* inspiration or genius.

What we have said thus far does not show with sufficient precision the connection which unites the Creator to the creature. Between man and God there is an abyss, an immense void, which is contrary to all that we know of Nature, who never proceeds by sudden leaps, from one centre to another, but by gradual transitions. Ought we not, then, to regard God and man as the extremes of a series, at each term of which we shall find, in ascending, that there are beings greater and greater, and more nearly approaching God? Thus the void will be filled up, and we shall comprehend how the infinite and the finite come into relation, since each Being, acting directly upon those which touch it above and below, will be strictly connected to all by the great chain of which the Deity is the first link.

There must then be above us a being, superior to us in such a degree that it will cause us to feel its immediate influence, which will mingle a portion of its own life with our life, which will partake our sorrows and divide our joys; a being which we can see and touch.

Can we not divine that this being is the Planet on which we were born?—the planet, which is admitted to be a body, and to which, without good motive, we have refused all intelligence and passion. We say, without motive, for our planet is not mere dead matter; it is a body wisely organized, with its aromal circulation, analogous to the circulation of the blood, and organs of the same nature for the manifestation of its will and desires, and its relations to the other planets.

The stars, according to this supposition, are intelligent passional beings, sustaining aromal relations to each other, and whose bodies are both ponderable and aromal. They obey the force of gravity, as we ourselves do, without resistance. In particular cases, as when they leave the cometary state to choose a convenient distance in which to circulate about the sun, they may draw from their aromas a force, which combined with gravity, will direct them in spaces as we combine muscular action with weight when we transport ourselves over the surface of the earth.

Thus, the distance of each planet from the sun will be owing to the will of the planet. Those who ascribe everything to chance, ought to be surprised at the discovery of the four small planets of our system. This was made while comparing the respective distances of the planets from the sun, by recognising the fact that these distances formed A SERIES, of which one term was wanting, and by seeking a place where that planet ought to be, in order that the defect might be supplied. They ought to wonder still more at that singular combination of double movement in every observed satellite, in consequence of which the satellite always presents the same hemisphere to its planet, whereas, according to all the calculations of probability, such a combination ought to be reproduced, only at infinitely rare intervals.

The globes then are beings like man, but superior to him, and one degree nearer the Creator. The soul of a globe will be united to it, till the moment of its decease, at which time, it will take possession of a newly-formed globe, drawing all its human souls after it, who will thus go to begin a new humanitary career, or a new series of existences.

Our solar system is a group, of which the sun is a pivot and chief. The aggregations of groups about suns, form a series of stars, a vortex of worlds, or a Universe, such as we now know. In this Universe, we see an intelligent and passional Being, two degrees superior to man, one degree superior to his planet, forming groups and series with other universes. The whole number of *universes* forms what Fourier calls a *Biniverse;* the Biniverses combine to form a *Triniverse*, and so on indefinitely, through *Quatriniverse*, etc., till we arrive at God, the *Infiniverse*, whose body comprises all matter, and whose intelligence includes all intelligences. This celestial hierarchy is admitted in all religions which speak of angels, archangels, seraphims, cherubims, thrones, dominions, principalities, powers, etc., etc.

God alone excepted, all beings are subjected to increase and decrease, and to death, which is only the abandonment of an old body for a new. At the moment of this transition, each soul draws with it the souls which are subordinated to it. Small souls are associated with great without losing their individuality, as our body which makes part of the body of the planet is nevertheless perfectly distinct.

All the beings of this hierarchy are made in the image of God, have a Reason not equal, but homogeneous with his, and passions that differ from his only in their intensity and modes of satisfaction. All beings, in effect, can have only one passion at bottom, Unityism, by which we mean the impulses toward Universal Justice and Truth, expressed in the desire to be happy ourselves and see all others happy. These beings are Immortals; their movement is eternal; and since it did not commence at any definite period, it has always been; so that Eternity extends both ways, behind as well as before us. The body of a dead star is decomposed to form matter for a new star.

It will now be easy to understand the thought of Fourier, when he says that Man, like his Planet, like the Universe, like everything that exists, is composed of three Eternal, Uncreated, Indestructible Principles:

    1st. MIND;*—the active or motor-principle;
    2d. MATTER;—the passive or moved principle;
    3d. MATHEMATICS;†—the neuter or regulating principle.

It is of little importance, as to consequences, whether God, the Active Principle, has caused the other principles to exist by his Will, or whether the three principles are the essence of God, co-eternal with him; for God, not being able to change, would submit to laws which he had dictated, as absolutely as though he were entirely independent of them, since they would only express his own nature.

These three principles show themselves in everything that we see, in all that it is possible to observe. Matter, the most inert in appearance, is yet subjected to molecular attraction and repulsions, to chemical affinities, and the influences of bodies with which it is in contact; it lives, and the matter which is abandoned by one individual life, enters into a more general life, to the influence of which it is more exclusively subjected. Thus, at the death of man, his body lives the life of the globe, and at the death of the globe, the matter which composed his body enters again into the life of the universe.

This perpetual *solicitation* of matter for mind, does not take place in an arbitrary manner; it is submitted to precise and rigorous laws from which it can not depart. Those laws constitute the third principle, the Regulating,—Mathematics, Justice,—without which it is impossible to conceive that anything should exist.

CHAPTER X.

UNIVERSAL ANALOGY.

"Finds tongues in trees, books in the running brooks,
Sermons in stones, and good in everything."—SHAKSPERE.

"The invisible things of God, from the creation of the world, are clearly seen, being comprehended by the things which he hath created and ordered—even his omnipotence and the other attributes of the Godhead."—ST. PAUL TO THE ROMANS.

WHEN a new word is used, or a special sense is attached to a word already known, the person or school who employs it, should define it at the outset. In this way, the world may know what is the whole doctrine taught, and criticism save itself much verbiage, as to the significance of terms.

The word *Analogy* is one of those to which Fourier gives a particular meaning, which we shall endeavor to explain.

Two homogeneous quantities, two things of the same nature, may be brought into relation; it is possible to compare them and find some common measure.

Between heterogeneous things are there also points of contact,—possible relations?

To this question, Science will be tempted to answer, No! but for a long time the instincts of the multitude have responded in the affirmative. All languages

---

* *Mind*, breath, spiritus, life, Passion.   † *Mathematics*, in physics, *Justice* in morals.

have words which have a *proper* sense and a *figurative* sense,—that is to say,—which are applied with equal fitness to things of a different order,—to physical properties, for example, and to moral qualities. Thus, the adjective *hard*, in its proper sense, expresses a physical property of solids,—a hard body. But the same adjective, in its figurative sense, expresses an accidental vice of the soul—as a *hard* character.

The reason of this is that there are felt to be between physical properties and moral qualities, a real relation, independent of all convention, that there is in physical hardness something which corresponds to moral hardness. This correspondence springs neither from chance nor from usage; and everybody is conscious that it would be absurd to seek to awaken an idea of the same moral quality by employing another physical adjective, by agreeing to speak of an inflexible man, for instance, as a *soft* character, the adjective soft preserving the same proper sense which it has in the phrase, a soft body.

There are, then, true relations even among things of a heterogeneous kind. These relations, very different from those which exist between homogeneous things, have been called by Fourier, the relations of Analogy. The profounder sense of the term will appear as we proceed.

Fourier divides the system of Nature into five branches or movements, four of which are *cardinal* movements, and one *pivotal* movement.

1st. *The Material Movement*, or the laws according to which God regulates the movement of matter, which Newton and the modern mathematicians have explained in the theory of gravitation, by effects but not by causes.

2d. *The Aromal Movement*, or the laws according to which God distributes the known and unknown fluids called Imponderable, such as light, heat, electricity, galvanism, etc., etc., which operate both actively and passively on all the kingdoms of creation, animal, mineral, and vegetable.

3d. *The Organic Movement*, or the principles according to which God distributes forms, tastes, colors, and other properties, to all the substances created or to be created on the different globes of the Universe.

4th. *The Instinctual Movement*, or the laws according to which God distributes the instincts and desires, passions and attractions, to all the beings of creation, past, present, and future creations, in the various globes of the Universe.

X.* *The Social Movement*, or the laws according to which God has regulated the order and succession of diverse systems of social organization on all the globes of the Universe.

These five branches of the system of Nature are governed by rigorous laws, which determine, in their respective spheres, all movements, all phenomena, all events.

But is it to be believed that these laws perform their functions, each in its own way, independently of all the others? that these movements are not, in any manner, related, combined, co-ordinated? Let us see what are the primordial properties of the Divine Nature,—the properties which must influence the Creative Power in all its manifestations:

Radical Attribute,	X.	INTEGRAL DISTRIBUTION OF MOVEMENT.
Primary Attributes,	{ 1st.	Economy of Means.
	2d.	Distributive Justice.
	3d.	Universality of Providence.
Pivotal Attribute,	⋈	UNITY OF SYSTEM.

These, we say, are the attributes which the Creator must have, as an infinitely wise and infinitely good Being, and which must govern Him in the regulation of the different parts of the system of the Universe.

If, then, there is *Unity of System* and *Economy of Means*, as there must be in all that the Divinity does, then we must suppose that the laws of universal movement are in some way closely connected, and correspondent to each other.

---

* In his classification, Fourier distinguishes his *pivots* by the sign X. Thus, in the classification of colors, he puts the X opposite the White, which is the Whole of the colors, and not an eighth color. The sign K relates to *transitions*.

Does not this appear, to our minds, the most simple, the most consistent, the most satisfactory mode, in which we can regard creation? Does not this interdependence furnish to man his most powerful means of investigation, since it allows him to compare one sphere with another,—to infer from the known to the unknown, and to elevate himself gradually to a knowledge of all the laws of Divine Government?

Unity of System and Economy of Means do not exclude variety. Only think of the modes of reproducing organized beings, from man to the humblest vegetable,—what an endless variety in the application of a single principle ·

We have seen that among heterogeneous things there exist natural relations. These relations are not an exception; they are not limited to a small number of cases, where they are seized instinctively, without protracted study; they are the rule; and everything that occurs, in one branch of movement, has its image or reproduction in the other branches.

The laws of passional or social movement are the laws of the cardinal movements. But, in each movement, the laws are translated into a special language, by particular effects. Thus Art, *which is one*, may render the same thought into different languages or modes of expression, as by form, by color, by music, by verse, etc.

Each phenomenon of passional movement, each effect of Passion in man, must be reflected in all the branches of the whole natural system. In the organic kingdom, for example, smells, tastes, colors, forms, properties, must be distributed in such a manner as to represent faithfully the play of the Passions.

This relation among the different modes of the manifestation of Life, this necessity that any phenomenon whatever, has everywhere its accurate image, should be reproduced under all forms, has been discovered by Fourier, and is by him named UNIVERSAL ANALOGY.

The life of an animal or vegetable is, in all its details, a consequence of the development which a passion takes, acting upon a given character, and in some one of the phases of human life. All that there is in it, tends to perfect the analogical resemblance, nothing is arbitrary, and a cause can be assigned for the most fugitive form of a petal or the lightest perfume of a flower.

Fourier has thus expelled Chance from all the points which it seemed to occupy. He shows that everything results from wise laws, from invariable principles. It was long since said, that there "are no effects without causes," but there has been only a half-faith in the truth. If the adage be absolutely true, the forms, colors, properties of a being, have a cause which man ought to investigate, which he is able to find, which he has virtually found in the law of analogy, since that law accounts for all in the most simple and satisfactory manner.

To show how faithfully Nature has traced her portraits, we shall take from Fourier some examples of the application of the Law. In order to find the particular analogy of a vegetable or an animal, Fourier gives the special analogies of each of its parts, of each of the characters which distinguish the individual. Thus, in the vegetable kingdom:—

Root.—Emblem of the principles which govern in the action of the Passion.
Trunk.—Emblem of the course followed by the Passion.
Leaf.—Emblem of the class or person depicted; then, an emblem of the cares (educational and others) which have prepared the effect of the Passion.
Calyx.—Emblem of the form in which the Passion envelops itself, and of the circumstances which influence it.
Petals.—Emblem of the kind of pleasure attached to a Passion.
Grain Seeds.—Emblem of the treasures amassed by the exercise of the Passions.
Pistils and Stamens.—Emblems of the product which the Passion gives.
Perfume.—Emblem of the charm which the Passion excites.

Fourier makes use likewise, in his calculations, of the analogy of colors, geometrical forms, musical notes, &c.,—as may be seen in the following table:

SCALE OF NATURAL RIGHTS WITH ANALOGIES.

Rights.	Number.	Passions.	Colors.	Curves.	Notes.	Metals.
Harvest.	1. Addition.	Friendship.	Violet.	Circle.	ut.	Iron.
Pasture.	2. Division.	Love.	Azure.	Ellipse.	mi.	Pewter.
Fishing.	3. Subtraction.	Familism.	Yellow.	Parabola.	sol.	Lead.
Chase.	4. Multiplication.	Ambition.	Red.	Hyperbola.	si.	Copper.
Interior Federation.	5. Progression.	Cabalist.	Indigo.	Spiral.	re.	Silver.
Freedom from Care.	6. Properportion	Papillon.	Green.	Conchoide	ta	Platina.
External Appropriation.	7. Logarthims.	Composit.	Orange.	Logarithmic.	la.	Gold.
MINIMUM.	* Y POWERS.	UNITYISM.	WHITE.	CYCLOID.	UT. H.	MERCURY.
Liberty.	X ————	Favoritism.	Black.	Epicycloid.	But.	————

Fourier has not explained all the parts of this table, but we shall attempt to show, in regard to the curves of the second degree, how *lines* may represent Passions.

Friendship and *Love*, which act in a circumscribed sphere, which are engaged exclusively with the present generation, with a limited number of individuals, are represented by the *Circle* and *Ellipse*, curves that are finite, closed, embracing a space precisely described

The *parabola* and *hyperbola*, on the contrary, are curves which do not terminate, which are prolonged indefinitely, like *Familism*, which thinks of its great-great-grand nephew, and *Ambition*, which dreams of the remotest posterity.

In the group of Friendship, there prevails equality and confusion of rank; in the circle, all the radii are equal, all parting from the centre, and returning to the centre.

The ellipse presents two foci or focuses. All that parts from the one is reflected by the other, which is an exact image of two hearts united by *Love*. If the plane of the Ellipse inclines more and more to the edge of the cone, one of the focuses is separated and loses itself in the infinite. Then the Ellipse is no more, and the curve becomes a *parabola*. Thus love leads insensibly into Familism, and the affection which expended itself on a single being, tends to expand itself, to embrace many, to stretch to the infinite in time, as the radii of the Parabola, go to seek the second focus in the infinite in space.

The radius parting from the focus of the *Hyperbola* ascends by separating itself from the axis, after having been reflected on the curve; it ascends the more, from having attained, from the first bound, a more elevated point. It is thus that the *Ambitious* person tends always to surpass the point at which he has arrived, and that his desires have grown with all his former successes.

The Hyperbola, as the Ellipse, has the Parabola for its limit, because Ambition, like Love, leads to Familism. The ambitious, when they have nothing more to hope for themselves, think of their descendants, of their house, of the name which they are about to transmit to future ages. In illustration of this, read the letter of Edmund Burke, the British statesman, where he bewails the loss of a son in whom his hopes had centred.

A few analogies from Fourier will show the method in which he treats this part of his great discovery.

In the animal kingdom the spider is an emblem of *civilized commerce*.—The spider must be guarded against incessantly, if we would not have it spread its net over every place not visited daily; commerce also builds its shop wherever it can be established, in the most filthy streets, against the most beautiful monuments; shops and spider-webs cleared away to-day, will make their appearance in the same spot to-morrow. Both also present all the varieties between the beautiful and ugly; some dirty and repulsive, others brilliant in their order and symmetry. In both, ingenious combinations of threads or of bells inform the owner of the presence of a stranger. This master-spider or merchant passes his life in a little corner of the world, which he reserves exclusively to himself; he opens his eyes and his ears, he looks and he hears, and that is his function. To move himself, to change his place, is an accident in his existence. Unfor-

---

* Y. Sign of the direct Pivot ; X. Sign of the indirect Pivot.

tunate the *biped* or *diptera* who approaches that mansion! The moment he touches that snare, his destiny is fixed. The merchant and the spider dart forth; they seize their prey; they wrap it in glutinous threads or softy sticky words; and when they have thoroughly despoiled it, they turn up their nose at the poor cadaverous thing! The spider has a head covered with eyes, an enormous belly, long and crooked paws; but the thorax is wanting, it has neither lungs nor heart. The spider devours its fellows, the female eats the male, and even her young ones, etc., etc.

The *toad* is an emblem of the mendicant. He crawls upon the roadside, showing his disgusting pustules, and overpowering all by his monstrous cries. The *frog* is a mendicant of a more polished exterior, who can penetrate into the interior of good families, and thus faithfully represents a higher kind of beggars or solicitors.

The *monkey*, with its tendency to imitate, its grimaces, its malicious and destructive disposition, its cynicism, is unfortunately a too striking emblem of childhood under the peculiar influence of civilized institutions and customs.

The *canary bird* is somewhere given by Fourier as a representative of the spoiled child, which demands to be fed on sweet things.

The *parrot* is an emblem of the false philosopher, who is dressed in a superb plumage of fine words, that in themselves are perfidious and absurd.

The most beautful analogies indicated by Fourier are those which are found in the vegetable world, his early and continued love of Flowers and Fruits having enabled him to seize upon the characteristics of plants with more of accuracy than he appears to have possessed in other cases. But we have no space for the details.

There are also many analogies of the Human Body,—which is a general table of society in the Combined Order,—that are given by Fourier. Of the bony structure, he says: the first view presents us twelve pairs of ribs, which tend to the three bones of the sternum. These are the emblems of the twelve passions, which, alike in both sexes, tend to the three focuses of Attraction before described. There are seven connected or combined ribs and five disconnected or incoherent ribs, just as there are seven spiritual passions, which reign in the Combined Order, and five material passions which reign in societies of an incoherent nature; a thirteenth rib, the Clavicle, surmounting the seven combined ribs, and figuring the thirteenth passion, Harmonism or Unityism, formed of the seven spiritual passions. This passion must be the principal lever of Societary Industry, and thus the clavicle is united to the arm, which is the lever of Corporal Industry.

This ordinance is reproduced partially in the bones of the skull, of which there are eight, of which seven represent the spiritual passions, and the eighth, the frontal bone, represents Unity, being of an order superior to the others.

These tables, Fourier says, can be repeated in all the solids and fluids of the human body; for instance, in the eight hundred muscles of man and woman, which represent the eight hundred characters of a Phalanx; in the ten pairs of nerves, which express the ten choeurs; and in the sixteen pairs of teeth, representing the sixteen choeurs and thirty-two quadrilles of the Phalanx. For the details, we must refer to Fourier's own works.

Other tables, equally interesting, are to be found in the heart, the liver, the viscera, the fluids, etc., by which there can be shown the closest correspondence between the play of the Passions and the human mechanism, down to the minutest details of anatomy.*

What we have here given is, of course, the most meager and unsatisfactory outline; but it is all that is consistent with the plan of this work.

Considerations of another order come to the aid of the principle of Universal Analogy, a principle which permits us to explain a fact, utterly irreconcilable otherwise, to the idea of an all-wise and provident Creator: we mean, the pres-

---

* We are aware how fanciful and inadequate these scattered instances must be. They may be wrong, even, without invalidating the principle.

ence on the globe of useless and hurtful animals, vegetables, and minerals—species in hostility to Man, who is the administrator and overseer of the Earth.

In the epochs of subversion, the human passions produce bad effects. Analogy, the faithful mirror, must represent these bad effects, no less than the good ones, in all the kingdoms of Nature. If the venom of calumny sullies all the relations of life, nature must paint its varied effects in the varied family of vipers, which conceal their hideous nature under brilliant and many-colored skins. If our roads are infested with brigands, our forests must be peopled with wolves, their exact resemblance. And here, let it be remarked, that civilization, which is beginning to deliver itself from brutal violence, purges the countries which it occupies, for the most part, from ferocious animals, the emblems of brutality; but it does not yet know how to keep itself safe from the emblems of the smaller vices that assail it—from the vile insects, the nasty caterpillars, locusts, wasps, etc., etc., which limit its power, and levy every year a heavy tribute upon the products of its industry.

During the infancy of the race, while the passions most commonly lead to disorder, the first creations, destined to form the materials of these unhappy epochs, furnish malignant species in great number; thus nothing could be more meager than our list of useful animals. Among insects, for instance, how few are the faithful servants, such as the Bee, the Silk-worm, the Cochineal, etc., compared with the almost endless multitude of those species which seem to exist only for our torment.

But science demonstrates that there has been already upon the Earth several successive creations, and there is no reason for supposing that the series of creations have reached their extreme term, that the future will not have its own, as well as the past.

The future creations, destined to furnish the materials of the ages of Harmony, will give, as emblems of those epochs, beneficent species in great number; animals useful in themselves, and useful because they will aid man in disembarrassing his domain of whatever is contained in it that is repugnant, malign, or odious.

Analogy is the enchanted prism through which Nature shows herself in the most graceful forms and most pleasing colors. By means of it, man finds a satisfaction for his apparently most futile inclinations, even for the love of the marvellous, which has haunted him in all ages, and to which he will surrender himself without fear of error, since the marvellous will then accord with the reasonable.

The study of the analogies of Nature is destined to become an exhaustless source of pleasure. The author or the journalist, instead of presenting his readers with a charade or an enigma, may ask the analogy of a plant or an animal, and thus amusement itself can be made to contribute to the establishment of Truth. The empty pleasure of deciphering a riddle can be replaced by the composite gratification of reading the lines inscribed by the finger of the Almighty on the great book of Nature.

In this respect, as in all others, God offers man the agreeable and the useful at the same time; for the law of Analogy is also a powerful means of comparison and investigation, besides that the knowledge of the analogies of a plant or mineral, will reveal all its hygiene, medical, or nutritive properties, etc., and discover every use to which it may be put.*

The law of analogy has something in it so captivating, that many persons have admitted it, even while rejecting other parts of Fourier's theory.

But having accepted a theory, it is absurd to shrink from the consequences which naturally flow from its admission. Fourier himself never regarded a principle as an empty word: he applied it always without hesitation; he pur-

---

* If, for example, the analogies of the poppy had been known, we should have been able to divine all the effects of opium, its product. Opium, the use of which degenerates into an irresistible temptation, the solitary intoxication of which produces a brutifying and mortal pleasure, is a sad, though indirect emblem, of a terrible secret vice, which is the scourge of youth in civilization.

sued it to its final consequences, even to attempting to determine the properties of beings in future creations. Some are startled by this boldness, but many more laugh at it; but, in both cases, the gainsayers prove only the timidity or falseness of their own minds.

Under a subversive system, a man is led into evil by his misdirected passions, and Nature paints the sorry result in some malevolent animal. Under a harmonic system, the same man, directed by the same passions, brings forth good alone, and Nature will give again, as an emblem of the happy transformation, some useful animal. Whoever, like Fourier, knows on one side the play of the Human Passions, and, on the other, the mechanism of all past, present, and future societies, has sufficient data for calculating the effect of a character upon each of these social systems, in order to determine the properties of the vegetables and animals destined to represent that effect.

Thus, in a barbarous society, ambition makes man a despot, of which he supposes the lion is the emblem. In Harmony, the same passion would lead man the opposite way, and the future creations, as an emblem of the inverse effect of the same cause, will give an animal the inverse of the lion—an animal good in all the qualities which render the lion dangerous, by its energy, by its activity, by its strength, etc., and which, for the present, may be called an Anti-Lion.

Anti-Lion, Anti-Tiger, Anti-Crocodile! There are many small wits, no doubt, who will be able to sustain their reputation for two or three days by the good things which they will say of these words!

Nature, which has shown, even in her malignant creations, infinite grandeur and variety of resource, shall she not be able to show us as great and wonderful a fecundity in her benevolent creations?

But how are the original generating couple of each kind, of each family, of each variety, to appear upon the Earth? Fourier has occupied himself with this question, and does not recoil from its difficulties.

We have said that a series of beings hierarchically distributed are interposed between man and God. These beings have the direction of the spheres over which they rule; they reign there as men reign over their more restricted sphere, without ceasing to be subjected to the superior laws of the Eternal.

Placed as the Master of the Globe, man presides over it to bring it to perfection, for the multiplication of its animals and vegetables; there, he ordains, he creates; there, God causes his power to be felt, but only by general laws which man can not resist without suffering.

Superior beings have a vaster empire to govern, an empire in which they represent God, as Man represents him upon Earth.

By this gradual delegation of a part of his power to all intelligent beings, Fourier explains how the Universe proceeds without an immediate relation between the Finite and the Infinite; we understand how each being can act directly on those which precede or follow it* at a short distance.

The nearest neighbors to Man, among the superior beings, are the planets. He sees, then, in the planets, his habitual purveyors, or the intermediates by which the benefactions of God are transmitted to him.

The planets, communing together by means of aromal organs, must find in the relations thus established, the satisfaction of all the passions, and consequently of the passion of Love, which is common to them, as to ourselves. For the physical action of love, the planets have sexual organs and can be fecundated. The products of these fecundations, will be precisely the first of each kind, the first parents of all the new animals, of all the new vegetables. The planets are necessarily androgenous, being enabled to fecundate and be fecundated. The fecundation of a planet by other planets of the system, will take place at certain epochs, signalized at each time by a creation of animal and vegetable

---

* The action of beings upon each other is reciprocal. It is felt in the ascending scale, as well as in the descending. Thus Man has an influence in the beings which govern him, but this influence is dispensed and weakened in proportion as it rises, so that it is infinitely small or nothing when it reaches God The Eternal, it has been sometimes suggested, suffers to a degree, with the sufferings of Humanity.

kinds or species. Planets formed in a regular series will give a regular series of products.

Each planet endowed with a particular character, will give products relating to that character, as emblems of the passions by which it is constituted. The satellites of a planet, connected to that planet by affinities of character, furnish emblems of the varied effects of the same passions.

A planet badly treated by its administrator, will yield in the act of fecundation only bad germs that will produce monstrosities and hurtful species representing the inharmonious play of the passions.

We advert to these higher speculations now, only that we may give a complete view of the whole of Fourier's doctrine, and not because his school deem them of direct and special importance.

Thus far, we have given Fourier's doctrine of Universal Analogy; but it is important to observe that he was not the first man of modern times who communicated this view. Emanuel Swedenborg, between whose revelations, in the sphere of spiritual knowledge, and Fourier's discoveries in the sphere of science, there has been remarked the most exact and wonderful coincidence, preceded him in the annunciation of the doctrine, in many of its aspects, in what is termed the doctrine of correspondence. These two great minds,—the greatest beyond all comparison in our later days,—were the instruments of Providence in bringing to light the mysteries of His Word and Works, as they are comprehended and followed, in the higher states of existence. It is no exaggeration, we think, to say, that they are THE TWO commissioned by the Great Leader of the Christian Israel, to spy out the Promised Land of Peace and Blessedness.

But in the discovery and statement of the doctrine of Analogy, these authorities have not proceeded according to precisely the same methods. Fourier has arrived at it by strictly scientific synthesis, and Swedenborg by the study of the Scriptures, aided by Divine Illumination. What is the aspect in which Fourier views it we have shown; we shall next attempt to elucidate the peculiar developments of Swedenborg.*

His fundamental position is, that there must be a Mutual Relation of Analogy between things material or natural, and things spiritual or moral.

1. In proof of this relation, he relies, in the first place, upon the fact that everything in a lower sphere of existence is produced for the sake of something in a higher; and that, if so, every higher thing for the sake of which any object of a lower kind is produced, is the Proximate Cause, by derivation from the First Cause, of the existence of the latter. There must, therefore, be an uninterrupted series of such causes and effects, each intermediate effect, becoming, in succession, a proximate cause of existence to something beneath it, from the First Cause itself, to the lowest of all. Every proximate cause, also, by the urgency, and for the sake of which, something beneath it was produced, is likewise the real essence, or ground of being, of such lower production, which, on its part, is thus an outward form manifesting the existence of such distinct essence. The lower order of objects must then answer to the higher, as certainly and immutably as the reflection in the mirror to its substance. Thus, for example, every lower thing that exists is produced to serve, either more nearly or remotely, to the use of man; this being the second cause of its existence, the thing itself is actually an image, under a different form, of something that is in man; and Man himself was produced to satisfy the Love of God—that there might be a being in the world capable of receiving, in a conscious manner, gifts from God, and of returning them to him in love and adoration. God himself thus being to Man both the Proximate and First Cause of his existence, man must be in a certain manner, an image of God. Accordingly revelation assures

---

* We derive the subsequent statement from the Rev. S. Noble's work on the Plenary Inspiration of the Scriptures.—one of the most masterly and convincing arguments that we ever read. In general, we have confined ourselves as near as might be, to his own language.

us that man was created in the image and likeness of God. If then, man altogether is an image of God, every particular thing which exists in man, is an image of something that exists in God.

2. The same truth is further sustained by Swedenborg and his disciples, by the consideration that Creation is but an Outbirth from the Deity, a production essentially distinct from the producing cause, but necessarily bearing to it an immutable relation. The Deity, in the work of creation, did not operate at random, producing things which have not in himself their divine prototypes or grounds of being. To produce such things he must have stepped out of himself, which is impossible. He formed everything after the pattern of the ineffable attributes and perfections which exist only in his own essence. The Universe, instead of being, as it is sometimes regarded, a result of mere caprice, little better than the offspring of blind chance, is the direct and faithful expression of the Divine Nature—a reflection of its essential properties. Man, therefore, being the image and likeness of his Maker, must reflect all these properties of his Original.

If the whole universe is thus an outbirth from the Deity, and bears in all its parts an immutable relation to Him who gave it birth, this relation is more immediately perceptible in the spiritual part of creation. It is generally acknowledged that the two leading attributes of divinity are Infinite Love and Infinite Wisdom, to which may be added their capacity of infinite creation, which is called Infinite Power. Now, the Will and Understanding of Man, are a certain image, however feeble, of the Will and Intellect Divine, and the endless varieties of thought and emotion of which the former are capable are only so many images of the variety of thought and emotion in the latter. In God, all that the mind conceives or the heart feels, have their inward ground and essence of being. The relation is more perfect, in proportion as Man receives into his will the love and goodness of the Lord, and into his understanding the divine wisdom. But even when he perverts his noble endowments, he still retains an image, though an *inverted* one, of his divine original. The faculties of Will and Understanding are still related to Divine Love and Wisdom, as *opposites*, the Will still being the seat of Love, though it is a love of evil, and the understanding being still the seat of thought, though it is the thought of error, which is held for truth.

The images of divine things, however, are not confined to the phenomena of the intellectual or moral world; they descend lower and display themselves on all the objects of outward and material nature; first, on the corporeal parts of man; next, on all the inferior animals; then, on the vegetable creation; and lastly, on the inert mass of earth and water, which forms the lowest plain of all.

It would consume too much of our space, to illustrate these principles fully, but we can not forbear indicating some of the analogies of the physical creation. As man has two faculties in his mind, which image forth, in an essential manner, the two great essential properties of his Creator, so he has organs in his body answering to the faculties of his mind. The life of his spirit for instance, depends upon his will and understanding, so the life of the body depends on the heart and lungs. Again: the whole body is made up of two constituent materials—the flesh and the blood—solids and fluids. The same analogy is continued, even till we come to the most shapeless masses of matter—the terraqueous globe, consisting of earth and water. Indeed it would be difficult to find anything in the whole circuit of creation, both in general and particular, which is not composed of two principal and constituent parts.

Man being an image of God, how evident is it, that the lower orders of creation, in their respective degrees, bear the same image, since the most cursory inspection shows that they bear an image of man? How strong the tendency to the human form among all the subjects of the animal kingdom, and, more remotely, among vegetables? The animals which differ most in external shape from man, have nevertheless nearly all the organs that are found in man, especially those which are essential to life, though all display them under endless varieties. All have heads, bodies, feet; in their heads, are eyes, noses, mouths, ears; and in their bodies hearts, lungs, and other viscera. As the animal descends in the scale of creation, the resemblance becomes less perfect; yet most of the species retain the principal organs; and where these cease, their place is supplied by something analogous which performs their office in a manner suited to the animal's nature.

Again: the similitude of the animal and vegetable kingdoms, is in many respects strikingly conspicuous. Vegetables, like animals, have a principle of life, are propagated from parents, increase to maturity, provide for the continuance of their kind, decay, die. They have a circulating system of arteries and veins; they have respiratory organs; and the developments of the sexual system, by Linnæus, have brought to light other wonderful analogies. The discoveries of modern science have gone farther, not only establishing general analogies, between all animals and vegetables taken respectively together, but between particular classes of animals and particular classes of vegetables;* and thus leading to the conclusion that every individual species in the vegetable kingdom has a species answering to it in the animal kingdom, each in its sphere discharging like functions in regard to the whole.

Similar observations may be made in regard to the mineral kingdom, where the tendency to offer an image of the higher creation is abundantly manifested. Crystallization, for example, is it not a mute prophecy of the coming vegetation? Or, take the inanimate globe, with its streams, and evaporations, and aromas of all kinds, and how like to the venous and respiratory system of the human body? But we can not dwell on these interesting details.

If the correspondence is thus obvious between the material forms of creation and those of man, how equally, if not more obviously, the relation between the mind of man and the moral qualities of animals. In the instincts, the propensities, the affections, the characters, in short, of the latter, we have a complete picture of the same impulses in man. Besides the common analogy, there are also analogies between every species and individual among animals, in particular, and something that there is in man. Even the savages who designate themselves with the names of favorite birds or beasts, have long since discovered this truth. How great is the contrariety between the wolf and the lamb, the lion and the ox! Yet how easy it is to see that the character of each is thus distinct, because it is formed by some specific affection taken, as it were, out of the human mind, and made the single governing propensity of the animal, without being modified by the innumerable variety of other affections with which in that wonderful aggregate of affections—the Human Mind—it is combined.

Similar analogies are traceable between the moral qualities of man, and the properties of objects in the vegetable and mineral kingdoms. How closely are the appetites and instincts, which in both animals and man tend to the preservation of the species, emulated in vegetables! They are provided with sets of vessels, which draw from the soil in which they grow, and the air which surrounds them, the juices and gases congenial to their natures; nor has Dr. Darwin in his poem called the "Loves of the Plants," or Dr. Thornton in his picture of "Cupid subduing the Vegetable Kingdom," proceeded upon mere fanciful grounds. Even minerals draw from surrounding substances the materials of accumulation, as the plant or animal selects its food, and under the influence of alternation and chemical affinity, rush, as it were, into each other's arms with impulsive yet discriminating mutual affection.

Who can not see, too, marked analogies between the moral qualities of men and animals, and the specific properties of vegetables and minerals? Between vegetables that afford pleasant and wholesome nutriment, the mild races of animals, and the unperverted feelings and thoughts of man, how evident the relation? And is it not equally so, between noxious minerals, noxious plants, noxious animals, and the malignant passions of our distorted souls? Thus, the attributes of the highest nature may be viewed as in a mirror in the lowest, and things invisible read in things which are seen.

* See "Remarks on the identity of certain general laws, which have been observed to regulate the natural distribution of insects and fungi," by W. S. Macleay, Esq., M. A. F. L. S. *Linnæan Transactions.*—Vol. 14, page 46.

We might illustrate these views further, by the common use of *figurative* language, by the ordinary instincts of physiognomy, &c., by which we judge of character, by the teachings of ancient mythology, and by the testimony of Scripture, but such a course would transcend our limits. We can, now, only again refer our readers to the original authorities which we have indicated.

If the doctrine of Universal Analogy be true, it is one of the highest importance. It furnishes us a means to unravel many of the mysteries of life and destiny, an instrument for the enlargement of our scientific knowledge, and a key to unlock the dark and deep sayings of Holy Writ. For example: 1st. It has puzzled the brains of philosophers why there should be so many races of destructive and venomous animals In the world: but the answer is found, as we have before stated, in the fact—that every inferior creature has its immediate antetype in man. If, therefore, man, by the abuse of the freedom of the will, with which he is endowed, perverts the divine gifts which he has received, images of such perversion and evil, by the continued action of the Divine Creative Power, must appear in the lower objects of creation. We are told by the scripture, that all things as they came from the hand of the Creator were *good*, because they were the visible manifestations of the All-Good; but when Humanity fell,

" Earth, through all her parts, gave signs of wo,"

and when Humanity shall have been redeemed, we learn on the same authority, that the " wolf shall dwell with the lamb, and the leopard lie down with the kid: and the calf, and the fatling, and the young lion together; and a little child shall lead them. And the cow and the bear shall feed, their young ones shall lie down together; and the lion shall eat straw like the ox. And the sucking child shall play on the hole of the asp; and the weaned child shall put his hand on the cockatrice's den." In this we find plainly taught, that when evil shall be banished from the moral world, it will cease to exist in the natural world, and that destructive and ugly creatures will disappear with the rectification of disordered passions.

2. Universal Analogy opens a new door to the cultivation of the sciences. When it shall be recognised that there is unity in all the works of God, that all parts of creation are but transcripts of each other, that truth is of universal application, a discovery in any branch of physics becomes the stepping-stone to a broad realm of analogous facts, and the laws which are now supposed to be limited to a few insignificant species or individuals will be found to be but links in the grand series of corresponding links that form the chain of the universe. At present our scientific men are too much engaged with minute and isolated facts; they dwell too exclusively upon microscopic analysis; and they are compelled to do so for the want of a rule for broad and magnificent generalizations. One result of this microscopic observation of facts has been that it has rendered science skeptical and timid, that it has banished faith from its walks, and that it has narrowed and belittled the intellectual vision of philosophers. If this class of men, would ever attempt to attain to the dignity of their vocation, they must elevate their minds to the higher interpretation of Nature than is to be found in the region of mere facts.

3. Universal Analogy, if true, throws a blaze of new and brilliant light upon the scriptures; and that it is true, seems to be proved by the researches of those who have studied the scriptures under this light, and tell us, that from beginning to end, they are found to bear a uniform and consistent construction, according to the principles of correspondence. They have higher meanings than the mere letter; they are sources of deep spiritual truths, that once perceived, illuminate the entire revelation as with a celestial torch. What are to us unmeaning narratives, what are rude and absurd ceremonials, what are insignificant events in the history of an individual, are found to be full of universal spiritual meanings. The Word and the Work of Deity are one; Science is harmonized with Revelation; the secret scroll of destiny is laid open; and God is worshipped no longer through fear, but through knowledge and faith.

CONCLUSION.

"A friendless warfare! lingering long,
Through weary day, and weary year,
A wild and many-weaponed throng,
Hang on thy front, and flank, and rear."—BRYANT.

WE have now fulfilled the task which we imposed upon ourselves, we have presented the conception of Fourier in its completeness, we have spoken not only of what he proposes for the present, but of what he conjectures for the futures, we have touched upon all questions, from the reform of the township to the modification which time must make in manners, from the education of the child to planetary influences, and the creation of worlds. We have, it is true, sketched only in the vaguest outline, but what we have done is sufficient to enable the reader to form an opinion of the Theory of Universal Unity. Will any one now dispute the grandeur and comprehensiveness of the genius to which we are indebted for such mighty generalizations? Are his notions unworthy of Man, or unworthy of God? Was there ever loftier conceptions of the dignity and glory of human destiny, or of the infinite wisdom and goodness of the Creative Power?

But, before we answer these questions, we are reminded that our work is not yet accomplished. The substance of Fourier's discoveries *as a science*, we have given; we have unfolded it to the extent in which it is developed in his published writings; but deeper questions remain behind. What relation does this science bear to the existing institutions of society; to the dictates of true Morality; and to the doctrines of Religion and the constitution of the Church? We shall attempt a solution of the difficulty supposed to exist on these points, in the form of an answer to the following objections:—

1. *That the new doctrine is dangerous to public order.*

By this it is meant, that our plans are revolutionary. They certainly are revolutionary, or, as the state of society now is, they would not be worth a moment's thought.

But the revolution they contemplate is not violent, nor unjust, nor destructive. On the contrary, it can be demonstrated that ours is the only universal and peaceful scheme of reform that is now agitated.

Society is at present divided into parties whose designs and wishes appear utterly irreconcilable, so that each of them in order to triumph, must desire the compression and ruin of all other parties. In this fact originates their deep and unrelenting mutual hostility.

Society is also composed of a class which wishes to preserve all that it has, and of another class that wishes to get much which it has not; the first thinks it can not yield without losing—the second that it can not gain without taking. For this reason, there is a perpetual and bitter hatred and war between the two ranks who look upon each other as natural enemies. The Conservative and the Reformer, the Tory and the Whig, the Democrat and the Aristocrat, have been at all times, and in every nation, in a state of vigilant and exacerbated antagonism.

The Phalansterian School ALONE, has nothing to do with any of these parties or classes, but presents itself in the midst of all with words of Positive Affirmation and Peace; it recognises the legitimacy of the desires of all; infringes the rights of none; it carries no torch to the temples of any; it offers to all at the same time, a doctrine which is capable of satisfying all.

It says to the higher classes that their possessions and their advantages are all theirs, and that it has no design of infringing them in the slightest respect. At the same time, besides this Right, it places a Right not less sacred, the Right of the laborer to his labor and its fruits, the assertion of which now menaces the existence of the rich and of social order, and will continue to do so, until it is recognised and satisfied.

It says to the lower classes that they will only suffer the more, by violently despoiling the wealthy, and thus impoverish others without enriching themselves; so that when all shall be miserably occupied in defending themselves against hunger, the sciences, the arts, all high and noble industry, will be abandoned, and the human race retrograde towards barbarism. At the same time, it sustains them in the sentiment that they are entitled to Labor, to Education, to Justice, and to Happiness.

It proves that a greater part of our evils spring from the misdirection of human energy, in fruitless enterprises and pernicious wars.

It proposes a plan for the organization of labor, by which the efforts of all classes shall converge towards a useful end,—the extracting from the Globe, an exhaustless reservoir, an amount of the elements of wealth and happiness amply sufficient for the wants of all, by giving to those who have not, and by adding to those who have.

The Social School demonstrates also that the masses have little interest in the irritating contests of politics; that the form of the government touches them only in a few points, since they are equally miserable (except when the accident of abundant land, as in this country, constitutes an exception) under all governments, and that their progress depends upon social reform,—the reform of the township, which on the diminutive scale on which it is essayed, can do no harm, if it could do no good.

How could such peaceful notions as these prove dangerous to public order? What sentiment is there to impel to disorder, men who know, *scientifically*, that every organic change, in a subversive state, short of a true and harmonious re-organization, is nothing more than a revolutionary perturbation? No: while we propose the reform of the whole world, we would not disturb the smallest corner of its broad domain. Peace is our motto; but it is a Peace, under the silent influences of which a new Earth would rise.

II. *That the doctrine is immoral.*

The Social School proposes to organize Labor; there can certainly be no immorality in that!

But they are accused of immorality, because Fourier has expressed the thought, that the manners of future societies, particularly in regard to the relation of the sexes, will be as different from those of our present societies, as ours are from those of the Patriarchs and Savages. We have already made a reply to this: if the conjectures of Fourier displease any, it is of little importance to us that they be rejected; they do not bear upon the project which we seek to realize. Our task is the organization of labor, and we leave to other generations the discretion of adopting such changes in their feelings and customs as superior intelligence, purity, and truth, may approve.

Again: we are accused of immorality, in that we urge men to indulge and not repress their Passions. Let it be understood, however, in what sense we use the word Passion, and to what does this objection amount? Why, that we inculcate that it is the duty of Man so to adjust his social relations, that his native impulses, which, freely indulged in the present state, only lead to evil, may be indulged in such a way as only to lead to Good!

Much error has been started in regard to Fourier's standard of morality, by the use of the word Passion, which has generally a bad sense in the present acceptation, but which was perhaps the best that he could find. He means by it, as we have before said, the springs of action in the human soul, the fundamental impulses, the affections, the motives of the Will. The passions, he says, have a right and a wrong development. The right development produces harmony, good, justice, unity: the wrong development produces selfishness, evil, injustice, and duplicity.

Sin, vice, and what are called bad passions, do not arise from any positive principle of evil infused from without into the mind of man, or having its original seat there; but are the false, disordered action of principles that are in themselves good. On the contrary, virtue and goodness are the true, harmonious, unitary action of all these faculties. Virtue is the integrity of a man's whole nature (*virtus*, *man*liness), and implies the due subordination, the perfect co-operation, the Unity of the Whole Man.

Fourier, in this view of human nature, is sustained by some of the most clear and profound of metaphysical thinkers. Bishop Butler, whom we regard as one of the acutest and large-minded of the able race of English divines, takes essentially the same view in his admirable Sermons. He defines Virtue as "the following of Nature," and vice as "deviating from it;" and proceeds to show that this is not "a loose way of talk." "Whoever," he says, "thinks it worth while to consider this matter thoroughly, should begin by stating to himself exactly the idea of a system, economy, or constitution of any particular thing or nature; and he will find that it is a One or a Whole" (Unity), "made up of several parts, but yet that the several parts, even considered as a whole, do not complete the idea, unless you include the relations and the respects which those parts have to each other. Every work, of both nature and art, is a *system*," etc. He then illustrates this by the *constitution* of a watch, and adds: "Thus it is in regard to the inward frame of man. Appetites, passions, affections, etc., considered merely as the several parts of our nature, do not give us an idea at all of the system or constitution of this Nature, because the Constitution is formed by somewhat not yet taken into consideration, namely, by the relation which these several parts have to each other," etc. (Unityism).

Again, in describing the nature of vice, he says: "Every work of art is apt to be *out of order*, which is true also of the human system or constitution." And after stating, from a deliberate survey of our nature, that "we were made for society, and to promote the happiness of it," proceeds as follows to state an objection: "But it may be asked, Has not Man dispositions and principles within which lead him to do evil to others as well as good? Whence come the many miseries else, which men are the authors and instruments of to each other?" In answer, he says, "there is no such thing as ill-will in one man towards another, emulation and resentment being away; whereas there is plainly benevolence and good-will; there is no such thing as love of injustice, oppression, treachery, ingratitude; but *only eager desires after such and such external goods* (what Fourier calls duplicity of action), which, according to a very ancient observation, the most abandoned would choose to obtain by innocent means, *if they were as easy* and effectual to their end; that even emulation and resentment, by any one who will consider what *these passions are in their nature*, will be found nothing to the purpose of this objection; and that the principles and passions in the mind of Man, PRIMARILY AND MOST DIRECTLY lead to RIGHT BEHAVIOR, with regard to others as well as himself, and only SECONDARILY and ACCIDENTALLY to WHAT IS EVIL."

It would seem, then, that Fourier's notion of the nature of evil and of virtue, is not unsanctioned by the highest authorities of Christendom.

Two remarks, however, are necessary to a complete understanding of his doctrine of obedience to the Passions.

The first is, that all the societies which have as yet existed upon the earth, being incoherent and disorganized, were subversive and false societies, and that the Passions of Man are subverted with them; hence, that compression and restraint are absolutely needed to prevent the race from degenerating into a still lower degree of degradation and suffering. In proportion to the extent of that subversion, is the need of more rigorous laws and restraints; but as society approaches a more organic state, the severity of its discipline may be relaxed, until finally, having attained Social Harmony, men may be left to their native

CONCLUSION. 113

Attractions, which are their only true guides, ever-present and permanent revelations in the soul of the Will of God.

Our second remark is, that owing to this fact of the *accidental* and *permanent*, or the false and true destinies, of society, the dictates of Morality are of two kinds: *relative* and *absolute*. There are certain duties which are duties for all men, of all ages or nations, and under all circumstances, such as the duties of Truth, Justice, Love, and Devotion to our Heavenly Father; these are absolute obligations, for the complete performance of which we are to seek all the aids that our position requires, from the energy of our own wills, and from the grace of God. There are other duties, which are duties exceptionally, under given conditions, and for the production of particular results, such as self-denial,* mortification, resignation, the endurance of suffering, fastings, contentment, etc. They are duties, because in incoherent society, they aid in controlling subversive passions, that would otherwise develop themselves to the injury of their possessors and others. Another reason is, that it would only be vain and irritating to indulge desires for the gratification of which society had made no provision —the love of wealth, for instance, which we are commanded to restrain, because it would only become a torment in societies where it is impossible for seven eighths of the people to have wealth.

That the present state of society is not its permanent state, and that the compression of the passions is not a permanent duty, is evident from the consideration that such compression is not, now, effectual, but only partial and temporary, and must continue to be of that character. No individual has ever succeeded in the attempt at a direct subduing and suppression of his passions. They are active and living forces, that will manifest their existence in one way or another, like the internal fires of the Earth, which, smothered in one place, speedily break out in another, generally made more intense by the feeble effort of resistance. The only method of eradicating a vice of the passions, is not suppression, but substitution, i. e. by changing the mode of their activity. Dr. Chalmers, the celebrated Scotch Presbyterian preacher, has an excellent sermon on " the expulsive power of a new affection,"—a phrase that recognises the truth that the best way of getting rid of an old affection is to get a new one, or in other words, to change the object of the affection. A healthful activity of all the faculties of our nature, which can only be procured in the Harmonic Order, is a better preservative against vice, than all the saws and commands of all the moralists from Confucius to Joe Smith. Only to the extent in which the means for such an activity has been presented by Society, have its manners and morals improved. This is a pregnant fact!

That the present state of society is utterly and abominably false, and needs a thorough organic renovation, is further evident since it imposes a restraint upon the practice of the *absolute* duties of life, almost as rigid and grievous as that which it lays upon the indiscriminate indulgence of the subversive passions. It is almost a matter of doubt, whether the world would be more disturbed and injured by the unbounded freedom of all the passions, or by the unflinching assertion of all the virtues. Suppose that Truth and Justice were at once applied to the existing ways and relations of Mankind! Could there be a more fatal supposition? What a universal uproar and distress among the plots of public men, the frauds of merchants, the tricks of politicians, the innumerable basenesses of industry, of legislation, of the press, of the pulpit, among secret dislikes and dissimulations in families, between man and wife, parents and children, the deceptions of Love, the ignoble conventions of politeness and law upon which society rests! Or, let Justice be done among men, and what devastations, what exposures, what overturnings, what horrors, would be the wild and cruel result?

---

* There is a sense, however, in which self-denial is of the essence of Religion. The law of life, according to Fourier, is this, " that God distributes to his creatures their particular attractions and desires respectively," and the particular exception to this law of distribution is, that man on Earth aspires to Heaven and a higher destiny than he can here enjoy. It is then, the link of Universal Unity which binds the soul of man, while on Earth, to Heaven, and every seventh function in material and spiritual life, should be religious, and diverge from earthly satisfaction to heavenly aspiration, as an act of devotedness and self-denial or sacrifice of self to God and Universal Unity.

8

War, pestilence, and famine, are hardly more dangerous to the physical welfare of our societies, than Truth, Justice, and Liberty, would be, if there were some Supreme Power, capable and ready to put them into instant action. Society itself admits this danger, every time it bristles so fiercely against some poor starveling, "indiscreet, imprudent, impracticable" reformer, who would only make a feeble application of some single bit of Truth or Justice; yet Truth, Justice, Liberty, are *absolute* in their requirements.

What becomes, then, of the charge that the doctrines of Fourier are immoral?

We admit fully the necessity of restraint in the subversive stages of society; we invade no recognised law of the present state; we would relax the discipline of coercion and force, only as the moral advancement of the race allowed and required; and we are the only reformers who have a practical faith in Absolute Virtues, because we are the only persons who can propose a social system in which they can find there true and perfect expression.

The truth is, that we are more moral than other people, because we know how to make morality available in the highest degree to the happiness of mankind. If individuals among the disciples of Fourier are immoral, they are so *in spite* of their creed.

III. *That the doctrine is irreligious.*

Those who make this objection, mean by it, that our views are exclusively moralistic or material, and that we hope to achieve the reformation of society by a mere internal mechanism, without regard to the teachings of religion.

We are not surprised at this charge, because the doctrine of Fourier has been taught generally in its scientific aspects, and Science, in a one-sided view of it, takes a position of antagonism to Revelation, although it is found in the end that they mutually support and illustrate each other—God being the author of both. Science is too much cultivated in the sphere of Necessity, and Revelation in the sphere of Faith, whereas they should be equally instruments of unfolding the mysteries of God's word and works. Astronomy, mathematics, geology, have all at times presented themselves in opposition to Christianity; but a larger knowledge of the facts of the one, and of the meaning of the other, have made them willing co-operators in the redemption of Man from ignorance and suffering.

Social Science, it will be seen in the end, so far from being hostile to true religion, is one of its best and highest expressions.

It would lead us into too technical and abstruse a metaphysical discussion to attempt to show the complete compatibility of every word of Revelation with the Doctrine of the Passions; but we believe we can do so, under the light of Universal Analogy, and may hereafter make the effort. At present, we confine ourselves to general affirmation and popular explanation.

We claim to be Christians, then, because we believe the gospel of Christ to be the highest revelation given to Man; and we believe that this religious dispensation will endure until it has been fully established by the creation of a New Heaven and a New Earth, described in the Book. And, again, we claim to be Christians, because we believe that the Providence of God is Universal; that it is both partial and general, and that he is a God of Love and Mercy, not a cold abstraction, but ever near to us, present in the mind and heart and senses.

We believe it to be our duty to obey the commandment of Love, and have perfect Faith in the promise of light given by the Savior.

"Seek ye first the kingdom of God and its Justice, and all these things [worldly comforts] shall be added unto you."

In obedience to this command, and in implicit faith in this promise, we seek that we may find the kingdom of God and its righteousness; and we are only afraid of those who say that nothing can be found by seeking; that the mystery of the Universe is impenetrable; that the curse of civilized duplicity and misery will last forever; that human nature is too bad to be redeemed; that the will of God can not be done on Earth, as it is in Heaven, though we are instructed to ask for this in daily prayer. We are afraid, we say, of such negations, and regard all persons who entertain them as infidels, whatever may be their *professions* or *creeds*.

We believe that every word of the Gospel is divine, but we believe also that no human understanding of that Word is perfect.

If, then, it be asked, what particular form of Doctrine we propose to teach, we reply that we have no mission to teach any one religious creed or preference to others. Individually, we admit all creeds in their peculiar spheres, inasmuch as they are all respectively, partial aspects of the one eternal truth of Revelation, in its infinite variety of aspects. We admit all views of truth, without denying any, and subscribe to every creed, but not exclusively; what is affirmative in each is, for the most part, true, while the error of each is in its negation and exclusiveism.*

Our object, in regard to Faith and Spiritual Light, then, is not to teach a new religion, but to point to That which has already been revealed, to show that men as yet have only grasped the shadows of that true Religion, in its various aspects, and mistaken these for reality. The various creeds and doctrines of religious sects are types of Unity, but the life and practice of these sects is not in Unity. It is a shadowy aspiration, more or less intense, but not a positive reality; for, while the truths of doctrine are embraced and held in veneration, practical life is steeped in discord and iniquity; and this must ever be the case, until the spirit of religious truth or unity be really *embodied* in the practice of daily life—the end we seek to realize.

We seek to effect this practical embodiment of religious truth and love, in daily life, by attractive industry and unitary combination; neither of which are in themselves alone Religious Unity, but the *body* or collective form in which alone the ordinances of Christianity, the spirit of religion, the Universal church, can be incorporated practically and incessantly, for without the Body, the spirit can not be manifested fully on Earth. We do not deny, then, the spiritual truth of Religion; we desire to organize a body to receive that truth; a practical reality, and not a mockery. And what is more, we hold that all religious creeds are true in their main features, and only need to be embodied in material organic Unity, to prove their beauty and utility respectively, and their indisputable claims to a true origin, ordained by Providence. It is the want of such a body which confines them to the realms of suffering spirits and discordant action: types and shadows in confusion struggling to become realities.

Religious truth is the *principle* of unity and harmony, but this can not be realized in *practice* universally, without a correspondent unity of action in the sphere of worldly interests; and thence it is that in the present state of disorder and discord in the world, though spiritual light and truth are the first in principle and importance, natural light and unitary combination are of primary interest as the practical foundation of a perfect superstructure; and to frown upon the science of industrial unity, as an inferior thing of mere material importance, is silly and thoughtless. The man must be emancipated from the degradation of the brute before he can be imbued with elevated views of God and a future life.

No one will deny, we hope, that society is much indebted to the progress of material art and science, for refinement and the spread of Christianity—the power of multiplying and diffusing Christian knowledge among nations. No one will deny that the ability of men to increase in knowledge, politeness, and friendship, is greatly promoted by the alleviation of their outward circumstances; and that comfortable apartments, freedom from care and drudgery, cleanliness, constant labor, and education, are efficient auxiliaries in the establishment of truth. Now, our only aim at present is to render the services of science and industrial activity, the handmaids of religion, more constant, more direct, and more effective. We wish to show, as society is now constructed, that there is no security for moral discipline and religious communion. Every one is left to act, without direct control, as his unbridled passions dictate; and as the interes*t*s

---

* See this matter treated at length in our following work, soon to be published.

of individuals are everywhere opposed to those of general society, temptation to iniquity is permanent and strong.

The Church has little or no hold on the minds of men (except to enslave their intellects); and never will have the power she ought to have, until society is organized materially on a plan of Unity, in which the light of Gospel truth can be conveyed in permanence, instead of being, as at present, wasted by dispersion among beings who are not sufficiently accountable to general opinion for their evil doing and neglect of duty. An appointed minister of light and truth has now no other function to perform but that of holding up the banner of religion to his flock, shut up in their purchased pens, called pews, for their speculative consideration, once in seven days, and then abandon them to all the snares of poverty and insecurity of worldly interests throughout the week; for if he undertake to visit and console his flock, between the intervals of Sabbath, he is quite unable to protect them from the many allurements and necessities of falsehood in the world.

This is not a system, then, by which religion can obtain sufficient influence over human conduct in the common walks of life; it is too loose and incoherent. It needs consistency and unity, in which the light of true religion might be ever present, to inspire the minds of individuals and control their actions. The problem, therefore, to be solved, is not so much the meaning of the Word of God, as the means of organizing worldly interests in harmony with truth, and spiritual light and love. The light of doctrine is already very great in the various branches of the Universal Church, but want of unity in worldly combination and material society, prevents that light from being always before the eyes of the laboring population, who are more or less dispersed in personal obscurity, deprived of aid and consolation, knowledge and security, and left alone, unguarded and abandoned to the recklessness of passion in the snares of iniquity.

This dispersion of the body of society, the unprotected, disunited, working classes, is the cause of darkness and depravity on earth, the reign of chaos and Satan. Not the absence of religious light, but the want of unitary influence and convergency, to save it from being lost and scattered in the dust of incoherent worldly interests. The spirit of religion wants a corporeal organism, to manifest itself in truth and permanent reality on earth, and this is what association is destined to prepare for it. The general delusion of society at present in regard to Religion is, to suppose that holding up the type of truth in principle and precept, once a week, to an unbanded congregation, is sufficient to prevent their backsliding all the week, in the midst of general depravity, that the Will alone of poor weak mortals is able to protect them from the temptations and delusions of the Adversary, that unfriended miserable men can alone sustain the conflict with evil, without the constant presence and aid of their fellow-men.

Association, then, is not designed to supplant Religion, but to be its servant in the accomplishment of the Redemption of the Earth. We look upon it as the mightiest auxiliary to Christianity that has ever been presented to men, because it is a direct outgrowth and manifestation of the Spirit of Christianity.

The object of Christ's mission on earth was to redeem mankind from sin and suffering, and reveal truths of peace and unity, that would confer inconceivable blessedness on all his creatures. No injunction occurs more frequently in the Bible than that men should make themselves One in faith, in love, in hope. Almost the last word upon the lips of the Savior when he separated from his sorrowing heart-broken disciples, was " Be ye one, even as I and my father are One"—a union the most intimate and most sacred.

Fourier did not set up any other name than that of Christ, and in one of the last chapters written by him, describing the triumphs of Universal Association, he exclaims, " These are the days of Mercy, promised in the Word of the Redeemer (Matt. v. 6). Blessed are they which do hunger and thirst after righteousness, for they shall be filled. It is verily in Harmony, in associative unity, that God will manifest to us the bounteous immensity of his Providence, and that the Savior will come according to his Word in all the ' glory of his father;' it is the kingdom of Heaven that comes to us in this terrestrial world; it

CONCLUSION. 117

is the reign of Christ; he triumphs; he has conquered evil. CHRISTUS REGNAT, VINCIT, IMPERAT. Then, will the Cross have accomplished its two-fold destiny; that of CONSOLATION during the reign of evil, and that of UNIVERSAL BANNER, when human reason shall have accomplished the task imposed upon it by the Creator. 'Seek ye first the kingdom of God and his righteousness,' the harmony of the Passions in Associative Unity. Then will the Banner of the Cross display with glory its device, the augury of victory; IN HOC SIGNO VINCES; for then it will have conquered evil, conquered the gates of hell, conquered false philosophy, and national indigence, and spurious civilization; *et portæ inferi non prevalebunt.*"

Thus, we have shown, in regard to the more important objections brought against the doctrine of Fourier—

1st. That it is the only doctrine which can conciliate all classes and parties, on a basis of mutual interest and harmony.

2d. That it absolves no man from the obligations of true morality, but insists upon it, as an absolute and permanent duty that every individual, being himself an image of God and of the Universe, must bring his faculties and life into accordance with the laws of Justice, Integrity, Unity, as well as he may in this state of duplicity and subversion. But

3d. That individuals can do this alone, only in rare cases; and that it is the direct effect of the attempt to make our own souls *at one* with God's Nature and Providence, to seek to bring the souls of others into the same divine state, for the accomplishment of which, no agency has ever been devised comparable in any degree to an organization of the whole of society according to the laws of universal gradation and harmony—the law of variety in Unity, which is the eternal fact of Creation.

INDIVIDUAL VIRTUE IS THE INTEGRITY, WHOLENESS, UNITY, of ALL the FACULTIES of THE INDIVIDUAL SOUL; SOCIAL VIRTUE, THE SAME INTEGRITY, COMPLETENESS and UNITY of ALL the PRINCIPLES of the Social Soul. *Each is necessary to the attainment of the other!!*

THE UNION OF BOTH SOCIAL AND INDIVIDUAL VIRTUE IS RELIGION!

If any man is able to make immorality and irreligion out of such doctrines, he is at perfect liberty to enjoy his discovery!

No: our immorality and irreligion consists in this, that the blind and corrupted growths of civilization do not comprehend that we are greatly in advance of them on all points of scientific and religious wisdom.

We have a morality which is not individual and selfish, and this they do not like. We have a religion which is not arrogant, narrow, and exclusive; which explains the mysteries of the Bible, which renders our hope, and faith, and charity, scientific, and our wisdom and truth religious; which promises to realize the Kingdom of God on Earth, and this they do not like. But we know that the future is ours, and thus we confidently look to God for the fulfilment of all his promises of blessedness to Earth.

"I saw the New Jerusalem, the Holy City coming down from God, out of Heaven, adorned as a bride for her husband. And I heard a great voice out of Heaven, saying, Behold the tabernacle of God is with men, and he will dwell with them, and they shall be his people, and God himself shall be with them and be their God."*

---

* The suggestion that those who do not like our views of human nature or of religion can form associations for themselves, is so obvious, that we have not insisted upon it; but we commend the *principle* of association to all sects, who are at liberty to adopt what *details* they please. The principle is practical Christianity.

NOTE.

"Fourier's science is not a system, but a demonstration of the principle of unity and order God has manifested in the systems of Creation, and the Word of inspiration, by which man is to be led from misery to happiness on earth and in a future state; and this science of universal unity, is nothing but a faithful Image, though perhaps but faint, of God himself.

God is, Himself, the law of universal harmony, and his Creation is an image of Himself. God is all in all, and there is nothing else for him to speak of in his word, or image in creation, but Himself; and God is a trinity in unity; from whence it follows that the law of order in the Word and in the Works of God is necessarily a *Trinity in unity*.

This is the system of Fourier, if it may be properly called a 'system' and simple as it may appear, it is the whole of his system. But then it is a Godlike system gifted with the power of infinite creation in the sphere of thought.

This principle of unity applied to general theology and science is, by Fourier, termed the 'series' or the law of order and of truth, which draws away the veil from mystery wherever it is taken as a guide in studying the word of God in scripture, and his works in nature; so that we may truly say, as Fourier says, that God himself explains all mysteries, and without him all is darkness and confusion. Christ is all in all, and unto him must all be gathered in the end: and this is what Fourier inculcates; for he has not made a system, but endeavored to explain the attributes of God, the law of universal unity, that all may live in God and God in all, and that the word of God may be fulfilled as it is written:—

'I am Alpha and Omega, the beginning and the ending, saith the Lord, which is, and which was, and which is to come, the Almighty.' Rev. xviii.

The System of Fourier, then, as far as it may properly be termed a system, consists in seeking for the law of God in every part of the Creation and the Word; which law of God is the image of God Himself and universal unity, the truth, the light, the life of all; and the fundamental principles of science and theology propounded by Fourier consist in what he terms the 'series' or the image of Divine Love and truth: the Trinity in Unity.

This Law of order is defined in various ways, according to the sphere of thought and action which engages our particular attention at a given time, and on a given subject; but the Universal theorem is, Trinity in Unity; the 'series,' or the 'Law of order;' which Law of order is the law of God; a picture more or less imperfect of Divinity and Universal unity. Applied to God Himself, as a definition of the Godhead, it stands thus:—

Scripturally	1 God the Father 2 God the Son 3 God the Holy Ghost	Trinity in Unity.
Analogically	1 The Active principle of life 2 The Passive principle of life 3 The Neutral principle of order	Trinity in Unity.
Providentially	1 Universality of Providence 2 Simplicity of action 3 Perfection of justice	Trinity in Unity.

God is Himself the Principle of Universal Unity. The whole and sole Governor of the Universe, the Lord of Heaven and Earth, and yet we are told in Scripture that the Devil is the God of this World. 2 Cor. iv. 4. This leads us to what Fourier terms the 'Law of exception, discord, and disorder which is not the law of order, but subject to that Law, as the Devil is not God, but subject to the Power of God. God, then, is the principle of order and of life; the Devil is the principle of death and darkness; God is the Law, Satan the exception; and yet God is all in all.

This is the principle of universal unity propounded by Fourier: God, the Law of order; Trinity in unity; the fountain and the life of all things; and Satan, the exception to the law of order, and the God of this world, as long as it remains under the curse of original sin. God is a positive Personality; Satan a negative, or no-thing but evil. Lucifer a fallen angel; and Diabolos a fallen man, or class of men.

The system of Fourier consists in keeping God before his eyes, in all his thoughts and actions, to discover what the law of order is in every sphere of life, and what is the exception. The Trinity in unity and its ambiguous counterpart. To scripture he applies this law; to Nature he applies it, and to the existence of Humanity. Wherever there is order in the universe, he finds the law of unity exemplified; and where disorder reigns, the law of discord, or the mere exception to the Law of order.

In man, he finds a trinity in unity; an intellectual or spiritual Trinity in unity subject to the law of death and darkness, as a mere exception to the law of universal life and Harmony. In universal nature he discovers the same law of order and existence.

The Solar System is a Trinity in unity, or a series of stars: 1st. Planets carrying moons or Satellites: 2dly. Planets which do not carry moons; and 3dly. *Satellites* revolving round superior planets; which trinity of orders is maintained in unity upon a centre called the Sun, which is itself neither a planet or a satellite, but the heart of all the system, and the apparent source of all their natural life and movement. But to this Law of order in the Solar System, there is also an exception in the movement of eccentric orbs called comets. The Sun is the centre of the three inferior orders of planets as the emblem of God who is the centre and the life of all spiritual aspirations, and when human nature as a trinity in unity abandons the true light of Revelation, it is lost in darkness like the comets that fly off into the vast infinity of space without a centre of fixed light and unity.

God is then, the principle of unity and order, and the system of Fourier consists in keeping God before our eyes in all our speculations; and when he treats of human science and society, the image of Divinity is what he terms the Trinity in unity; the law of order; the 'Series.'"

"This is a speculative abstract of 'Fourier's system' or more properly, his method, and the aim of what he terms the 'theory of Universal unity' is

Unity of man with God.
Unity of man with Man.
Unity of man with the Universe.

The first of these unities is what is commonly called Religion, though Fourier includes everything in universal or religious unity. He refers us, however, to the Word of God for full instruction with regard to spiritual unity, or unity of man with God, and for the laws of natural unity, or unity of man with man collectively on earth, he refers us to the Book of Scripture and the Book of Nature conjointly as the double source of Revelation in which we are to seek the laws of God and righteousness, ' Seek ye first the kingdom of God and His righteousness, and all these things shall be added unto you.' Matt. vi. 33.

It is in obedience to this command, and with implicit Faith in the Promises of God to man in Scripture, that Fourier undertook to seek the laws of universal order and the science of social harmony, or unity of man with man; and this science is what may be deemed especially ' The System of Fourier,' as he has dwelt upon it more than upon other branches of universal unity. In his science of ' universal analogy' he treats of all the unities, but in Religious dissertations he treats principally of the unity of man with God ; in his cosmogony, he treats of the unity of man with the Universe, and in his Science of Society, he treats of the unity of man with man.

He has not published much of his cosmogony, because he thought it might be deemed conjectural and fanciful by superficial minds, and though his works are eminently theological he has not written much on school divinity because he deems the Church the proper teacher of divinity, and he believes that she will grow in light as fast as the people are prepared to receive it, for Christ has said to the Apostles, ' Upon this Rock I will build my Church, and the gates of Hell shall not prevail against it.' Matt. xvi. 18. ' If thy brother neglect to hear the Church, let him be unto thee as a heathen man and a publican. Matt. xviii. 17.

And in Revelation, xxii. 16, etc., it is said, ' I, Jesus, have sent my angel to testify unto you these things in the Churches. I am the root and the offspring of David, and the bright and morning Star.'

' And the Spirit and the bride say, Come. And let him that heareth say, Come. And whosoever will, let him take the water of life freely.'

' For I testify unto every man that heareth the words of the prophecy of this book, If any man shall add unto these things, God shall add unto him the plagues that are written in this book; and if any man shall take away from the words of the book of this prophecy, God shall take away his part out of the book of life, and out of the city, and from the things which are written in this book.'

Fourier, then, has neither added to the book of Revelation, nor taken away from it, by forming a new religious creed of faith and doctrine. He refers us constantly to the Word of God as the true standard of Faith, and reconciles all partial creeds and doctrines based upon the Word without preferring any one exclusively. Partial creeds or sects he looks upon as fragmentary; a ' taking away from the whole Word,' certain parts to form a special creed distinct from other partial creeds derived from other fragments of the Word ; which breaking of the word, and of the Body of Christ, he looks upon as an exceptional law of progress in false unity, to be restored to true unity again, when all are gathered under Christ the Prince of Peace, when the following Revelation shall be realized:—

' And he showed me a pure river of water of life, clear as crystal, proceeding out of the throne of God and of the Lamb. In the midst of the street of it, and on either side of the river was there the tree of life, which bare twelve manner of fruits, and yielded her fruit every month, and the leaves* of the tree were for the healing of the nations.'

' And there shall be no more curse ; but the throne of God and of the Lamb shall be in it; and his servants shall serve him; and they shall see his face, and his name shall be in their foreheads.' Rev. xxii.

As the word of God contains all partial creeds derived from it in truth, Fourier admits the truths of all; and as all are destined, he believes, to grow more perfect, until they are all absorbed in one religious creed of catholicity embracing the whole word of God, and not a part only of that word, put forth as special articles of Faith exclusively ; his policy of peace and reconciliation is, to conform to the Established Church in every christian country, whatever be the special creed or articles of faith put forth authoritatively in particular branches of the Universal Church of Christ respectively. His creed and that of his particular partisans being that of the whole word of God, they can consistently conform to any partial creed, but not exclusively; for catholicity is the universal creed, embracing all, rejecting none, receiving all, and purifying all as partial streams are purified by entering the sea. That is the creed of Fourier and his followers in Christ. They neither add to nor take away from the articles of Faith contained in the word of God ; and believing that word to be perfect, they make unto themselves no fragmentary creeds, or special articles of faith selected by mere human wisdom from the universal Word.

Nor is there any impropriety in our conforming to the special creed of any one branch of the universal church, Greek, Anglican, or Roman, for Christ has said in one of the articles of His universal creed, ' Again I say unto you, that if two of you shall agree on earth as touching anything that they shall ask, it shall be done for them of my Father which is in heaven. For where two or three are gathered together in my name, there am I in the midst of them.' Matt. xviii. 18, 19.

It is, however, in the name of Christ alone, we can unite, and not without a name, or with a heathen name, or a Mahometan. Heathens are to be converted before they are accepted, and Christ must be acknowledged universally as the sole head of the Church.

In the twenty-sixth chapter of Matthew, there are several important articles of the universal creed, in which we are enjoined to feed the poor and clothe the naked, to visit the sick and give shelter to the stranger ; and this is the special object of Fourier's ' system.' It is not a new creed, but a new method of attending to the articles of the everlasting creed of Christ, and of his universal church : one God, one Church, and one Holy Catholic Faith; universal unity ; material and spiritual unity.

HUGH DOHERTY."

* In the science of universal analogy, according to Fourier, the leaves of trees and plants are symbols of industry ; the flowers being emblematic of the pleasures of attractive occupation, and the fruit of the results.

DEMOCRACY,

CONSTRUCTIVE AND PACIFIC.

BY

PARKE GODWIN.

"These volumes will show that the author feels strongly the need of deep social changes, of a spiritual revolution in Christendom, of a new bond between man and man, of a new sense of the relation between man and his Maker. At the same time they will show his firm belief that our present low civilization, the central idea of which is wealth, cannot last forever; that the mass of men are not doomed hopelessly and irresistibly to the degradation of mind and heart in which they are now sunk; that a new comprehension of the true dignity of a social being is to remodel social institutions and manners; that in Christianity and in the powers and principles of human nature, we have the promise of something holier and happier than now exists. It is a privilege to live in this faith, and a privilege to communicate it to others. [Dr. CHANNING's *Preface to the last edition of his Works.*]

New-York:
J. WINCHESTER, XXX ANN-STREET.
1844.

INTRODUCTORY.

Ours are new words; they express new thoughts; yet, we hope, that the newness, either of words or thoughts, will not prevent the reader from giving what we are about to say, a calm and profound attention. If we employ language that to many may be strange; if we utter thoughts that have the appearance of novelty; we still intend that our phrases and meaning shall be as clear as the nature of our discussion will allow. We are about to speak of Democracy, but in no party sense; not as it is spouted in ward meetings, nor slavered through the columns of newspapers; but of Democracy as a God-ordained principle of social government, which will give to every individual his precise place in society, which will develope and perfect all the elements of human nature, which will recognize the inherent rights and spiritual majesty of man, and which, in the end, will make the "kingdoms of this Earth the kingdoms of our God, and of his Christ." It is of a kind, this Democracy, which has not yet been treated of in Presidents' messages: it has made but small figure on the floor of Congress; neither of our great parties sets up claims to the exclusive ownership of it; while, at the same time, it is broad and benevolent enough to take in all parties and all creeds, however different their tenets, or apparently irreconcileable their aims. We mean not the Destructive and Revolutionary Democracy, which has done so much to change the world—but the Constructive and Pacific Democracy, which is destined to do infinitely more in a still nobler change.*

---

* In the general outline of the few following sections, we have closely followed the profound and eloquent "Manifeste" of the Démocratie Pacifique written by Victor Considerant; but we have not scrupled to modify that paper in many ways so as to adapt it to the state of opinion in this country. The writer is alone responsible for what is here said

PART FIRST.

§ I.—ANCIENT AND FEUDAL SOCIETY.

History makes us acquainted with various societies in the Past. These are distinguished from each other by many diverse traits, yet they have have many characteristics in common. In Judea, in Egypt, in Greece, in Rome, the life of society had phases peculiar to itself in each, although in many respects a broad similitude is traceable through the manifold developments of all. Alike in all, the only acknowledged principle of action was force; war was their only politics; conquest and glory their chief aim; while slavery, or the subjection of man to man, in the most thorough, inhuman, and barbarous manner, was the great feature of their national economy. Slavery was the base and War the summit of their whole social structure. The producer, or in other words, the Worker, was universally a slave; the Freeman, whether plebeian or patrician, alone was allowed to make war and to consume. The sentiment of humanity was bounded by the narrow horizon of a creed or country. To the Jew, all things beyond Judea, were unclean; to the Greek and Roman, the term foreigner was a synonym for barbarian. In all old civilized societies, then, we see only implacable domination abroad; only tyranny, and the insuperable distinctions of caste at home.

The feudal order, though an improvement on the ancient societies, retained some of their worst abuses. Feudalism, being an effect of conquest, became very soon a mere organized conquest. War remained its leading fact—war, and the traditional but permanent consecration of the distinctions of primitive conquest. It was relieved, it is true, by some few meliorating influences; it called forth, as even the worst arrangements have done, some few virtues: it developed in a few, a manly sense of personal worth and individuality: its system of economy was a trifle less severe and brutal in the subjection of man to man. The sentiment of humanity, too, warmed by the first rays of the rising sun of Christianism, began to stretch beyond the contracted limits of country. Nations and races began to feel the ties of fraternity, and to connect themselves in closer bonds, though still in obedience to the laws of feudal hierarchy. Throughout Europe, the nobles, legitimate heirs of the first conquerors, regarded themselves only as equals, while they trampled to the dust the clowns and commoners, whom they scarcely looked upon as belonging to the same species. But the latter everywhere enslaved, grew to regard each other as brothers, and thus unconsciously, in the darkness and distresses of the Present, prepared the way for that Future of justice and truth which was destined to wrest from their haughty oppressors, the privileges which had been so long withheld. The spirit and right of the feudal times, was the spirit of aristocracy and the right of the nobles; and both continued to exist, until the French and other fearful revolutions, gave them a blow that sent them howling in the agonies of death.

§ II.—THE NEW OR CHRISTIAN AND DEMOCRATIC SOCIETY.

On the ruins of the old and feudal society, there has gradually grown up the elements and forms of a new order. A change has been wrought which is manifesting itself in the development of industry, science and art, in the silent and irresistible conquests of mind over force, in the genius of creation triumphing over the genius of destruction—in the substitution of noble, sacred Work, for base, unholy War. The right of modern societies has come to be the general right; their principle is the Christian principle of the specific unity of the whole human race in humanity, whence the political dogma of the equality of all citizens before the state; and their spirit is the spirit of democracy. True, in the older nations, the division lines of former days are still drawn; the badges of caste are still worn; the privileges and honors of nobility are perpetuated. But they are perpetuated mostly in form. They cannot be said to be the controlling spirit of the present times. The French Revolution in the old world, the American Revolution in the new, struck a battle-axe into the rotten timbers of past institutions which has shattered them into slivers. The better classes, the nobility, the monarchs may govern—but they do so virtually in the name, with the consent, and for the welfare of the people. THE MASS is a new word that has crept into all modern languages, and which indicates the existence of a new fact. The mass, through so many weary years, the despised and spoliated hewers of wood and drawers of water, have proclaimed their equal manhood. They assert that they are an essential element in the community. They stand before us with the honest faces, the broad shoulders, the hard muscles, the swelling hearts of men; they demand of us that they be admitted into fellowship: they claim their younger brothers-share of the patrimony of the common Father. With haggard and malignant looks, their eyes darting fiery impatience and their hands grasping the red torches of fury; through streets flowing with blood and plains strewed with the dying; in the midst of agonizing cries and wild maniac rejoicings, they have fought their way to where they now stand, and there dwells not on this, nor any side, of Heaven, the power for whom it would be safe to resist their just appeals. The existence of the mass, we say, is a new fact, demonstrated in an irregular wild way—but with somewhat of significance and emphasis.

§ III —SEPARATION OF THE DEMOCRATIC PRINCIPLE FROM THE REVOLUTIONARY.

In several of the more liberal and recent European constitutions of government; in all the constitutions, we believe, of the United States, the universal and equal Right of man is broadly asserted.

This new Right, this democratic Right, having entered into the world by revolution, having been proclaimed, established, and defended by revolution, advancing from triumph to triumph by revolution, is it at all surprising that the principle of democracy and the principle of revolution should have been confounded?

The new Right might have been incarnaced in society by the consentaneous and progressive action of reform and organization, which would have completed, by peaceable means, the natural transformation of the past society in all its departments.

But this natural movement, this absorption of the old (and secretion of the new, which constitutes the healthy growth of all the organized creation, and which might have wrought the quiet and unobstructed renewal of society,) not having been seconded and directed with intelligence by those in authority; the new spirit not having been wisely and liberally guided in its mighty expansion, the work of change was left to the arbitrament of explosive violence.

It has almost invariably occurred in the contests of adverse interests, that the usurper grows selfish and the wronged furious. A wild assault and reckless repulse is followed by long years of relentless battle,—by the impetuous shock of armies under whose tread the earth shakes to its centre,—until slow Time decides an issue which had long before been decided in the eternal laws of Providence.

When the hour has come for the Past to yield its abuses and be changed, its resistance only provokes warfare and makes its defeat the more signal. The new principle, by being resisted, instead of proceeding to the task of infusing itself into existing arrangements, is exclusively absorbed in the fight with the Past; it wastes its energies in unnecessary expenditures of strength, and it confounds itself with, and takes the character of, a manifestation of mere Violent Protest—Revolution—War. This is a most grave error. It leaves the whole task of organizing the New Order, a thing to be done.

Now, this is the task which is committed to our epoch—this the problem which the genius of Destiny has summoned us to solve. With the vigorous arm of a lusty youth, we have shattered what was bad in the Past. We have gone through with the terrible work of destruction. We have broken into the ancient domain of Authority and Oppression. We must now add the infinitely higher work of true democratic construction and adjustment.

§ IV.—THE REVOLUTIONARY WORK FINISHED, THE DEMOCRATIC WORK HARDLY BEGUN.

Our modern democratic revolutions, though they have accomplished some good, have chiefly exhibited the new principle of the Rights of man, in its abstract and negative aspects: They have swept away the last remains of the Feudal system, founded upon war and the aristocratic distinctions of birth; they have established a representative system in politics, which, inasmuch as it reposes on a principle of election independent of the accident of birth, is a decided advance upon pre-existing systems; they have rendered elementary instruction more accessible to all classes of the people; and they have called into life, under the inspiration of Christianity, a deeper sense of the worth and dignity of the individual soul. This is their good. But oh! how much they have left undone!—how much is there which they could not do! They have left without organization, without direction, without rule, the whole immense sphere of Industry! They have abolished the wardenships, the guilds, the corporations of the ancient time,—all of which answered the purpose in a feeble way, of a partial organization of Labor—but they have not supplied their place by a better organization. They have opened to a *laissez-faire* the most absolute, to a competition the most anarchical, to a war the most blind, and consequently to the Monopoly of great capitalists, the whole social and economical Workshop of the World,—the vast field on which is effected the Production and Distribution of Universal Wealth! Here is their grand defect; here is their radical weakness; here is the practical vice which condemns the entire machinery of revolution as inefficient and unsound.

The imperfect state in which revolutionary and destructive, or rather negative Democracy, has left its work, keeps open a sluice by which a deluge of wrongs is let in upon mankind. In spite of the supposed liberality of our new principles, in spite of the destruction of old abuses, in spite of the constitutional equality of citizens, in spite of the abolition of exclusive privileges in the sphere of commerce and trade, the actual social order, in this most democratic of countries, is a hateful and pernicious aristo-

1*

cratic order,—pregnant with injustice and suffering—*not in principle nor law*, BUT IN FACT. We are apt to imagine in our overweening vanity that we have left behind us the odious distinctions that prevailed among our ancestors. We sometimes pride ourselves upon the equality of condition and happiness that marks the society of the United States; and to a certain extent this pride is just. Yet it is only to a certain extent. Theoretically, constitutionally, legally, there are no privileged classes in this nation; the odious laws of caste are annulled. But, practically, positively, really, we still live under a regime of caste, we are still governed by classes, all our social helps and appliances are still distinguishing, partial and confined to the few. It is not so much our legislation, though that is somewhat to blame; it is not the law, it is not political principle, that erects barriers between the different categories of the American people,—it is our economical arrangements, or to speak more accurately, our complete want of social and industrial organization. Let this be noted!

§ V.—THE RAPID FORMATION OF A NEW FEUDALISM,—THE COLLECTIVE SERVITUDE OF LABOR.

A striking phenomenon is beginning to show itself in these days, even to the eyes of those least observant of such things. We refer to the rapid and powerful constitution of a new Aristocracy, of a commercial and financial Feudality, which is taking the place of the ancient aristocracy of nobles and warriors, by the annihilation and impoverishment of the lower and middling classes.

After the grand explosions of the American and French Revolutions, after the overturn of the ancient political system, after the abolition of feudal property, of laws of primogeniture, of trading guilds and commercial corporations, and the bold proclamation of the great doctrine of free-trade, society has believed itself forever emancipated from the domination of aristocratic and exclusive powers. It has supposed that it had achieved the enfranchisement of every individual, that it had bequeathed to the universal race of man the opportunity for a full development of all its faculties.

There never was a greater mistake, as the result most abundantly proves.

An essential element in the calculation has been overlooked. Now that the agitation caused by the first onset of destruction has somewhat subsided, when matters begin to assume their regular places, it is found that individuals indeed enter upon the new race of life, with perfect *freedom* to use themselves and their natural powers as they please; but upon what very different conditions have they entered? They are free to run the same race, but on most unequal and disadvantageous terms. The same course is open to all, but each one, to continue our sporting metaphor, carries different weights. Nay, they cannot be said to have been started at the same starting-place. Some were already provided with facilities to carry them swiftly and surely along their way,—they had fortune, talents, education, high and influential positions, —and the accumulated experience of ages; others, and these are the most numerous, had none of these things; they had, nor fortune, nor rank, nor talents developed by anterior education, none of the aids and spurs by which the more favored rise; they are banished to the outer borders of civilized existence, they welter in the lowest pools of corrupt and stagnant companionships.

What must result in such a state of things, from that industrial liberty on which we reckoned so much—from that famous doctrine of free-trade, which was the peculiar glory of the new science of political economy, and which we fondly thought the last best expression of the democratic theory? What result? Let facts answer the question! They will point us to the general subjection of the masses—of the class without wealth, talent or education—to the class which is well-provisioned and equipped!

"The lists are open," say you, "all men are called to the combat, the terms are equal for all capacities." Hold! you have forgotten one thing! It is, that on this great field of battle, some are trained, disciplined, caparisoned, armed to the teeth an impenetrable hauberk and shield is round their bodies, swords and spears are in their hands—and they hold the advantageous places for assault or for flight; while others, despoiled, naked, ignorant, famished, are compelled to live from day to day, and support their wives and children, on the meagre pittance extorted from their adversaries or picked by piecemeals from the streets. Oh! most benevolent free-trader, what sort of equality is this? What fight, what resistance even, are we of the many-headed multitude to make? Your absolute liberty is only an absolute abandonment of the unarmed and destitute masses to the charity of the well-fed and well-armed few. Your democratic civilization, which began in aristocratic feudalism—the progress of which has emancipated the working-classes from direct and personal servitude only—will end in a moneyed aristocracy will lead to a collective and indirect servitude just as oppressive as that from which we have been so lately relieved. "Gurth," says Mr. Carlyle, "born-thrall of Cedric, the Saxon, has been greatly pitied by Dryasdust and others. Gurth with a brass collar round his neck tending Cedric's pigs, in the glades of the wood, is not what I call an exemplar of human felicity; but Gurth, with the sky above him, with the free air and tinted boscage and umbrage around him, and in him the certainty of lodging and supper when he came home,—Gurth to me seems happy in comparison with many a Lancashire and Buckinghamshire man of these days, not born-thrall of anybody! Gurth's brass collar did not gall him; Cedric deserved to be his Master. The pigs were Cedric's, but Gurth too would get his parings of them. Gurth had the inexpressible satisfaction of feeling himself related indubitably, though in a rude brass-collar way, to his fellow-mortals on this earth. He had superiors, inferiors, or equals. Gurth is now "emancipated" long since; has what we call "liberty." Liberty, I am told, is a divine thing. Liberty when it becomes the liberty to die by starvation is not so divine." There is much in that fact. Mr. Carlyle!

§ VI.—THE CONDITION OF THE LABORER DETERIORATING, THROUGH THE DEPRECIATION OF WAGES, &c.

But while this incoherence of trade, of which we have spoken, has tended and is tending to subject the workman to the capitalist, the proletaire possessing nothing to the patrician possessing all things, let us consider that it has at the same time awakened a most disastrous competition among workmen themselves. It is setting proletaire against proletaire in an almost deadly industrial war. Where laborers abound, which is everywhere, the necessities of existence, under any system of competition, compel them when they go forth each morning in the pursuit of employment and a master, to lower their wages to the lowest possible sum. The rate of wages, in other words, everywhere tends to be reduced to the lowest possible sum consistent with the mere continuance of the laborer in life. This, when it is thought of, is an awful statement,—but it is not exclusively our own. We find it taught in the leading political economists of the day as one of their fundamental doctrines. "The wages of simple labor," says Say, "seldom rise in any country much above what is absolutely necessary to subsistence! the quantum of supply always remains on a level with the demand; *nay, often goes beyond it.*" In Adam Smith, in McCullough, in Malthus, in Wayland, there are a multitude of passages to the same effect. Well, what is the obvious inference from such a statement? Why, that the least fluctuation in the demand for labor must inevitably doom a large portion of laborers to starvation—to death! These very writers are cold-blooded enough to state that inference. "Where laborers," says McCullough in his dainty language, "where laborers are already subsisting, as in Ireland" (and he might have added other countries) "on the lowest species of food, it is of course impossible for them to go to a lower in a period of scarcity, and should their wages sustain any serious decline, *an increase would necessarily take place in the rate of mortality.*" What a coldly dignified and stately way of telling us that thousands of fellow-beings would die by a most painful and lingering death! *The rate of mortality would increase,* says the philosopher, with as much *sang froid* as the surgeon amputates a limb, heedless of the agonies of his victim! At the same time a brother philosopher, Monsieur Say, tells us, but with more feeling, that wages are liable to "most calamitous oscillations." "War or legislative prohibition," he continues, "will sometimes suddenly extinguish the demand for a particular product, and reduce the industry employed upon it to a state of utter destitution." "The mere caprice of fashion," says another, the famous Malthus, "is often fatal to whole classes. The substitution of shoe-ribbons for buckles was a severe blow to the population of Birmingham and Sheffield." Indeed, the whole of Malthus's celebrated doctrine of population, viz: that the increase of laborers outruns that of the means of subsistence, and that therefore, wars, pestilences, famines, storms, that depopulate whole kingdoms, and the direst afflictions of mankind, are beneficial—is founded on the melancholy fact in the condition of the working classes on which we are dwelling. We might, were not the fact itself most glaring in every nation, fill a volume with corroborative citations from the essays of the political economists. On one side, we see competition among laborers reducing the wages on which they and their dependent families must subsist; on the other, we see competition among employers, forcing them, how great soever may be their generosity, to yield only the lowest rates of pay, (since no employer, without running the risk of certain ruin, could afford to pay his workmen higher wages than what was paid by his competitors;) and thus the detestable maxims of our modern economy break all the laws of justice and humanity. Free-trade, by which we here mean competition without organization, is distinguished by the execrable mark, that it always and everywhere tends to the reduction of wages. After plunging the toiling masses into the gulf of misery, it grinds them with a weight that is forever growing heavier. In Ireland, in England, in Belgium, in Italy, in France, in our own country, wherever competition reigns, where nothing arrests the action of a disorganized and incoherent industrialism, the working classes are inevitably becoming more miserable and more abject. They not only work against each other, but against machines that cost nothing, yet dispense with the labor of an hundred men.*

We state this not as an opinion of our own—not as a logical deduction from premises existing in our own minds,—but as a fact, proven by statistics, declared by official records, and confirmed by innumerable observations made by missionaries of benevolence and enlightened and liberal statesmen. What means that significant dispute that has put the more recent of political philosophers on the continent, at loggerheads? Whence the awful fact, that in the midst of an increase of general riches, the condition of the laboring classes is growing worse,—a fact in the solution of which they are all so much puzzled? Sismondi, one of the most brilliant successors of Jean Baptiste Say, though of another school,

---

* The question of the influence of labor-saving machines is a great one, which we may hereafter undertake to discuss.

was so painfully impressed with this fact, that his whole work may be considered as a prolonged wail over the miseries of the working-classes. " His cry of alarm," says the distinguished professor of political economy at the University of Paris, M. Blanqui, " has been solemnly and eloquently repeated; it is re-echoed by whole populations in manufacturing cities, amid the tumult of insurrection." Again, says the same able and profound writer, in criticising Adam Smith, " Why is wealth so unequally distributed in society? Why are there so many starving beings in civilized nations? What is the natural relation between population and subsistence? *Why does misery increase amongst the laboring classes in proportion to the increase of wealth in the nation?*" Again he says, "This doctrine," the doctrine of Adam Smith, that private interest left entirely to its own management, will always direct capital to those channels which are best adapted to public welfare, "this doctrine, which has prevailed in England and given most extraordinary impulse to industry, has commenced nevertheless to produce the most alarming effects; it has produced unbounded wealth among capitalists and wretched poverty among the lower classes; it has enriched the nation, but at the cruel expense of industry." To the same effect M. Rossi, professor of political economy in the College of France, and a learned writer regarded by Guizot as "the wisest representative of the science," in an introductory discourse remarked, " A great problem occupies all minds; it is the coexistence of two seemingly conflicting facts; on the one hand, a general increase of national wealth; on the other hand, growing misery and distress among the greater part of workmen. A solution has been demanded of political economy, but it has not yet been found. This solution, when it shall have been made, will be the greatest social discovery of the day." If we were in a position to consult authorities, we could cite many more confirming paragraphs of the same nature. But Heaven knows, that we have written enough on this head. Our hearts begin to sicken with the details which our inquiry forces upon us!

§ VII.—REDUCTION OF THE MIDDLING CLASSES.

Alas! this is not all; the evil is not merely confined to the lowest classes of laborers. Analogous symptoms are showing themselves among the possessors of small means—among master mechanics and farmers. If the first effect of our monstrous modern system of competition—competition, we mean, on conditions so unequal,—has been the subjection of the workmen, its second effect will be the progressive ruin of the poorer class of employers. Small properties—master-mechanics on a small scale—inferior branches of commerce and art—are destined to be crushed under the gigantic weight, the colossal wheels of larger properties and enterprises. We may see this tendency of things even in this country, where the possession of inexhaustible tracts of land gives so fine an opportunity to the individual to resist the tendencies of society. Already, in almost every branch of industry, great capitals, great enterprises give the law to the smaller. Steam, machinery, large manufactories are everywhere supplanting the meaner kind of workshops. Employers are sinking into the class of the employed, which only renders the supply of work the more uncertain and less in amount to the latter class. Our cities are vast commercial vortices that are drawing the whole country within their fatal circle. Commerce, which should be the dependent handmaid of Agriculture and Manufactures, has become their absolute master. It rules the world with the omnipotence of a despot. It makes all industry, and art, and science its tributaries. It is a vast insatiable parasite sucking the life-sap of Production. It is a monstrous vampire that preys with remorseless appetite upon the energies of nations. It absorbs all property, in regulating values by means of its banks; it concentrates wealth in the hands of a few men in a few central places: it is the source of innumerable frauds, fluctuations, bankruptcies and commercial crises; and it is fast laying its hand upon the land, by means of agricultural loaning companies,—and upon government, by means of national debt.*

Now, Commerce, be it remembered, is the legitimate offspring of our competitive system of industry.

---

* We pass hurriedly over Commerce, because we intend giving it a full criticism hereafter.

§ VIII.—DIVISION OF SOCIETY INTO TWO CLASSES—ONE, POSSESSING ALL—THE OTHER, NOTHING

Thus, in spite of the abstractly democratic principle of industrial freedom, or rather in consequence of that freedom, (false and illusory as all simple unorganized liberty must be,) capital gravitates around capital in proportion to its mass, and is gathered into the hands of a few of the wealthiest men. Society tends to a division, more and more distinct, into two classes,—a small number possessing everything, or next to everything, absolute masters of the entire field of property, commerce and art,—and the great mass, possessing nothing, living in a forced dependence on the owners of capital and of the instruments of labor, and compelled for a precarious and decreasing return to hire out their muscles, their skill, and their time to their new feudal lords.

This is no dream; it is no prophecy; it is a piece of contemporaneous history. We are advancing with rapid strides, we repeat, toward the constitution of a new aristocracy,—one as odious as it is ignoble—one which, unconsecrated by hereditary remembrances or actual deeds of valor, derives its only distinction from the ineradicable baseness and tenacity of its love of money. The fact characterizes our whole modern civilization. It is a phenomenon, not peculiar to any one civilized nation, but which is developed in every State in a degree corresponding to the advancement of its industry. It follows, step by step, in the tracks of commerce and manufactures. Great Britain presents the most signal example of the concentration of capital in the hands of a few, but the awful contrasts of her social condition are fast being rivalled by Belgium and France. Our own country abounds in the symptoms of the disease. Already the mere commercial dependents of England, we begin to exhibit traces of her vicious and corrupting spirit of aristocracy. Commerce is the controlling power in the country. It is enslaving every other branch of business. It is making every class of men its subsidiary. One of our most sagacious statesmen, Mr. Benton, long since had the sagacity to perceive this, although he did not have wisdom enough at the same time to discover the reasons of it, nor the remedy. Our political battle, said he, is a battle between Man and Money. The

Republican party caught up the saying, and has struggled desperately to resist the stream of moneyed influences that is bearing it onward to death. But, not knowing why nor wherefore, it has struggled blindly; the very means of reform which it often proposed, if carried out, would only have exaggerated the evil. It was not the Whig policy that was so much in the wrong; it was not because the law sanctioned banks that they suffered; it was not protective tariffs nor internal improvements that provoked the curse. These were bad enough; but lying back of them was a cause which was vastly more pernicious than either of them or all. For they all had their origin in the unorganized state of industry. To have repealed all monopolies, to have unloosed exclusive laws, to have given free scope to the existing energies of trade, in the want of such organization, would have aggravated the disorders of society. It could only have made the rich richer and the poor poorer. It would have accelerated the formation of that Aristocracy of Wealth which we are deploring, and against which so fierce a war has been justly but blindly waged for ten years.

§ IX.—THE INFEUDATION OF GOVERNMENT.

Yet the fact that the laws are made to sanction and sustain the overgrown monopolies of trade, is one of the most melancholy evidences of the extent to which the new feudality has advanced. So strong is it, that it is even strong enough, at this early period in its career, to grapple and overcome the strongest governments on earth. To what point soever in the civilized world we turn our eyes, we see that the Money Power is mightier than the Legislative Power. No matter what the form of the government, it is compelled to strike its colors before this formidable enemy. Monarchs, aristocrats, and republicans have alike fallen victims to the huge Juggernaut of Money. On the continent of Europe, we are told by good authority, that the canal and railway companies often rise in resistance of the designs of the government. But it is in this nation, where there are fewer restraints upon the insolence of the money power, (for the very reason that it is more democratic than any other,) that its manifestations have grown to an oppressive and overshadowing enormity. To such a height has its unbridled audacity been carried, that we can hardly find language in which to describe the excess of its evils. Our general government, as well the governments of every individual state, has been made to succumb to its influences. What has been the aspect of our legislation for the last twenty years, nay, ever since the origin of the nation? Has it not been one unceasing struggle on the part of the possessors of wealth, either to secure past immunities, or to acquire additional privileges? Have not our legislative bodies been beset, day after day, and year after year, by the insinuating arts of the applicants for exclusive charters of all kinds? Has not the invention of selfishness been exhausted in devising schemes for robbing the mass for the sake of the few? What plans have been left unbroached,—what iniquities untried? Banks to be controlled by the few; tariffs operating solely for the benefit of the few; private enterprises to be paid for out of the public purse; hypothecations of national stock in behalf of individuals or corporations; the borrowing of money to carry on works of partial or local character; these have constituted the staple topics of our legislative discussions. Our states, which in their origin were christened, and which we still call, Independent Sovereignties, have degenerated into menial train-bearers to stock-jobbing merchants and fraudulent speculators. All their pride and dignity have been sacrificed to the selfish whims of the Mammonites. Their infeudation is well-nigh complete. They are becoming, and in many respects, have become the vile, miserable vassals of their superiors,—the Money-Lords: bound hand and foot by the heavy chains of debt, and sold, body and soul, to the capitalists, either at home or abroad, who are their owners and masters. Bankrupt in purse; bankrupt, many of them, in honor; their future time and labor, their very sinews and muscles, are alienated and pledged. Was there ever a serf, a vassal, a slave less free? Oh! it was no irony that which dubbed our knights of the bank-counter, with the title of Rag-Barons; or rather it was the keen and biting irony of strict truth! Nor was it a mere far-fetched party ruse to liken the famous Nicholas of the Bank to the *autocrat* Nicholas of Russia. He was one of the mightiest of autocrats, and the name stuck because it fit. No despots in the old world wield a more tyrannic power than the despots of our commercial system; there are none whose commands are more imperatively issued, or more speedily or more slavishly executed. The waive of a small metallic wand in Threadneedle street, London, will send an electric shock to the remotest corners of the globe. A handful of men, gathered in a back parlor of the Bank of England, paralyze the industry of millions, living thousands of miles off, and for a half century to come. Was there ever monarch who could do as much as this?

We well remember reading, a few years since, in one of the most respectable organs of the Democratic party,* an article on the identity of the modern banking and the ancient feudal systems. It was a convincing demonstration of the likeness. It showed a close resemblance in every feature of the two systems, only that it made the banking system the ugliest. Yet what has that party done, or what can it do, to alter the fact?

§ X.—DANGER OF SOCIAL REVOLUTIONS.

A condition of things such as we have been describing, cannot long continue. Universal monopoly cannot, in the age in which we live, be endured by the oppressed and suffering working classes. The notion of individual and equal rights which has fastened itself so deeply in the minds of men within the last few centuries, will prompt the people to rise against the institutions to which they ascribe the existence of this frightful evil. The growing hatred of the poor for the rich—a hatred which it is useless to deny—will every day grow more intense. Already among the chartists of England, a "black mutinous discontent," a hot feverish hatred of the wealthy is springing up. They are getting restless under their long discipline of a thin diet and hard labor. A notion is fermenting in their brains that society is bound to do more for them than to provide dusky poor-houses and bastiles. It will be a terrific explosion this fermenting notion will make, unless the weight of their superincumbent misery be removed. Let it be looked to in time.

Human beings are not mere commodities, whose price augments and diminishes with the supply in the market. Society owes them a guaranty of life and work. They possess a right to labor, which is the most sacred of all rights. Labor is their property; the highest form and source of all property. They have intel-

---

* The Democratic Review.

lectual and moral faculties which must be developed. God has placed them on the earth, to advance. What shall they do, then, with that society, which not only prevents them from advancing, but which degrades and brutifies them into natures worse than those of beasts? We say worse than beasts, because to the stupidity and unreasoning violence of animals, they often add the malignity of demons.

§ XI.—THE SOCIAL HELL.

Thus we have stated that blind competition tends to the formation of gigantic monopolies in every branch of labor; that it depreciates the wages of the working classes; that it excites an endless warfare between human arms, and machinery and capital,—a war in which the weak succumb; that it renders the recurrence of failures, bankruptcies, and commercial crises a sort of endemic disease; and that it reduces the middling and lower classes to a precarious and miserable existence. We have stated, on the authority of authentic documents, that while the few rich are becoming more and more rich, the unnumbered many are becoming poorer. Is anything further necessary to prove that our modern world of industry is a veritable HELL, where disorder, discord, and wretchedness reign, and in which the most cruel fables of the old mythology are more than realized? The masses—naked and destitute, yet surrounded by a prodigality of wealth; seeing on all sides heaps of gold, which by a fatal decree they cannot reach; stunned by the noise of gilded equipages, or dazzled by the brilliance of splendid draperies and dresses; their appetites excited by the magnificence of heaped-up luxuries of every climate and all arts; provoked by all that can gratify desire, yet unable to touch one jot or tittle of it—offer a terrible exemplification of Tantalus, tormented by an eternal hunger and thirst after fruits and waters, always within his reach, yet perpetually eluding his grasp. Was the penalty of Sisyphus condemned to roll his stone to a summit, from which it was forever falling, more poignant than that of many fathers of families, among the poorer classes, who, after laboring to exhaustion during their whole lives, to amass somewhat for their old age or for their children, see it swallowed up in one of those periodical crises of failure and ruin which are the inevitable attendants of our methods of loose competition? Or the story of the Danaides, compelled incessantly to draw water in vessels from which it incessantly escaped, does it not with a fearful fidelity symbolize the implacable fate of nearly two thirds of our modern societies, who draw from the bosom of the earth and the workshops of production, by unrelaxing toil, floods of wealth, that always slip through their hands, to be collected in the vast reservoirs of a moneyed aristocracy? Walk through the streets of any of our crowded cities; see how within stone's throw of each other stand the most marked and frightful contrasts! Here, look at this marble palace reared in a pure atmosphere and in the neighborhood of pleasing prospects. Its interior is adorned with every refinement that the accumulated skill of sixty centuries has been able to invent; velvet carpets, downy cushions, gorgeous tapestries, stoves, musical instruments, pictures, statues and books. For the gratification and development of its owner and his family, industry, science, and art have been tasked to their utmost capacity of production. They bathe in all the delights, sensuous and intellectual, that human existence at this period of its career can furnish. They feel no cares; they know no interruption to the unceasing round of their enjoyments. Look you, again, to that not far distant alley, where some ten diseased, destitute and depraved families are nestled under the same rickety and tumbling roof; no fire is there to warm them; no clothes to cover their bodies; a pool of filth sends up its nauseousness perhaps in the very midst of their dwelling; the rain and keen hail fall on their almost defenceless heads; the pestilence is forever hovering over their door-posts; their minds are blacker than night with the black mists of ignorance; and their hearts are torn with fierce lusts and passions; the very sun-light blotted from the firmament and life itself turned into a protracted and bitter curse! Look you, at this, we say, and think that unless something better than what we now see is done, it will all grow worse! Oh heaven; it is an oppressive, a heart-rending thought! How well has one of our noble young poets uttered:

> I do not mourn my friends are false,
> I dare not grieve for sins of mine,
> I weep for those who pine to death,
>   Great God! in this rich world of thine!

So many trees there are to see,
    And fields go waving broad with grain,
And yet, what utter misery,
    Our very brothers lie in pain.

These by their darkened hearthstones sit,
    Their children shivering idly round;
As true as liveth God, 'twere fit,
    For these poor men, to curse the ground.

And those who daily bread have none,
    Half-starved the long, long winter's day,
Fond parents gazing on their young,
    Too wholly sad, one word to say.

To them, it seems, their God has cursed,
    This race of ours, since they were born;
Willing to toil, and yet deprived
    Of common wood or store of corn.

I do not weep for my own woes,
    They are as nothing in my eye;
I weep for them, who starved and froze,
    Do curse their God, and long to die.

§ XII.—SOMETHING TO BE DONE—AND WHAT?

What, then, in a world like this, is to be done? The question of questions is this! Either we are to close the shells of our selfishness around us, sinking down into the mire, with stupid indifference, or we are to address ourselves, at once, like noble and true-hearted men, to the solution of the difficulty. The fact of human misery is a broad and glaring one, written in characters of fire and blood across the whole earth. What is to be done with it? We iterate the question.

1. We remark that little or nothing is to be done by any form of political action, that we know of, using the word political only in its common application to the movements of government. And there are two reasons for this; first, that politics have accomplished all that it is required of them to accomplish; and second, that their sphere is so limited, that they cannot be made to touch the source of the evil. We wish to say nothing here against any of our great political parties; but we do assert that the doctrines of either of them, carried out to the hearts' content of the most sanguine advocates of them, would achieve nothing in the way of social

reform. The Whigs, by the system they propose, would only consecrate by law those abuses and distinctions which are the evidence and result of our rapid tendency to a commercial feudality. On the other hand, the Democrats, by the repeal of all restraining laws, would only give a broader field for the freer development of the elements of disorder—they would only deepen and widen the breaches in society opened by the operation of the principle of unlimited competition. The truth is, that there is everywhere spreading a secret dissatisfaction with the results of our political contests. Among our best minds, there has long been a conviction that the strife of politics was an utterly inane and useless one, fit only, like the bull-baitings and carnivals of older nations, to amuse the coarser tastes of the populace; while the people themselves are conscious of a growing indifference to the magniloquent appeals of statesmen and editors. It is now more than half a century since the controversies of our politics begun, and it would require the sharpest optics to discover in what particular they had advanced. There has been infinite labor with no progress. The same questions have been argued and reargued, without coming to a decision. We have heard speech after speech; we have seen election after election; the bar-rooms have resounded with appeals; the streets have reëchoed with clamorings; now this faction has triumphed, and now that; victory and defeat have alternated more swiftly than the changes of the moon; legislatures and senates have met, and Presidents have fulminated; yet it does not appear, after all this noise and commotion—after all this everlasting talk and expense, that we are at all nearer to a conclusion, in these days of John Tyler, than we were in the days of Thomas Jefferson. If any one would be impressed with this view, let him compare the daily newspapers of the two epochs; he will find that with the change of a few names and dates, the articles of one might well answer for the pages of the other. Our long discussion seems to have been afflicted with the curse of perpetual barrenness. This protracted struggle, this ever renewed debate, has resulted, when all is told, to the net quotient—zero.

But let us not be understood as saying that there has been no progress in American society. God forbid! How could we say it, when we know that the mighty muscles of the human hand, the mighty powers of the human mind and heart, have been at work? How could we say it. when giant miraculous Labor has been felling the forests, and turning the glebe, and whirling the spinning jennies, and putting down its thoughts in words and deeds; when the spires of an hundred thousand school-houses point to the skies; when the fires of truth and self-sacrifice have glowed in many more thousand breasts; when the noblest aspirations were ascending from millions of noble souls? Yes, we thank God, there has been progress: but it has not been by means of, so much as in spite of, our politics. We mean that our politics has never been thorough enough to touch the root of our social distress. It has now no vitality. All the sap has dried out and withered from our discussions. The old straw has been thrashed and rethrashed until it is reduced to the merest impalpable powder—out of which nothing can be made, not even snuff strong enough to tickle a grown man's nostrils. Something deeper—more searching, more comprehensive, more true—is wanting, to raise us from the slough into which we have lamentably fallen.

2. Our help, if any is to come to us, is to be found in the better adjustment of our social relations. The vice for which we seek a remedy is in the heart of society, not its extremities; and it is to the heart that we must apply the cure. What that cure may be, is partly indicated by the whole tenor of this essay. We have shown that capital and labor are at open war. The field of industry, in all its branches, is an eternal field of battle. Either capital tyrannizes over labor, or labor, driven to extremes, rises in insurrection against its oppressor. One or the other of these effects inevitably follow the working of the system of unrestrained competition. How obvious the suggestion, then, that this competition must be brought to an end? If we can introduce peace, where there was before war—if we can make a common feeling where there was before antagonism and hatred—if we can discover a mode of causing men to work for each other instead of against each other—then, we say, we have advanced a most important step toward the solution of the problem.

Now, the power which is able to effect this change, which can turn opposition into accord, divergence into convergence, contest into coöperation, is the principle of the ORGANIZATION OF INDUSTRY ON THE BASIS OF A UNION OF INTERESTS,

§ XIII.—UNITY OF INTERESTS.

The three productive elements of society, the three sources of its wealth, the three wheels of industrial mechanism, are Capital, Labor, and Talent. Is it not conceivable that these three powers could be wisely combined so as to be made to work together, that these three wheels could be made to roll into each other with a beautiful harmony? Can we not suppose that for the anarchical strife of blind competition; that for the war of capital against capital, labor against labor, workman against workman and against machinery; that, for general disorder, the universal shock of productive forces, and the destruction of values in so many contrary movements, might be substituted the productive combination and useful employment of all these forces? Most assuredly such an arrangement can be supposed; and why not accomplished? At any rate, does it not become our first and most imperative duty to seek out the conditions of industrial reconciliation and peace?

There is no radical antagonism in the nature of these things; there is no eternal and necessary repulsion between the various elements of production. The frightful combats of capital against capital, of capital against labor and talent, of laborer against laborer, of masters against workmen and workmen against masters, of each against all and all against each, is not a remorseless and inexorable condition of the life of humanity. They pertain only to the actual mechanism of industry, to the system of chaotic and unregulated competition, to that false liberty of whose triumphs we have boasted with such hollow and ill-timed joy. A better and truer mechanism, a nobler organic liberty, to which these awful evils do not adhere, can be found. The wisdom of man is able to discover, if it has not already under God discovered, an outlet to this labyrinth of suffering—a pathway upward from this dark, disordered, howling abyss.

This is what we mean by true democracy—a state in which the highest rights and interests of man shall be the means and appliances of a full development; and this Democracy, constructive and pacific in its character, becomes the object for which every benevolent and conscientious man should labor. How far we have already advanced toward the realization of it, and what yet remains to be done, shall be our topic in some future inquiry. Meanwhile, look to it, O ye people!

PART II.

In the first part of this Essay, we came to the conclusion, that the only remedy for the existing distresses of society, and particularly of the working classes, could be found in some plan for the uniting of material interests. We said, that it was possible for the intellect of man to devise means by which Labor, Capital, and Talent should be made to work together and for each other, instead of against each other, and through which every man would labor for himself while laboring for his neighbor. But thus far, our argument has been mostly critical; we shall now attempt to make it constructive.

§ I.—ORGANIZATION.

One fact, as much as any other, strikes us, when we consider the material creation of God. It is, that this whole universe is made according to a law of organization; that there is nothing in it incoherent or at loose-ends; that from the planet to the plant, from the stars which are the suns of worlds of unimaginable magnitude, to the insect whose body is three million times less than a visible point, amid the endless variety of forms and existences that link by link supply the interval, there is an organic law pervading the whole. Beginning with the rude masses of the mineral kingdom, which seem like mere accidental conglomerations—the primitive elements out of which the higher kingdoms are to grow—we soon see in its tendency to crystallization, the mute faint prophecies of the more definite organization of vegetable nature. At the summit of the vegetable series, we again discover the outlines of the more intricate and finished structure of animals. While in man, the crown and chief of the material world, we behold the consummation of an organism, perfect in all its parts, and perfect as a whole. It would be delightful to inquire into this law of organization, and to show how, by the organic SERIES, the Creator has distributed the harmonies of the universe; but it is sufficient for our present purpose, to point out its existence. This immutable and eternal fact, is impressed on all we see, that nothing is perfect which is not organized.

§ II.—MORAL ORGANIZATION.

Men appear to have been aware of this law, in the efforts which they have made to carry into effect their various religious, literary, and social projects. At least, we infer so from a superficial reading of their history, from the earliest time down to the present moment. Nearly all the controversies which have shaken the world, have related to the question, as to what was the best mode in which men could organize themselves, either as a State or a Church. The question of government, which has been the bone of contention at all times and with every people, resolves itself into a question of organization—*that is*, how the political relations of mankind can be best adjusted into a system, which would give the largest liberty to the individual, and, at the same time, preserve the unity and strength of the community. The question of the outward establishment of the Church has been a mere question as to the right method of organizing the spiritual relations of priests and people: and indeed, nearly all the enterprises that men undertake, seem to centre and end in an effort after a more complete organization. When a man, a sect, or a party have any new idea to propagate, it is common to begin by organizing some body which is charged with the task. Or we might rather say, that the very existence of sects and parties is a proof of the strong tendency of the human mind toward combination and organic effort. Thus, we have armies, instituted for works of destruction, which do their work most effectually; we have missionary societies, which send their agents to the remotest regions of the earth, regardless of tropic heats or arctic colds; we have academies of music in which are developed concords of sound the most grand and the most melting; we have institutes of learning, where the accumulated literature and science of three thousand years are made available to any capacity; we have Bible and tract societies that scatter religious truth like seed on the wings of the wind; we have trading and banking corporations, that lay the wealth of the world under tribute, and heap up for their projectors vast untold treasures; in short, on all hands, we see the giant miraculous effects of systematic and regulated co-operation. Yet these instrumentalities are meagre and incomplete developments—mere aggregations of men, like the simple cohering particles of rude matter—hardly approaching a formal organization, yet demonstrating, with resistless force, how great would be the vigor of a true and living organism! For if such things are done in the green tree, what shall be done in the dry?

§ III.—INDUSTRY ALONE WITHOUT A PLAN.

And here we are struck with a notable anomaly in the midst of all these arrangements. It is, that while men have resorted to associated effort in the execution of almost every kind of enterprise, it has never occurred to them to organize the human forces, the vital energies by which alone all useful results are brought about. We mean that it is a strange oversight in the possessors of these forces that they have never thought of combining them for their own benefit. It is true, that military leaders, that governors of states, that capitalists and speculators, have well known the secret of the mighty power of united labor, and have availed themselves of its advantages. But the wonder is, that the men of industry themselves, have at no time, unless in the most narrow and feeble way, arranged that cunningness and strength of muscle, which has been their only wealth, which indeed is the only source of wealth to mankind, into something like an organization. In the sphere of labor alone, has the world remained in the state of isolated, incoherent, cut-throat individuality and competitive antagonism. The simplest forms of mere aggregated effort have scarcely been applied to it, save under the domination of some severe task-master or despot. But why should not industry be organized? Why should not laborers band together for the accomplishment of their ends; not as a class merely, not as a political party, not for selfish or temporary purposes, but as the great, collective, eternal POWER OF PRODUCTION? Will any one say that such a thing is impossible? Can any one point out in what respect industry is incapable of being united and harmonized? No; the impossibility is in continuing it in its present condition of duplicity and discord—inefficient in its movements, at war with itself, monotonous, convulsive, repugnant and dishonorable! The time has arrived, when it must either come to an end in violence, or receive into itself a higher law. Now, what that law may be, is precisely the question of this epoch; it is the question on which we are engaged; it is the vital all-important problem, on which hangs the fate of our modern societies. We have got so far into the future, that we can say boldly, that labor must be organized—one way or another, the thing must be done. It is the impregnating principle of the coming time. As the personal Christ of old, who is our redemption, sprung from the family of the Carpenter, so do we most earnestly believe, that his second coming in spirit, for the salvation of our poor, decrepit, diseased and wretched societies, will be through the family of Labor.

§ IV.—PRACTICAL EXAMPLES.

We have said that Industry alone has remained incoherent, but we are reminded of one or two instances to the contrary, which may be regarded in the light of those exceptions which confirm the general truth. We refer now particularly to an exemplification of unity of interests that grew up among the cheese-makers of Jura, and a still more remarkable instance discovered by Dr. Urquhart, among the Turks of Ambelakia. The former case is told us by M. Considerant, of France, who speaks from his own knowledge, to this effect. In the mountains of Jura, where the climate interdicts the cultivation of the vine and grain, and where milk cannot be sold in its pure state owing to the distance from the cities, it is converted into cheese. It was the custom not long since, in every village of this region, where there were some twenty or thirty families, owning some two hundred cows, for each family to make its cheese for itself, and to send to market for itself—thus every day making use of some twenty or thirty utensils, some twenty or thirty dairies, and of the labor of some twenty or thirty men, both in producing the article, and conveying it to market. And in most cases, to say nothing of waste, the cheese produced was of an inferior quality; while each family coming into competition when they entered the market, was obliged to sell at the lowest possible price, so that none gained by the sales, while the majority were losers. What did these brave mountaineers do in these circumstances? Why, they fell upon the very rational principle, that it was not wise in them to be picking each others pockets, and would be much better could they assist each other as good friends and neighbors. So they hired a small house in the centre of the village, composed of two rooms—one of which they converted into a shop, and the other into a dairy In the shop they erected a huge brass kettle, large enough to receive the daily milk product of the two hundred cows, which milk was made into cheese by the labor of a single man called the fruiterer, without further trouble on the part of its owners. The quantity of milk deposited by any family each day was notched upon two pieces of wood, one of which was kept by the fruiterer, and the other taken by the family; by which simple method the strictest account was kept. When the cheeses were sold, they were sold by wholesale, without losses through competition, and with a comparatively slight charge for conveyance to market. From the general sum received for them was subtracted the rent of the house, the price of fuel, instruments, carriage, and of the work of the fruiterer, after which the remainder was divided among the families of the village, in proportion to the amount of milk contributed to the dairy. Thus, with one-thirtieth part of the labor, and a thirtieth part of the expense, they were enabled to receive a thirty-fold return for their product. This practice begun in the hamlet of Salines, is now the common custom through all the higher provinces of the Alps. It is a simple but most significant illustration of a great truth.

The other example, for the details of which we must refer to Dr. Urquhart's noble work, "The Spirit of the East," is found in the commercial municipality of Ambelakia. There, with a population of four thousand people, all the manufacture and trade was carried on according to a joint stock principle—no distinctions of interest existing between capitalists and laborers. It grew rapidly in importance; its fabrics became so celebrated, as shortly to absorb the best markets; and it annually divided from sixty to one hundred per cent. upon all its investments. Thus a weak, insignificant hamlet, in what is commonly called one of the most despotic of nations, without a single field in its vicinity, with no advantage of position, with no local industry, with no commercial connection, in the neighborhood of no manufacturing movement, neither situated on a navigable river nor on the sea, accessible by no road except a goats'-path among precipices, its industry unaided by the secrets of chemistry or combinations of mechanical power—did, by the simple fact of a union of interests, and a union of sympathies, rise to a degree of outward prosperity and internal harmony, unparalleled in the history of commercial enterprise. External causes of violence, and the invention of spinning jennies in England, contributed to the dispersion of this hive of labor and productiveness.

§ V.—SUGGESTIONS AND PROJECTS.

Is there any reason why similar combinations should not take place among the workmen and capitalists of this day, when industry is so much more developed, and the facilities of intercourse so many and important? Is it not the plainest matter imaginable, how immeasurably the laborers of any trade or craft would be the gainers, if, instead of working against each other as they do now, they should contrive to concentrate their energies in obedience to some law of mutual interest?

We can easily conceive of a variety of modes in which the principle of a common interest might be realized. The shoemakers, or any other class of mechanics might, without much difficulty, form themselves into an union, under discreet and liberal laws, for the prosecution of the different branches of their trade. With a single large building, somewhere in the centre of trade, with a proper distribution of labor, allowing each man a payment proportioned to the kind and amount of his work, with the advantage of having all the departments of the art conducted near to each other, with the best tools and materials, buying by wholesale, and at all times commanding the markets for its sales—such a league would inevitably lead to the fortune of all its members. But the advantage of an industrial formation like this would be greatly extended, if the club of shoemakers should be so enlarged as to embrace all the dealers in leather. How much could be saved in house rent, fuel, waste of material, loss of time in passing from one place or one pursuit to another? Or take the business of newspaper publishing, as an example of what might be accomplished by a right division and combination of employments. Let the editorial department constitute one group of laborers, the composing and printing department another, the publishing and financial department another; and then let each member of the firm be paid according to the skill, capital, or labor which he brings to the concern—think you, that such an enterprise would not soon grow into an extensive and wealthy establishment? Next, let there be added to it, a department for making paper, and a department for casting type, (so that what was before only an *aggregation*, would now become a GROUP,) and its economies would increase with a corresponding increase of efficiency. Yet a simple group, of similar pursuits of this kind, would be nothing compared with a SERIES of groups, with all the additional force that would be derived from the enthusiasm of contact and rivalry.

Now, it is a series of co-operations that we propose, as the means of our social reform. It is not a mere league on the part of the followers of a particular calling—it is not a treaty of amity between the members of distinct classes—not the promiscuous commingling of all branches of trade, that we vindicate: but it is the voluntary union of the whole of Humanity, on definite and scientific grounds. We contend for the solidarity of the race in organic forms; we desire the universal association of man, according to an universal principle: we aim at the thorough reorganization, not of a segment, but of the whole of society, on a basis of individual independence and freedom, and collective harmony and progress.

§ VI.—ORGANIZATION OF THE TOWNSHIP.

This object can be attained, we think, by the organization of the township. Let us suppose, that in a district composed of some three hundred families, (about eighteen hundred souls) the inhabitants should call a public meeting, to consider their social condition, and after the maturest deliberation, should adopt the following resolutions:

1st. An association is formed between all the inhabitants of this township, rich and poor; the capital to be composed of the fixed property of all, and of the furniture and goods which each one may see fit to contribute, at an appraised valuation.

2nd. Every associate shall receive in exchange for what he brings, a certificate representing the exact value of the capital relinquished to the society.

3d. Each share shall be a mortgage upon the fixed property which it represents, and upon the general property of the Association.

4th. Every associate, whether he have contributed fixed property or not, shall be allowed to take part in the productive use of the common funds, for the employment of his labor and talent.

5th. Women and children enter the society on the same terms as the men.

6th. The annual income, the common expenses being first liquidated, shall be divided among the members on the following terms:

(a) A first portion shall go to pay the interest on stocks.

(b) A second portion shall be divided among the laborers, according to the difficulties of their work, and the time devoted to it by each.

(c) The third and last part shall be distributed among those who have distinguished themselves, in various labors, either by intelligence, activity, or vigor.

Thus, each man, woman, and child, will be entitled to a share in each division, proportional to their respective concurrences in the production, by their three productive faculties of Capital, Labor, and Talent.

Let us suppose, further, that the inhabitants of this township, instead of remaining in their isolated houses, should agree to dwell in a large building, or rather, in a row of buildings, separated from each other so as to secure the privacy and independence of each family, but at the same time, so connected as to render available the obvious economies of fire, light, cooking, cellars, &c. &c.: that all the different branches of labor were distributed among groups of workmen best adapted for the execution of each, including in the term of labor, domestic avocations, agriculture, mechanical art and instruction; and that each group should have the entire control of its special department, subject only to the advisory direction of a more general and superior group; we say, let this be supposed, and we shall have the outline of the simple, but most important re-organization of society which we propose.* We do not here assert that an organization of this kind, is the true organization for society, although we hold that the position can be proved beyond a cavil: we merely wish to show, that Society, if it would escape from the terrible evils under which it now groans, must resort to some similar organization as the next step in its progressive career. We assert that Association by townships, as here delineated, if not *the* right way, at least leads toward the right way, and is the best approximation to a Perfect Constitution of Society, that has been presented to mankind. We assert that it is the most easy, the most feasible, the most safe, the most rational, and the most desirable phasis in which we can look at the great question of Social Reform. We assert this upon the subjoined brief views of

§ VII.—ITS CHARACTER AND ADVANTAGES.

1st. *It begins with the beginning.* It begins with the organization of the township, where sagacious minds have long since discovered that all reforms, to be efficient and practical, must begin. Napoleon, whose overwhelming energy of action so absorbs our minds, when considering his character, that we are led to forget his deep-searching practical insight, has said in a note, addressed about 1800 to his brother Lucien, then Minister of the Interior, that "if he had not been distracted by war, he should lay the foundation of the prosperity of France in the organization of the commune (*il commencerait la prosperete de la France par les communes, s'il n'etait distrait par la guerre.*") Thomas Jefferson, one of our most profound, and at the same time, most sagacious minds, writing to one of his friends, insists that all true political reform must begin with small districts. The framers of the Federal Constitution felt this when they were so careful to distinguish and secure the rights of the states. A consolidated government, extending over so wide a field of influence, would either

---

* Our object has been to give only the most elementary view—to suggest, rather than describe. We can prove scientifically that the organization here sketched, is the one designed by God.

fall to pieces from internal conflicts, or be smitten with the death-stroke of immobility. State action is the life of the Republic, such life as it has. Again: the new class of political reformers, lately sprung up in this State, demanding an amendment of the constitution, are impressed with the necessity of a still further extension of the districting principle; and urge as one of their fundamental tenets, that the enormous power now held by the State, shall be taken away from it, and returned either to the school districts, counties, or towns.

Now, these politicians are right for once. Experience has taught them that nothing is to be done through the cumbersome legislation of a too extensive territory. The government of a vast nation is too huge and unwieldy to make any active progress. You need the quick brain and nimble limbs of a smaller organization. A state, comprising, perhaps, millions of individuals, distributed over a wide extent of land, and embracing a thousand diverse interests, has too many wills to consult, to attain true concert and harmony of action. Buffalo, for instance, either from ignorance or indifference, will not consent to the local reforms necessary in the city of New York. Thus, legislation is injuriously delayed, or becomes grossly corrupt. The disgraceful system of *log-rolling*, which obtains in all the larger States, has its origin in the source to which we refer. Men are compelled, as we see annually at Albany and Harrisburg, to buy their palpable rights, by the meanest compliances, or the most unblushing bribery.

It is well, therefore, that our Constitutional Reformers, would restore the usurped power of the state, to its legitimate sphere, the township. Let one township be successfully organized—and the reform would soon expand, like the concentric circles of the water, till its circumference embraced the world. Give us one example of a political community founded upon correct and progressive principles, and we will answer for the universal adoption of it—and that right soon.

In no other mode, can a system of universal reform be begun. Nature, in the formation of the manifold and wondrous series of series that go to make up her Whole, begins with a small centre of vitality, around which the parts in their beautiful and divine order, are arranged according to the glorious law of Variety in One—which is the Eternal Fact of Creation. Well, would it be for man, did he not presume to be more wise than his Maker.

2d. *It is peaceful.* As it only contemplates voluntary action, the only force which it could use, is the force of truth and moral suasion. No man's rights would be infringed by it, but on the contrary, every legitimate right would receive an additional security. It makes no violent war upon the just privileges of any class, proposes no wholesale destruction of the property of the rich, no forced distribution of goods already acquired, deals in no bitter and malignant denunciations of any party or sect. It welcomes all ranks of people, it accepts all creeds and doctrines, and shows the basis upon which all can be harmonized in variety. Good-will, the sentiment of human brotherhood, the love of the neighbor are the only feelings to which it appeals.

When we look back upon the history of the world, we see how great a thing this feature of Peace is, in any reform. Christ, in that holy moment, when he separated from his poor heart-broken disciples, said, "My Peace I give unto you—My Peace I leave with you," as though it were the grandest legacy which Omnipotence could bequeath But the world, in mockery of the divine words, would not have Peace but War. Even the professed followers of Jesus, have propagated their faith by violence. They have burned Error at the stake, in the persons of its deluded worshippers, (burning much Truth with it,) and they have spread Truth with flashing bayonet and roaring guns. It is heart-sickening to think how Humanity has only advanced, through fightings, confusions, explosive overturnings, and volcanic uproar—how it has marched forward only amid the horrible discord of trumpet-clangors and cannon-vollies—how the masses, to establish their rights, have been compelled to wade through seas of blood, and trample out the hopes and hearts of their fellow men in the dust! The picture seems the more frightful, when we consider that at no time has this terrific slaughter been necessary, to accomplish its aims. God, while he permitted it, never designed it; and Man only has been guilty.

At any rate, let us now hope that the period of violence, whether necessary or unnecessary hitherto, is past. Let us hope that Mankind, in its modes of growth, will imitate Nature in her growth, and expand and enlarge by silent expulsion of the Old and the silent absorption of the New. One of our own poets has sung this spirit of Peaceful Reform in his noblest strains, where describing the havoc and desolation of "The Winds," he exclaims·

" Yet oh ! when the wronged spirit of our race,
    Shall break, as soon he must, his long-worn chains
And leap in freedom from his prison-place,
    Lord of his ancient hills and fruitful plains,
Let him not rise, like these mad winds of air,
To waste the loveliness that time could spare,
To fill the earth with wo, and blot her fair
    Unconscious breast with blood from human veins.

" But may he like the spring-time come abroad,
    Who crumbles winter's gyves with gentle might,
When in the genial breeze, the breath of God,
    Come spouting up the unsealed springs to light;
Flowers start from their dark prisons at his feet,
The woods, long-dumb, awake to hymnings sweet,
And morn and eve, whose glimmerings almost meet,
    Crowd back to narrow bounds the ancient night."

3d. *It is positive.* By this, we mean, that the reörganization we propose, does not rest upon any mere critical exposition of the evils of the present state, but that it is founded in the knowledge of a higher and better state. Our criticisms proceed from our constructive principles. We condemn, not according to any imperfect, one-sided, fragmentary, variable standard; but according to what we esteem to be a perfect and universal standard. Having discovered what we think the real formula of progressive organization, we feel prepared to animadvert upon all conditions which are a departure from the truth. The defect of all other methods of Reform, is in the fact that they are for the most part negative. They see the Wrong, without seeing the Right. For instance: there is a class of men who mourn over the desolations of Intemperance, and they denounce the dealers in spirituous liquors, but they have no positive remedy for the evil, and therefore their appeals and denunciations have had only a temporary effect. There is another class of brave and warm-hearted philanthropists, whose sympathies and convictions are shocked by slave-holding, yet, in the midst of their burning invectives and persuasions, they have only spread their sentiments, without producing any positive practical change. There are societies of tender-hearted females, who would rescue the thousands of their debased sisters whom circumstances have driven to the sullied haunts of vice, but for the want of positive plans, they excite only ridicule and sarcasm from the more sagacious world. There are associations for the reform of juvenile delinquents; there are work-houses for the relief of poverty; there are a thousand agencies for the extinction of crime; yet delinquency, pauperism, crime, cover the face of society, and seem to be rather on the increase. The truth is, that these, and various other projects of Reform, are smitten with perpetual barrenness, for the want of an impregnating principle. They undoubtedly do good; they keep alive a tender and benevolent sentiment; they remove individual cases of suffering; they impress the scoffing world with the conviction that something is ever to be done for our fellows; but, measured by the large scale of what they ought to do, they are most lamentably partial and inefficient. They are a few drops of oil spread upon a sea, to still a tempest. They are a withe of straw held against the raw and cutting east wind. Shakspere has said, with hardly more beauty than literal truth:

"As far as the little candle throws its beams,
So shines a good deed upon a naughty world."

Verily; your good deeds, your plans of reform are a small candle light in a vast world of darknesss, duplicity, and discord. You need a deeper insight—a broader groundwork—a mightier principle of positive vitality. In the midst of such influences as are now around you, a powerful stream of tendencies dragging you downward to evil; the poor, as we have shown,[*] growing more poor and debased, and the rich, more rich and corrupt; misery spreading and multiplying; cheerless homes and inviting grog-shops; the wages of sempstresses ten cents per day, while the wages of sin are as many dollars per night; political parties absorbed in selfish schemes; and the church, chewing the husks of a dead theology, or lapped in luxurious indolence; and all the while your greatest leaders proclaiming that most abominable, most cruel of political maxims, that "each man is the best judge of his own interest, and therefore must take care of himself"—a maxim proceeding from the first born Cain—under such circumstances, it is impossible that your slender, meagre, fragmentary plans of reform should succeed. No—you must walk at once into the heart of the matter; you must see that the root of all this wrong lies in the false constitution of Society; you must know that there is a better constitution; and then, laying aside your partial schemes, plant your foot firmly upon positive universal ground. None but universal ideas are, at this day, worthy of attention Our plan is thus universal, for

4th. *It fulfills all the duties and answers all the ends of Society.* Man has a right to a living off of the Earth, or he would not have been sent here; and, for the same reason, he has a right to use all those elements which are necessary to his full growth and development. The possession of these rights, imposes corresponding *duties* on Society. It is the primary, fundamental, most important and imperative duty of Society to guaranty his rights to every human being. But, no society that ever existed, no society that now exists, has discharged this duty. A majority of men have had hard work to get even bread and water enough to keep them alive, under the old arrangements, to say nothing of the higher wants of the mind and soul. Indeed, a theory has gone forth, and is earnestly vindicated in high places, that all society has to do, is to protect the person and property of the individual. A despicable theory, if it were even carried into practice! But unfortunately, this duty, small as it is, has not been met. Society has not protected property. It is true, the property of the rich has been hedged around with the thick-set fences of all law, learning and public opinion. Accumulated Labor in the shape of Capital, is the golden fruit, watched by many-headed dragons; but living, breathing Labor, which is the poor man's only property, is flung loose to the winds, left to shift for itself, without guaranty, without protection. Yet, society pays a fearful penalty for this neglect of its duty. Its armies of paupers, its alms-houses, its prisons, its soup and clothing charities, its taxes, demonstrate with vivid clearness, how much better it would be for it to stop evils at their source. This can only be done by the thorough reorganization which we propose—an organization which would secure to every man, woman, and child, (1.) the means of comfortable subsistence, such as a clean house, wholesome food, decent clothes, and the privacy of their families; (2.) the opportunities of education, in elementary branches of knowledge, in the business of life, in the positive sciences, and in the general principles of fine arts; (3.) and facilities of intercourse with their fellows, with a position to be affected by all the gentler and more refined influences of learned and polite conversation and deportment.

It is because we believe that an organization, according to our principles, would secure these ends, that we have ventured to speak of Democracy. Never was there a word more abused—never was there a word more profoundly significant. It does not mean that ferocious spirit of levelling, which, in the French Revolution, crumbled the entire Past, and even plucked God from his throne; nor yet the wild, dirty, and turbulent mobism, which, in this country, covers with the slime of its filthiness, every character that is purer and nobler than itself: but it does not mean a condition of society in which the least individual shall have his rights acknowledged, and the means and opportunities for the fullest expansion of his faculties guarantied. It means a social state, where the whole of life, for nine-tenths of the people, shall not be a suicidal struggle for life—where the finer essences of the soul shall not be ground out to furnish bare nutriment for the body—where none of its families shall esteem it a curse to have children born to them—where honesty and diligence, not impudence and falsehood, shall be the measures of success, and where noble thoughts and generous emotions shall not be trampled out, because forsooth, they are not what the worldly-wise deem practicable or prudent. But the great fact of the Brotherhood of Man shall be recognized—that Humanity is a living organism, of which every individual is a member—each in his sphere, bound to his fellows and the whole, as the arm or the foot is bound to the body—a partaker in their wrongs—a sufferer of their diseases—a sharer in their felicity, and a co-worker with them for good and evil. Then, in the arrangements of the State, the reconciling maxims of distributive equity shall take the place of the insane and destructive doctrines of positive equality—the slavery of pauperism and vice shall be succeeded by rational freedom—and the palsying stagnation of hopeless and remediless conservatism give way to the healthful agitation of conservative progress.

5th. *It is a direct manifestation of the Spirit of Christianity.* No fact in the life of Christ, (and he was the highest form of his religion,) strikes us more forcibly than the comprehensiveness of his benevolence. Reinhard, in his admirable work, " The Plan of Jesus," attempts to prove his divinity by the very fact that he was thus universal. His utterances, his prayers, his miracles, all evince the depth and tenderness of his sympathy with Man. He took the little children into his arms; he multiplied the wine at the festivities of Galilee ; he fed the poor believing crowd, not so wise as the prudent Pharisees ; and he washed the feet of his sorrowing disciples, that he might show how much he loved all his fellow-men. He wished to testify that it was our chief duty to minister to each other, to call no man master, to lord it over no man, to make life a perpetual scene of mutual helpfulness and service. Such was his spirit—and this spirit he intended should be manifested in the organization of society. The outward must ever be an expression of the inward, if we would be true to our principles. The form must correspond with the in-dwelling law —the external tenement with the idea of its inhabitant.

What then is the law which Christian Society ought to embody or incarnate : " Thou shalt love the Lord, thy God, with all thy heart, and with all thy mind, and with all thy soul. This is the first and great commandment : and the second is like unto it— Thou shalt love thy neighbor as thyself. On these two commandments hang all the law and the prophets.—(Matt. xxvii. 57.)

A new commandment I give unto you, that you love one another; as I have loved you, that you also love one another.—(John, xii. 34.)

All things whatsoever you would that men should do unto you, do you even so to them ; for this is the law and the prophets.— (Matt. vii. 12.)

Seek ye first the kingdom of God and its justice, and all worldly things shall be added unto you.—(Matt. vi. 33.)

Ask and it shall be given you ; seek and ye shall find ; knock and it shall be opened. Come unto me, all ye that labor and are heavy laden, and I will give you rest. Ye are all one, as I and my father are one.—(John.) For as the body is one—so also is Christ. For by one Spirit are we all baptized into one body, whether we be Jews or Gentiles, bond or free, &c. That there should be no schism (disunity) in the body; but that the members should have the same care one for another. And whether one member suffer, all the members suffer with it ; or one member be honored, all the members rejoice with it,"

CONCLUSION.

We have hinted in the course of this essay at the following points, any one of which might be easily expanded into a volume:

1. That there is, in civilized society, a rapid increase of population, without any due provision by society for its employment or support.

2. That the working classes, who are a majority everywhere, by the present system of blind competition, are picking each others pockets and cutting each others throats.

3. That, according to the admission of nearly all the distinguished political economists, the condition of laborers is rapidly deteriorating.

4. That the continued invention of labor-saving machinery is still further tending to the reduction of all laborers for the sake of the capitalists.

5. That Capital is more and more concentrating in the hands of the few, who are thus forming an oppressive Money-Feudalism.

6. That no political party has as yet proposed any measure that in the remotest degree touches the root of these evils.

7. That some plan for the unity of the material interests of men is the only one that can prevent our downward tendencies.

8. That this plan is presented in the doctrine of Association, on the basis of Attractive Industry.

These principles we present to the public. Individually we have nothing to gain or to lose by their adoption or rejection. Our only interest in seeking to spread them, is derived from our strong conviction of their truth, and our urgent hope that something will be done for humanity. We know that we shall excite prejudice: we know that ridicule and scorn has been heaped upon us without measure; but we know, at the same time, that we act in sincerity, and we leave the rest to God. We are confident of victory. Already the white light of the rising sun is caught upon the mountain-tops—already we see the streaks of the coming day. Whence the present unusual ferment of the public mind? Why are the deepest religious feelings of the soul, the oldest religious institutions, undergoing such sifting and earnest controversy? Is it not that the world is travailing in the birth-throes of a mighty and better Future? Even the ephemera of literature are seized with the common sympathy, and become unconscious prophets of the days about to be. Why do your Eugene Sues probe the sores and secret wounds of your diseased society, and hold all nations captive by their pictures of Humanity in her hunger-stricken, straw-covered lairs? Why tingles the blood, when the pen of Dickens—lately so false to his own genial nature—exposes the want, and wretchedness, and cureless griefs of the poor? It is because you know in your hearts, that all is wrong with your miserable death-struck societies, and that you inwardly long for the Better Time. It is because you would like to join in some practicable and generous movement for the extirpation of pauperism and crime. That movement is at hand! The field of battle is before you; but, oh! how different the weapons and objects from those of former warfares. Our weapons are truth, justice and religion Our objects, universal conciliation, and universal love. Unity and Peace are the banner-words of our host.

Says Mr. Carlyle, in his last and greatest work, "Past and Present," "Not on Ilions or Latium's plains; on far other plains and places henceforth, can noble deeds be now done. Not on Ilion's plains; how much less in Mayfair drawing-rooms! Not in victory over poor brother French or Phrygians; but in victory over Frost-jotuns, Marsh-giants: over demons of Discord, Idleness, Injustice, Unreason, and Chaos come again. None of the old Epics is longer possible. The Epic of French and Phrygians is comparatively a small Epic; but that of Flirts and Fribbles, what is that? A thing that vanishes at cock-crowing, that already begins to scent the morning air."

"But it is to you, ye workers, who do already work, and are as grown men, noble and honorable in a sort, that the whole world calls for new work and nobleness. Subdue Mutiny, Discord, wide-spread Despair, by manfulness, Justice, Mercy and Wisdom. Chaos is dark—deep as Hell: let light be, and there is instead a green flowery world. Oh! it is great, and there is no other greatness. To make some nook of God's creation a little fruitfuller, better, more worthy of God; to make some human hearts a little wiser, manfuller, happier—more blessed, less accursed! It is work for a God. Sooty Hell, of Savagery, Mutiny and Despair, can, by man's energy, be made a kind of Heaven; cleared of its soot, of its Mutiny, of its need of Mutiny; the everlasting arch of Heaven's azure overspanning it too, as a birth of Heaven; God and all men looking on it well-pleased. Unstained by wasteful deformities, by wasted tears, or heart's blood of Men, or any defacement of the Pit, noble, fruitful Labor, growing ever nobler—will come forth, the Grand Sole Miracle of Man."

THE END.

APPENDIX.

DEPRESSION OF LABOR.

The Industrial System, which has transformed the serf into the operative, and prepared the way for Modern Feudalism, which we insist is no advance on the Feudalism of the Middle Ages, is beginning to attract the attention, not only of radicals and socialists, but of politicians and statesmen. Its effects in reducing labor to a state of complete servitude to capital, and, therefore, the operative to the proprietor, is beginning to be seen, and to be felt, in the unspeakable misery and distress of the laboring classes. The great fact can be no longer concealed or denied, *that the present economical system of what are called the more advanced nations of Christendom, places labor at the mercy of capital, and every increase of wealth on the part of the few is attended by a more than corresponding increase of poverty and distress on the part of the many.* Here is the fact. Men may gloss it over as they will, ascribe it to this cause or to that; but here is the fact. The richest nation in the world is the poorest; abundance superinduces want, and, with the general increase of wealth, the mass of laborers find themselves reduced to the starving point, and rapidly falling *below* it. This is the fact our social reformers see, and seek to remedy. Our own labors for twenty years have been devoted almost exclusively to the great work of ascertaining the means by which labor may be emancipated, and the acquisition of wealth prevented from becoming a public curse.

Brownson's Quarterly Review, for April, 1844.

RICH AND POOR IN ENGLAND.

A candidate for Parliament stated that all the arable lands in England were owned by thirty-three thousand proprietors. I called on the officers of the Statistical Society in St. Martin's Lane, in London, to ascertain the truth of this statement. At their request I committed several interrogatories to writing, which they said should be answered when the results of the census, then in press, were known. Three months thereafter they told me that the statistics of England did not afford the information required. A similar statement was afterward made by a member of Parliament; and, as it was never contradicted, it may be regarded as true—that the cultivated lands from which the English are fed, belong to thirty-three thousand persons. The chief among them are the members of Parliament, and the hereditary nobility, born to power as well as to riches. They have established a code of laws for their own benefit, the most inhuman known in the annals of legislation. Not only are their own estates exempt from general taxation, but the cultivation of them is forced upon the people by prohibiting the importation of every article of food from abroad. The poor laborer is at their mercy; from them he receives his bread; and his wife and children must be fed on such terms as they prescribe. There is no escape; ignorant and destitute, he cannot take refuge in foreign countries, where his proud oppressor cannot pursue. He is starved to the lowest point of endurance; yet life is spared. Sufficient strength to till the earth is kept up by gruel and potatoes, provided by the poor laws or the landlords themselves, as oats are given to horses that they may bear the burthens heaped upon their backs. There is policy in oppression; if the cords were drawn too tight, the poor peasant would die, and thus the greediness of the rich would consume themselves.

There are five millions of laborers who cultivate the earth, and six millions of operatives engaged in manufactures, who possess no land, no, not a mole-hill; no vote, no home but at the will of a landlord; are hungry from morning till night, and sleep and die on straw. If to these be added three millions of paupers fed at the public charge; the beggars that frequent the streets and highways; the poor mechanics and journeymen, prostitutes and laborers of every description, it may be safely affirmed, that out of the twenty-six millions that inhabit the three kingdoms, twenty millions—men, women and children—daily feel the yearnings of unsatisfied appetite. There is not a day that the newspapers do not tell some piteous tale of destitution, and too often has the surgeon's knife proved starvation to be the cause of death. In 1842, the poor of Preston cut and eat the flesh of a cow that died of disease, which they dug up from the common where it had been buried. The fact was published without contradiction in all the leading prints of the kingdom.

The English are, indeed, a great people. They hold two sceptres, by sea and by land; they have stretched their vast dominions to the outer limits of the earth; they have reached the summit of human glory; but it is glory in rags. Of all nations, they are at once the richest and the poorest; the proudest and the most servile, the wisest and the most ignorant. Five thousand persons, titled of right and by courtesy, are provided for by their constitution; a few professional men, manufacturers, merchants, and tradesmen, have provided for themselves; they spend their lives in a perpetual gorgeous holiday, while the naked, needy multitude live in a constant struggle for bread.

APPENDIX. 49

During the years 1841-2-3, I entered 122 cottages in Somersetshire, Devonshire, Lancashire, Warwickshire, Surrey, Middlesex, and Kent, always with a view to understand a subject in which I felt a deep and abiding interest. My first visit to Somersetshire disclosed the whole truth; I had nothing further to learn, thanthat the same wretchedness, the same round of potatoes and salt, the same appalling picture of wretchedness and rags, prevailed throughout the kingdom.

Judge Carlton, in the Democratic Review.

FEELINGS OF THE POOR TOWARD THE RICH.

No man ever hears of a laboring peasant rising into an owner of land. The feudal system binds them as tightly to the soil as ever they were bound. They are as much *adscripti glebœ*, as in the Conqueror's time, with this difference, that when old age disables them, instead of a place below the salt at their owner's table, they have the work-house to retire to. They are the Pariahs of English society. And, as a consequence of this miserable and benighted condition, in which the whole mass of society appears to them one cruel, heartless jest, the well-being of the upper classes 'the arch fiend's mock,' they burn corn stacks and farm steadings, and would, doubtless, burn *chateaux*, too, like the French peasants in 1793, if they dared. It is now established, beyond the possibility of any reasonable denial, that feelings of the bitterest hostility to their masters, and of desperate disaffection to the present order of things pervade the peasantry; that in most instances of wilful fire raising, the whole neighboring population are accessories after the fact; that they look with apathetic indifference, if not with gratified revenge, upon the wanton destruction of life and property.

Liverpool Mercury.

NO REMEDY FOR THE SUFFERING POOR.

At the last meeting of the London Statistical Society, a remarkable paper, which touches the internal condition of Ireland, was read by Mr. Chadwick, the author of the *Sanitary Reports*, that have attracted attention in both hemispheres. This paper is included in *The Supplementary Sanitary Report*, worthy of being studied by every political economist and municipal administrator. The primary purpose of the author is to correct the *mistake*, as he deems it, of Dr. Price and other statistical writers of authority, by whom "the proportions of deaths to the population, and the average age of death, are treated as equivalent." The London Morning Chronicle describes the paper thus:

"The whole document is replete with interest, and shows that there is a process of *deterioration* going on among our population, which no mere palliative can possibly check. Even *emigration*, by itself, will only aggravate the evil, because it would tend to accelerate the rate at which a *stunted, youthful, miserable* population is rapidly growing up in the very midst of the greatest *sickness* and *mortality*. We are here taught the strange, wonderful, and appalling fact, that insufficient shelter, insufficient food, insufficient means of living, instead of being checks to population, constitute one of its *worst* stimulants; because under such a state of things we have a greater number of births, a larger amount of early deaths, and a more deplorable condition of *mortality*, than where the people are well-fed and well-housed. The subject is one of the very gravest importance."

This, however, is not the first time that the fact has been proclaimed; nor is it so strange or wonderful. The results of the absence of moral checks on the increase of population were long ago indicated, and those of physical destitution and misery on the ages of death are quite obvious. Mr. Chadwick explains and works out his position, first, by reference to the actual experience among nearly two millions of English population, or upward of forty-five thousand deaths in thirty-two districts, equivalent to as many populous towns—which the Registrar-General had enabled him to examine for the year 1839. But the most impressive details are those which he has extracted from the latest returns of the census from Ireland. He proves by them that "where the pressure of the 'causes of mortality is the greatest—where the average of death is the lowest, and the duration of life the shortest, there the increase of population is the greatest.'" And, besides, there the proportion of children, always dependent on the thinned adults, is necessarily greatest.

Washington National Intelligencer.

POVERTY IN THE STATE OF NEW-YORK.

An abstract of the annual returns from the Superintendents of the Poor, submitted by the Secretary of State to the Legislature, appears in the *Albany Argus*. These returns embrace every county in the state, and reveal an extent of pauperism which we did not suppose to exist, and which must astonish our readers. From this statement of the Argus, it appears that, in 1843, the number of county paupers relieved or supported, was 78,233; paupers of town, 4,521. Whole number of regular paupers, 82,754, or about 1 to 30 of every inhabitant in the State. But, in addition to these, there were 62,047 paupers *temporarily* relieved by the public officers, making an aggregate of paupers in the State of New York of 144,801, or about 1 to every 17 of the inhabitants.

The whole expenditure for the poor, during 1843, is..............$592,353 29
But the value of the labor of the paupers, amounting to...............58,658 85

Must be deducted, and the net expense is.........................$533,694 44
which is raised by direct taxation.

During 1842, the expense was.......................................$517,738 02
Deduct pauper labor..57,133 30

$460,604 72

Thus showing an increase of pauper expenses of the year 1843 over those of 1842 of $72,989 72, or an increase in a single year of over 15 per cent. in the expenditures. The average weekly expense of each pauper during the year

   1843, was...................58 cents and 2 mills.
   1842, was...................64 " 6 "

This shows that the expense of supporting each pauper has decreased 8 per cent., and yet the whole aggregate of expenses has increased 15 per cent. This solely arises from an increase in *the number* of paupers. This increase was 21,314 over the preceding year.

It will be remembered that the large numbers of poor families relieved by various charitable societies and private benefactions, are not included in these returns. If, therefore, the number of those who are in the habit of receiving aid from the German, Scotch, Irish, Italian, Welsh, Benevolent and Emigrant Societies, from the funds of different churches, created for purposes of pauper relief, from the various Clothing and Sewing societies, instituted by benevolent ladies, and from the donations of individuals, were added to the number of State paupers, we have no doubt that the ratio of paupers to other inhabitants would be greatly increased.   New-York Evening Post.

New-York is one of the richest, if not the richest, agricultural state in the Union, yet 1 in 17 of its inhabitants are supported by charity. In the city of New-York, the Alms-house have administered relief, in the year 1843, to 40,000 persons! This is at the rate of 1 to 7½ of the population.

THE VAMPYRE OF COMMERCE.

We find, in a Michigan paper, the following statement of the distribution of the annual wealth of this country. It is taken from a Letter addressed by Mr. S. Denton, of Michigan, to a State Farmers' Convention.

"*That wealth is but the accumulated creations of labor,* is a cardinal and obvious truth, which none will pretend to deny. But how is it, that those who *create* it all, are enabled to retain so little for their own share, is a phenomenon which requires explanation.

What sum in dollars will represent the value of the annual products of the United States in all branches of production?

Different answers have been given to this interesting question by various statisticians, some estimating them as high as 1300, and others as high as 15 or 1600 millions of dollars.

But in these estimates, I have found that several large items have been twice and others thrice reckoned. For instance, our wool is first estimated, and then it is again reckoned in our manufactured woollens, and just so of our cotton and cotton goods.

Our grain is first estimated, and then reckoned over again in the products of our flouring mills. The annual value of our lumber, bricks, and lime, is first put down and then it is all re-estimated in the value of the buildings annually erected. The lumber, metals, cordage, &c., are first estimated and then reckoned over again, in the annual value of ships built, and the cordage, sails, &c., had been estimated once previously in the value of the flax and hemp crops; and thus we might go on through a very large catalogue. It will be readily perceived that this mode of analysis, will reduce the estimates of some economists very much.

We have deducted one item more from our estimates, viz: the *necessary subsistence* of the laborers. Food, clothing and lodging are indispensable, even for slaves: and all that is *absolutely necessary for that object*, we have excluded in our calculations, and thus make the aggregate annual products of industry, of all the laboring classes of the United States, over and above so much food and clothing, as a master in the pursuit of his own interest, would allow his slaves, amount to $1,046,186,000.

Now, it is obvious, that all the wealth which any man, or any class of men in the United States obtains in any way, is derived directly or indirectly, from this original sum.

Now, if we can arrive at the sum which each class of non-producers annually receives, the remainder will be the amount left for distribution, among those who create it all.

For this purpose we have gone into a very thorough and minute examination, to ascertain the amount annually distributed to each of the non-producing classes, in the United States, viz:

THE AMOUNT DISTRIBUTED TO THE LAWYERS, AND ALL OTHERS ENGAGED IN THE ADMINISTRATION OF THE LAW;

THE AMOUNT DISTRIBUTED TO THE BANKERS AND BROKERS, &c.;

THE AMOUNT DISTRIBUTED FOR TOWNSHIP, COUNTY, STATE, VILLAGE, TOWN, CITY AND NATIONAL GOVERNMENT PURPOSES;

THE AMOUNT DISTRIBUTED TO OUR MERCHANTS;

THE AMOUNT ADDED TO THE PUBLIC BURTHENS, CONSEQUENT UPON THE PRESENT MODE OF COLLECTING THE UNITED STATES REVENUE, &c. &c.

These aggregate sums amount to $889,087,409, leaving for distribution among the laborers, $157,097,591. This is the laborers' portion over and above such necessaries as a prudent master would provide for a slave, when acting in conformity to his own interests.

But for the sake of being on the safe side in these calculations and for the purpose of reducing the figures to round numbers, I will call the latter sum 206 millions, and the former sum 900 millions of dollars, making 1100 millions of dollars in all."

MACHINERY vs. MEN.

The subjoined is an extract from a report, read to a meeting of workingmen, held in this city, in March, 1844. It will be a significant fact to many, to state that the remedy hinted at in the same report, was *an equal division of the land.*

" Having made due inquiry into the facts, the committee are satisfied that there is a much larger number of laboring people congregated in the seaboard towns, that can find constant and profitable employment. Your committee do not think it necessary to enter into statistical details in order to prove a fact that is not disputed by anybody.

The result of this over-supply of labor is a competition among the laborers, tending to reduce wages, even where employment is obtained, to a scale greatly below what is necessary for the comfortable subsistence of the workingman, and the education of his family.

It appears to your committee, that as long as the supply of labor exceeds the demand, the natural laws which regulate prices, will render it very difficult, if not altogether impossible, to permanently improve the condition of the working people.

Our inquiries, therefore, were naturally directed to ascertain how far existing causes are likely to affect the supply and demand of labor—whether those causes tend to lessen, or increase the evil under which the working classes are now suffering.

As tending to lessen the evil, we find an increasing home consumption of articles produced by mechanical skill—we also anticipate an increase, to some extent at least, of our export market.

But we believe that this additional demand is by no means likely to keep pace with our accumulating powers of production. First, we find in our cities and factory stations, an increasing population, the great majority of whom depend for a subsistence on mechanical labor; and secondly, we find the new-born power of machinery throwing itself into competition with our working population. Indeed, if we judge of the next half century, by the half century just past, there will be, by the end of that time, little mechanical labor performed by human hands.

We find, on consulting authentic data, that *machinery* has taken almost entire possession of the manufacture of cloth. That it is making steady—we might say rapid—advance upon all branches of iron manufacture. That the newly invented machine-saws, working in curves as well as straight lines—the planing and grooving machine, and the tenon and mortice machine, clearly admonish us that its empire is destined to extend itself over all our manufactures of wood. That while some of the handicrafts are already extinct, there is not one of them but has foretasted the overwhelming competition of this occult power. We can clearly perceive that while the laws of population tend to steadily increase the supply of mechanical labor—so does the improvement of machinery tend to, not merely lessen, but almost annihilate the demand.*

This result—this triumph of MACHINE LABOR, and ultimate prostra-

---

* In spinning cotton, Baines informs us that one man can now produce as much yarn as 25,300 men could have done under the old systems. "This machine-spun yarn," says Dr. Ure, "possesses a more uniform twist, and is, in every respect, superior to hand-spun yarn. As in spinning, so in weaving. One water-wheel, or engine, will set 1,000 looms to work. One of these looms will make about as much cloth as four looms worked by the hand; one female superintends several looms, merely to supply full bobbins, and mend threads that happen to break in the process of weaving.

"Nails," says Dr. Ure, "are now manufactured with little or no aid from the human hand." "The making of nails," he continues, "is no longer a handicraft operation, but belongs to a Dictionary of Arts."

Not long ago bread stuffs were ground in a handmill. Two men might be able with great labor, to dry and grind a bushel of grain in a day. Now, one watermill will turn out 1,000 bushels in twenty-four hours.

In bookbinding, Ure informs us, that a machine has been recently invented by an Englishman, named Hancock, which dispenses, entirely, with the operation of stitching, sewing, sawing-in and hammering the back, or the use of paste and glue.

Calico printing was long a tedious handicraft operation. It is now performed by cylindrical machines revolving with the rapidity of light.

In manufacturing steam-boilers much of the labor is now performed by machinery. Thus we see the iron monster, like other monsters, has the faculty of reproducing itself.

The employment which our lakes and rivers promised to afford to a numerous population, will be almost wholly superseded by the steam engine afloat.

In the crafts of boot and shoemaking, machinery is beginning to show itself—and we may not estimate the progress it will make in this department, even in our own day. Certainly skill in this handicraft will afford a very insecure dependence to our children.

"Machinery," says Dr. Ure, "is ready to accomplish everything in the manufacture of hats;" but he adds that it is kept down for the present, by what he calls " a lawless combination of the journeymen." This is in Britain, and the Doctor predicts that this combination will soon be broken down before the genius of machinery.

In ropemaking, the machine has taken almost entire possession. The recent improvements enable 4 or 5 men to do the work of ten times that number of regular hands. Such is the distress and desperation that this change has created among the working men, that several " machine-houses " have recently been destroyed in the neighborhood of this city, by incendiary fires. They were, however, immediately rebuilt, and are now in full operation.

A machine for making brick, is now at work in Washington. It can mould 30,000 bricks, by the power of a single horse. These are turned out perfectly dry—ready for burning. At several points on the Hudson machines are in operation for the purpose of preparing clay for bricks—a laborious process that used to give employment to great numbers of laborers.

Even our bakers are not safe—a powerful kneading machine is coming into extensive use in England.

Two-thirds of our carpenter-work is now performed by machinery. To this also is it coming with our ship-builders. The letter press printer belongs, almost, to a past order of things, and machinery is even trying its hand at type-setting. In currying leather they use a machine which actually makes one hide into two. Heavy cloth garments of an elegant style, are now made in England by the hatting process, thereby dispensing with the thimble and shears. Steam coaches now navigate the streets of London to the great dismay of cabmen—our very scavengers are jostled out of the way by the same power—and while the Yankee Paddy moves the hills with all the ease of a Titan, the same power is hard at work in another quarter cutting out the precise machinery of Yankee clocks.

tion of HUMAN LABOR—can not, in the opinion of your committee, be averted. We may wrestle with the monster, as the toilers of England wrestle, till myriads of us perish in the unequal strife. But your committee are of opinion, that all this will be only so much strife, and so much suffering wasted in vain. As well might we interfere with the career of the heavenly bodies, or attempt to alter any of Nature's fixed laws, as hope to arrest the onward march of science and machinery."

The author has cut these paragraphs from the newspapers, &c. of the day, while the body of his work was in press. He might, with a little labor, add ten thousand more confirmations of the views he has advanced.

THE AMERICAN UTOPIAN ADVENTURE

sources for the study of communitarian socialism in the United States 1680–1880

Series One

Edward D. Andrews THE COMMUNITY INDUSTRIES OF THE SHAKERS (1932)

Adin Ballou HISTORY OF THE HOPEDALE COMMUNITY from its inception to its virtual submergence in the Hopedale Parish. Edited by W. S. Heywood (1897)

Paul Brown TWELVE MONTHS IN NEW HARMONY presenting a faithful account of the principal occurrences that have taken place there during that period; interspersed with remarks (1827)

John S. Duss THE HARMONISTS. A personal history (1943)

Frederick W. Evans AUTOBIOGRAPHY OF A SHAKER and revelation of the Apocalypse. With an appendix. Enlarged edition (1888)

Parke Godwin A POPULAR VIEW OF THE DOCTRINES OF CHARLES FOURIER (1844) DEMOCRACY, CONSTRUCTIVE AND PACIFIC (1844)

Walter C. Klein JOHANN CONRAD BEISSEL, MYSTIC AND MARTINET, 1690–1768 (1942)

William J. McNiff HEAVEN ON EARTH: A PLANNED MORMON SOCIETY (1940) With "Communism among the Mormons," by Hamilton Gardner

Michael A. Mikkelsen THE BISHOP HILL COLONY. A religious, communistic settlement in Henry County, Illinois (1892) With "Eric Janson and the Bishop Hill Colony," by Silvert Erdahl

Oneida Community BIBLE COMMUNISM. A compilation from the annual reports and other publications of the Oneida Association and its branches, presenting, in connection with their history, a summary view of their religious and social theories (1853)

Marianne (Dwight) Orvis LETTERS FROM BROOK FARM 1841–1847. Edited by Amy L. Reed (1928)

Robert A. Parker A YANKEE SAINT. John Humphrey Noyes and the Oneida Community (1935)

A. J. G. Perkins & Thersa Wolfson FRANCES WRIGHT: FREE ENQUIRER. The study of a temperament (1939)

Jules Prudhommeaux ICARIE ET SON FONDATEUR, ÉTIENNE CABET. Contribution à l'étude du socialisme expérimental (1907)

Albert Shaw ICARIA. A chapter in the history of communism (1884)